PACIFIC NORTHWEST

TRAVEL ✦ SMART®

Second Edition

Jena MacPherson

John Muir Publications
Santa Fe, New Mexico

Acknowledgments
Many thanks to my editors, Jill Metzler, Krista Lyons-Gould, Heather Pool, and Cassandra Conyers, for their good humor, patience, insights, and hard work. And to the countless Northwest travel and information specialists who helped over time and with this book—especially David Blanford and Margaret Monfert; to Deidre Campbell, Heather Day, Erika and Peter Durlocher, Barbara Glover, Laura Jobin, Eileen Mintz, Victoria Pratt, Sally Sederstrom and Karen Runkel, Laura Serena and Derek Hemmes and their staff, Laura Street, Debra Wakefield, Carrie Wilkinson-Tuma, and Tamara Wilson. Thank you to Nancy Davidson, Steve Lorton, and Jim McCausland, who taught me to capture and shape ideas, and Dick Bushnell, whose early unrelenting efforts helped me craft them. Jerry DiVecchio, Sinclair Philip, Jon Rowley, Kasey Wilson and Anthony Gismondi—food and wine professionals who've shared their vast knowledge and shaped my tastes. Opinions and errors herein are mine, but special thanks for generosity of spirit go to these many fine people.

Thanks to Joanne and Leah Otness, Megan Chance, Elizabeth DeMatteo, Melinda McRae, Liz Osborne, and Sharon Thomas for everything. To Jim and Molly for their constant love and support. And to my father, Jamie Philip Shedd, who found poetry in a harsh landscape and music in words.

John Muir Publications, P.O. Box 613, Santa Fe, New Mexico 87504

Printed in the United States of America.
Second edition. First printing March 1999.

ISSN 1099-9892
ISBN 1-56261-455-X

Editors: Jill Metzler, Krista Lyons-Gould
Graphics Editor: Heather Pool
Production: Janine Lehmann
Design: Janine Lehmann, Linda Braun
Cover Design: Janine Lehmann
Typesetting: Diane Rigoli
Map Style Development: American Custom Maps—Jemez Springs, NM USA
Map Illustration: Kathleen Sparkes, White Hart Designs
Printer: Publishers Press
Front Cover Photo: top—© John Elk III (Seattle's Space Needle with the Monorail)
                 bottom—© John Elk III (Mt. Baker with Chain Lakes)
Back Cover Photo: © John Elk III (Cape Kiwanda on Three Capes Drive, Oregon Coast)

Distributed to the book trade by
Publishers Group West
Berkeley, California

HOW TO USE THIS BOOK

The *Pacific Northwest Travel•Smart* guidebook is organized in 18 destination chapters, each covering the best sights and activities, restaurants, and lodging available in that specific destination. Thanks to thorough research and experience, the author is able to bring you only the best options, saving you time and money in your travels. The chapters are presented in geographic sequence so you can follow an easy route from one to the next. If you were to visit each destination in chapter order, you'd enjoy a complete tour of the best of the Pacific Northwest.

Each chapter contains:

- User-friendly maps of the area, showing all recommended sights, restaurants, and accommodations.
- "A Perfect Day" description—how the author would spend her time if she had just one day in that destination.
- Sightseeing highlights, each rated by degree of importance: ✩✩✩✩ Don't miss; ✩✩✩ Try hard to see; ✩✩ See if you have time; and ✩ Worth knowing about.
- Selected restaurant, lodging, and camping recommendations to suit a variety of budgets.
- Helpful hints, fitness and recreation ideas, insights, and random tidbits of information to enhance your trip.

The Importance of Planning. Developing an itinerary is the best way to get the most satisfaction from your travels, and this guidebook makes it easy. First, read through the book and choose the places you'd most like to visit. Then, study the color map on the inside cover flap and the mileage chart (page 12) to determine which you can realistically see in the time you have available and at the travel pace you prefer. Using the Planning Map (pages 10–11), map out your route. Finally, use the lodging recommendations to determine your accommodations.

Some Suggested Itineraries. To get you started, six itineraries of varying lengths and based on specific interests follow. Mix and match according to your interests and time constraints, or follow a given itinerary from start to finish. The possibilities are endless. Happy travels!

SUGGESTED ITINERARIES

With the *Pacific Northwest Travel•Smart* guidebook you can plan a trip of any length—a one-day excursion, a getaway weekend, or a three-week vacation—around any special interest. To get you started, the following pages contain six suggested itineraries geared toward a variety of interests. For more information, refer to the chapters listed—chapter names are bolded and chapter numbers appear inside black bullets. You can follow a suggested itinerary in its entirety, or shorten, lengthen, or combine parts of each, depending on your starting and ending points.

Discuss alternative routes and schedules with your travel companions—it's a great way to have fun, even before you leave home. And remember: don't hesitate to change your itinerary once you're on the road. Careful study and planning ahead of time will help you make informed decisions as you go, but spontaneity is the extra ingredient that will make your trip memorable.

© John Elk III

The Oregon Coast with Mt. Humbug

Highlights of the Northwest Tour

It would take three weeks to spin through this itinerary. But if a driving tour is what you're after, this gives you the best of sights and scenery.

❼ Vancouver (Stanley Park, Robson Street, Granville Island, Museum of Anthropology)

❹ Victoria (Butchart Gardens, Royal British Columbia Museum, the Empress Hotel, Government Street)

❽ San Juan Islands

❾ Bellingham and Northwest Washington (North Cascades National Park)

❿ Leavenworth (Cascade Loop Drive, Lake Chelan)

❶ Seattle (Pike Place Market, Seattle Art Museum, Ballard Locks, Museum of Flight)

❷ Olympic Peninsula (Hurricane Ridge, Port Townsend, Hoh Rain Forest, Cape Flattery)

⓰ Oregon Coast (Oregon Dunes National Monument, Oregon Coast)

⓲ Portland (Oregon Zoo, Japanese Garden, Oregon History Museum, Portland Art Museum, Columbia River Gorge Loop, Maryhill Museum)

Time needed: 3 weeks

Nature Lovers' Tour

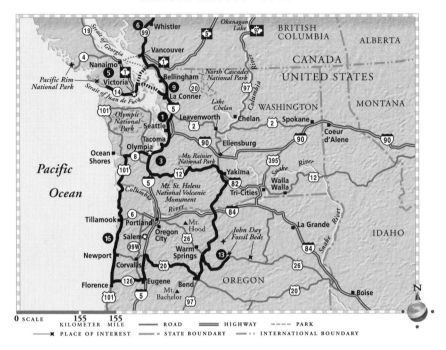

Nature lovers can be happy just about anywhere in the Northwest. Here are some high-interest destinations.

❻ Whistler (Brackendale Eagle Tours)

❺ Cowichan Valley and Up-Island (Pacific Rim National Park)

❾ Bellingham and Northwest Washington (Whalewatching boat tours from Bellingham and La Connor)

❶ Seattle (Seattle Aquarium, whalewatching boat tours from Everett)

❸ Tacoma and Mt. Rainier (Nisqually Delta)

⑯ Oregon Coast (Oregon Coast Aquarium in Newport, Oregon Dunes National Recreation Area in Florence)

⑬ Central Oregon (John Day Fossil Beds)

Time needed: 2 weeks

Arts and Culture Tour

Opportunities to enjoy arts and culture are concentrated in the larger cities; out-of-the-way exceptions are noted here as well.

⑦ Vancouver (Granville Islands artisan studios, Vancouver Art Gallery, Museum of Anthropology)

⑤ Cowichan Valley and Up-Island (Chemainus Island history in murals)

④ Victoria (Royal British Columbia Museum)

① Seattle (Seattle Art Museum, Seattle Asian Art Museum, Henry Art Gallery, Museum of Flight)

③ Tacoma and Mt. Rainier (Tacoma Art Museum, Washington State History Museum, Broadway Performing Arts Center)

⑱ Portland (Portland Art Museum, Maryhill Museum on the Columbia Gorge)

⑮ Willamette Valley (End of the Oregon Trail Interpretive Center)

⑬ Central Oregon (High Desert Museum, the Museum at Warm Springs)

⑫ Washington's Wine Country (Yakama Reservation Museum, Toppenish history in murals)

Time needed: 2 weeks

Family Fun Tour

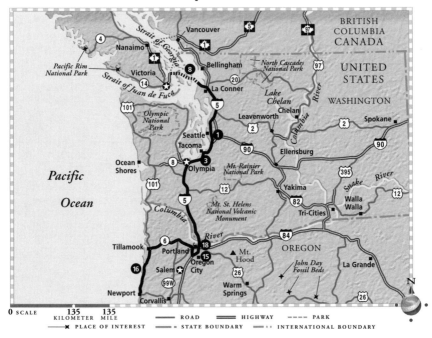

Many of the Northwest's outdoor activities—boating, hiking, beach exploring—are fun for the whole family. Here are some special stops that will please folks in all age groups.

❽ San Juan Islands (ferry rides, whalewatching, kayaking, and canoeing)

❶ Seattle (Seattle Center, Hiram M. Chittenden Locks, Museum of Flight Woodland Park Zoo)

❸ Tacoma and Mt. Rainier (Point Defiance Zoo and Aquarium, Northwest Trek Wildlife Park, Children's Museum of Tacoma)

⑱ Portland (Oregon Zoo, Oregon Museum of Science and Industry)

⑮ Willamette Valley (End of the Oregon Trail Interpretive Center in Oregon City)

⑯ Oregon Coast (Oregon Coast Aquarium, Tillamook cheese factory)

Time needed: 10 days

Wine Regions Tour

The wine regions of Oregon, Washington, and British Columbia are magnets for good living. The balmy-to-hot summer weather in the areas of the Willamette, Yakima, Columbia, and Okanagan valleys, as well as the recreation and food choices you'll find here, make for richly varied destinations.

❾ Bellingham and Northwest Washington (Nooksack Valley)

❼ Vancouver (International Wine Festival, wineries)

❺ Cowichan Bay and Up-Island (small wineries with tasting rooms)

❹ Victoria (wine festival)

❽ San Juan Islands (winery on Lopez Island)

❶ Seattle (wineries on Whidbey Island and around Seattle)

⓬ Washington's Wine Country (Yakima Valley, Columbia Valley/Tri-Cities area, Walla-Walla tours and wine festivals)

⓯ Willamette Valley (valley wineries, Oregon Wine Tasting Room)

⓮ Medford, Ashland, and Southwestern Oregon (wineries in Roseburg)

Time needed: 10 days

Summertime Mountaintop Tour

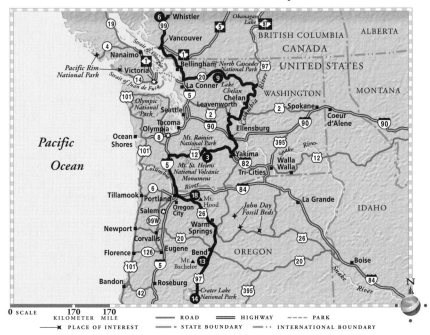

Touring the mountaintops of the Northwest in summer offers great views and a different way to look at the mountains. It's also a treat for non-skiers. Atop many mountains, you'll still find patches of snow, even at the height of summer. The roads down many of these slopes are favorites with mountain bikers.

- **Whistler** (horseback riding and hikes to Harmony Lake on Whistler Mountain, hikes through wildflowers on nearby Blackbob Mountain)
- **Bellingham and Northwest Washington** (Mt. Baker's Artist Point, hikes and interpretive center at Heather Meadows)
- **Tacoma and Mt. Rainier** (Mt. Rainier's classic Paradise Lodge with restaurant and lodging)
- **Portland** (Mt. Hood, with classic Timberline Lodge restaurant and lodging, Mt. St. Helens volcanic monument and interpretive center)
- **Central Oregon** (bicycling or in-line skating down Mt. Bachelor)
- **Medford, Ashland, and Southwestern Oregon** (boat tours of Crater Lake, Crater Lake Lodge)

Time needed: 2 weeks

USING THE PLANNING MAP

A major aspect of itinerary planning is determining your mode of transportation and the route you will follow as you travel from destination to destination. The Planning Map on the following pages will allow you to do just that.

First, read through the destination chapters carefully and note the sights that intrigue you. Then, photocopy the Planning Map so you can try out several different routes that will take you to these destinations. (The mileage chart that follows will help you to calculate your travel distances.) Decide where you will be starting your tour of the Pacific Northwest. Will you fly into Seattle, Portland, or Vancouver, or will you start from somewhere in between? Will you be driving from place to place or flying into major transportation hubs and renting a car for day trips? The answers to these questions will form the basis for your travel route design.

Once you have a firm idea of where your travels will take you, copy your route onto one of the additional Planning Maps in the Appendix. You won't have to worry about where your map is, and the information you need on each destination will always be close at hand.

Crystal Garden

The Pacific Northwest abounds with wildlife.

Pacific Northwest

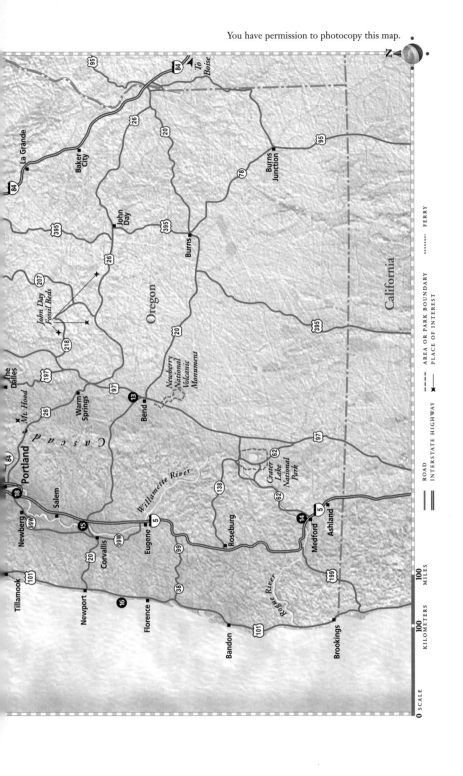

PACIFIC NORTHWEST MILEAGE CHART

	Seattle	Port Townsend	Vancouver, BC	Whistler, BC	Tacoma	Bellingham	Yakima	Spokane	Bend	John Day	Ashland	Crater Lake	Eugene	Brookings	Portland
Port Townsend	60														
Vancouver, BC	140	130													
Whistler, BC	210	200	70												
Tacoma	31	87	174	244											
Bellingham	88	78	52	122	122										
Yakima	142	194	273	343	166	223									
Spokane	278	331	412	482	303	360	205								
Bend	325	364	468	538	296	416	219	384							
John Day	408	461	541	611	433	490	267	329	153						
Ashland	466	504	609	679	437	557	478	644	196	349					
Crater Lake	424	463	567	637	395	515	325	489	104	257	104				
Eugene	289	328	432	502	261	380	301	467	115	250	182	140			
Brookings	525	564	668	738	497	616	537	703	297	486	147	205	241		
Portland	170	208	313	383	141	261	185	351	158	285	289	247	112	348	
Astoria	174	188	317	386	145	265	222	445	252	379	393	351	216	340	97

WHY VISIT THE PACIFIC NORTHWEST?

The Pacific Northwest is home to Microsoft and Starbucks, Boeing and Nike, the Dawgs and the Ducks, the venerated Oregon Shakespeare Festival, Vancouver's sparkling contemporary Ford Centre—and much, much more.

Whether you come in summer to cruise the San Juan Islands, hike the West Coast Trail, or golf the plethora of courses around Bend; or in winter to cross-country ski the Bavarian-style village of Leavenworth, snowboard the slopes of Mt. Hood, or spend a Dickensian Christmas eating plum pudding and sipping tea in Victoria, you'll find a richly complex region with diverse arts, ethnic groups, landscapes, and options that excite the imagination. This is, after all, where cultures as ancient as the legend-rich native peoples, and as forward-looking as Bill Gates' software universe, merge.

Yes, it rains here. That's why much of the region is a delicious, emerald green. And why storm-watching is a favorite wintertime sport. Yes, you might face congested roads or long ferry lines to reach the gem destinations dotting the thousands of miles of saltwater coastline. That's what keeps those spots quiet and delightfully low-key much of the year.

These few drawbacks are simple reminders that here Nature rules. Strictures of weather and terrain are part of the trade-off for a vast, masterful blueprint that melds forests, waters, mountains, deserts, volcanoes, and creatures—from eagles to orcas—in a vital, awe-inspiring way. Bona fide Northwesterners, be they transplants or natives, happily adjust. Besides, if it gets too wet or crowded on the coastal side of the region, you can always head east to the dry, less populated side. And if you really don't want to wait in a ferry line, you can hop a float plane to your waterfront destination and arrive in minutes rather than hours. There are choices.

Oregon, Washington, and British Columbia have plenty of them. They also have more in common than their coastal connection and the watery swath of the mighty Columbia River. Erase the international boundary and you'll find a cohesive region where breathtaking mountains crisscrossed with trails, rise high in the Cascades and Coastal Mountain ranges. You'll find a region where fishing villages lie on saltwater bays and elaborate wine regions perfume fertile, produce-rich valleys. The bounty of all this inspires the work of talented chefs and provides succulent menu choices in the grandest restaurants or the simplest cafés.

And last, but perhaps most important, you'll find people, born here or drawn here from many other parts of the world, who love this place passionately.

So, naturally, come visit. But be forewarned. There's so much to see that even those of us who've been here all our lives—and try to see and experience everything we can—can't see it all. The following chapters and suggested itineraries on pages 3 to 8 will help you choose the best from all that's here.

HISTORY AND CULTURES

The first people to come to the Northwest walked across a bridge of land from Siberia when the continents were connected north of the Bering Strait. And that was thousands and thousands of years ago. They survived the Ice Age and the volcanic turmoil of the region. They thrived on fish, berries, and roots, made utensils of shells, wove baskets of bark and reeds, and built shelters and canoes of wood. They worshipped the mountains, the creatures, and the bounty of the land, and passed on their history and values in their legends. While there were many tribes, there were basically two groups. Those who lived in relatively stable communities along the rivers and shores west of the Cascade Mountains and were a fishing people; and those of the interior plateau, who adopted use of the horse and were more nomadic like the Plains tribes. The largest group in the region lived along the coast.

Signs of the native peoples—now commonly referred to as Native Americans in the States and First Peoples or First Nation in Canada—are visible all over the Northwest. You'll see totem poles of the Northwest coast peoples pointing toward the heavens in wilderness areas and cities of the coastal regions, particularly of British Columbia. The whole town of Duncan, on Vancouver Island, is an outdoor museum to the totem pole; at the excellent Cowichan Native Village, you can often see totem carvers at work, as well as knitters making the prized Cowichan sweaters. British settlers taught the Cowichans to knit their fisherman-style sweater in one piece, and over time the knitters added designs, like animals or snowflakes, to individualize the natural, rustic, and very warm garments.

You'll see teepees, signs of the lifestyle of the interior plateau peoples, at the Yakama and Warm Springs reservations. Visitors can camp in these native-style dwellings on both reservations.

There are noted collections of art and artifacts not to be missed by the serious student, especially at the Museum at Warm Springs reservation in Oregon, the University of British Columbia's Museum of Anthropology in Vancouver, and the Royal B.C. Museum in Victoria. There are also outstanding tribal heritage centers on reservations, like those of the Makah at the northwest tip of the Olympic Peninsula, and the Yakama in eastern Washington. And there are many other displays, exhibits, galleries, and events around the region, some of which are mentioned in upcoming pages. You'll also see the modern gaming casinos of the tribes, which range from modest structures to very elaborate complexes with restaurants and art stores.

While the native peoples revere traditions, they are very much of the modern world. Examples of this are the brightly colored lithographs, artwork, and innovative glass work you will see. One of the most stunning examples of modern native art is the *Spirit of Haida Gwaii*, by the late Canadian artist Bill Reid. The sculpture of a large canoe is filled with legendary creatures of Haida mythology more often found on totems—Raven, Eagle, Grizzly, Mouse Woman, Beaver, Frog, and Wolf. It is located in the new Vancouver International Airport, and worth a trip whether you are flying or not. Books of all sorts have been written about the history of the Northwest's native peoples and their totems, masks, basketry, fishing, customs, and legends. See "Recommended Reading" on pages 27 through 29 for starters.

While the native peoples' heritage goes back centuries, white settlement came recently—in the last few hundred years. In 1778 British Captain James Cook explored the coast of what is now Oregon, Washington, and British Columbia. Captain George Vancouver charted Puget Sound in 1792, and that same year the American Captain Robert Gray arrived at the mouth of the Columbia River and named the river after his ship. In 1803 Lewis and Clark charted the way west, opening it for thousands to follow along the Oregon Trail. Then gold had its impact on many communities. The Fraser Canyon Gold Rush brought droves of miners north from the fields of California in the 1850s as well as from other parts of the globe, and the Klondike Gold Rush of the late 1890s made wealthy merchants out of Seattle provisioners and set the community on a road of future growth and prosperity.

The Chinese who labored on the railroads and in the fishing industry established residential and commerical districts in Vancouver,

Victoria, Seattle, and Portland; most still thrive. You can still see the homes of wealthy English sea captains and merchants who built picturesque homes in the oldest Oregon and Washington seaports of Astoria and Coupeville; and the influences of Scandinavian settlers who formed the fishing village of Poulsbo on the Kitsap Peninsula west of Seattle. Dutch dairy farmers settled Ferndale and Lynden in northwest Washington; Scots came to farm the Willamette Valley, bringing names like Dundee to their new settlements; the Basques brought sheep and their cuisine to eastern Oregon. All imprinted their cultures on the region. There are the more recent migrations—the Japanese who brought their horticulture techniques, the Hispanics who arrived in the 1930s and '40s and worked the newly irrigated fields of the interior, and prosperous Chinese from Hong Kong into Vancouver and other parts of British Columbia. These examples don't encompass everyone, but certainly show the rich ethnic diversity here.

And then there's the modern-day culture creature produced by the region itself: the quintessential Northwesterner. Here's a thumbnail sketch. He or she has at least one pair of hiking boots and a knapsack (from REI), fishing gear in the closet, well-worn gardening gloves, a favorite neighborhood restaurant hangout (too many to list), stacks of books around the house from a favorite bookstore (Powell's in Portland, Elliott Bay in Seattle, Munro's in Victoria, or Duthie's in Vancouver), a four-wheel-drive vehicle, and owns or is friends with someone who owns a sail- or motorboat. And despite all this outdoorsy stuff, there could be formal wear in the closet to attend arts and philanthropic functions. The best kind of Northwesterner is a Renaissance person making the most of this Renaissance region.

THE ARTS

Music, dance, theater, and the visual arts thrive in this environment of natural beauty. Special museums—the Seattle Art Museum, designed by Robert Venturi; the Vancouver Art Gallery with its collection of Emily Carr paintings; unique Maryhill Museum, overlooking the Columbia River with its unexpected Auguste Rodin sculptures; and the Northwest Museum in LaConner, Washington, focusing on Northwest School artists Mark Tobey, Morris Graves, and others—all contribute to the rich fabric of the region. Notable Northwest artists include glass artist Dale Chihuly of Tacoma, whose work is exhibited all over the world, including the Louvre. The new

International Glass Museum, to open in 2000 in his hometown, will showcase his art.

Besides glass, a lesser known specialty of the region is the work of Northwest woodcrafters. It is considered some of the finest in the world. In woodworking galleries in Portland, Seattle, and smaller towns, you will see one-of-a-kind pieces crafted primarily from maple, walnut, and cherry. Styles spring from classics like Shaker, Craftsman, Asian, and Scandinavian furniture, or are a product of the artist's vision, like sculpted figures or organically designed shapes. The Northwest Gallery of Fine Woodworking, a Seattle area cooperative, is considered to be the most successful cooperative in the country, exhibiting such artisans as David Gray, Judith Ames, Hank Holzer, Michael Peterson, and Thomas Stangeland, to name a few of the hundred or so Northwest craftsmen who exhibit here and elsewhere.

There are also excellent painters, potters, and artisans. Many gravitate to small towns along the Oregon coast, to central Oregon around Bend, or to Puget Sound, the San Juans, and the Gulf Islands. You will find galleries and evidence of the artists' work (and open houses or art tours at different times of the year) when you visit these areas. Granville Island is unique in that it is a whole community of top craftsmen and artisans' studios, along with the prestigious Emily Carr Institute of Art and Design, in the midst of urban Vancouver, British Columbia. Another surprise is the eastern Oregon town of Joseph, where three foundries make bronze and other metal sculptures for patrons around the world.

Live theater is also dynamic—perhaps in Seattle most of all, but also in Vancouver, Tacoma, Portland, and Ashland (home to the Oregon Shakespeare Festival). And there are many community theaters. There are dance companies here—like the Pacific Northwest Ballet in Seattle—and music of all kinds.

CUISINE

Too much food, too little time. You won't believe all the wonderful food experiences there are to be had in the Northwest! You'll just have to taste-test yourself. Food folks debate the issue of whether or not there is a "Northwest Cuisine." There is. In my view, it's based on bountiful seafood, fresh (often organic) produce, simplicity, and preparations that include specialties of the region—like salmon, Dungeness crab, mushrooms, and Walla Walla sweet onions. Asian overtones are common. For years running, the Wild Ginger restaurant, near Pike Place Market in Seattle, with its satay bar and creative Pan-Asian menu, has topped the list of favorites for locals and visitors alike. And Vancouver's food scene, recently enriched with an infusion of talented chefs from Hong Kong, makes Chinese food a must-have on any visit. In Northwest cities and increasingly in rural areas there's a rich pool of culinary talent and a growing variety of restaurants. Your only problem will be deciding what kind of food you want to experience.

To get the best the region has to offer, here are some hints. Be prepared to indulge yourself in seafood. The salmon, prepared simply for centuries over outdoor fires, is still best grilled, although most restaurants offer it poached or baked as well. Dungeness crab is sweet and succulent and with a little butter, heavenly; Penn Cove mussels in a simple garlic wine broth (for dipping crusty bread) can often be found in haute cuisine restaurants and on modest bar menus. Then there's the mysterious and strange-looking geoduck (pronounced "gooey duck")—if you see it on the menu, try it. Do you like its sur- prising sweetness? Ditto on the elusive razor clams, which are usually breaded and lightly sautéed. Their season is random and short so try them when you can. And finally, oysters—dozens of varieties ranging from sweet tiny Olympias to earthy European Flats—are all raised in waters that are cool and remarkably clean. There are plenty of oyster bars (you'll find the most in Seattle) where they are shucked fresh and served with regional microbrews (Portland is the capital of brews) and wines (see "Wine Regions Tour" on page 7). Note, too, that seafood vendors will often ship their product around the country; Pike Place Market fishmongers are known for this.

Then consider menu choices that include other of the region's classics. The cheeses: Oregon blue, Bandon's cheddar, Tillamook Vin- tage Reserve (white and gold cheddars), Cougar Gold—that scrump- tious, nutty white cheddar–like cheese produced by Washington State University's creamery—and the handcrafted goat or sheep's cheese made by artisans like Sally Jackson in Washington and David Wood of Saltspring Island. The specialty produce: hazelnuts from the Willamette Valley, lamb from Ellensburg in Central Washington, and salmon candy and farmed venison in British Columbia.

The fruit? Washington apples, Rainier cherries, pears from the Hood River Valley, peaches from British Columbia's Okanagan Valley, grapes from the Yakima and Columbia Valleys, cranberries from coastal bogs, and other berries from lush growing areas all over, abound.

To get the best of the region, ask your server "What's fresh? What's in season?"

FLORA AND FAUNA

From sea kelp and tide pool critters to high mountain wildflowers and eagles, the nature lover has plenty to see. There are rain forests draped with moss and wetlands crowded with birds, verdant sedge-rich deltas and sagebrush-dotted high deserts. The mix of climate and soils here makes this the best place in the world for conifers to grow. And fortunes as well as houses have been built with Douglas fir, cedar, and pine. So many, in fact, that there are few old-growth trees left, and certain ones, like those in Campbell Grove near Lake Quinault Lodge on the Olympic Peninsula, have become tourist destinations in themselves. In spring, showy rhododendrons fill home and public gardens alike. In fall, deciduous maple trees and blueberry bushes turn the dark green forests brilliant red and gold, and the highways near spots like Tumwater Canyon outside Leavenworth in Washington's Cascades become thick with leaf-lookers.

LAY OF THE LAND

Surprise. A preponderance of mountains and evergreens is what you'll notice most about the Northwest, especially if you fly into Portland past Mt. Hood, into Seattle by Mt. Rainier, or into Vancouver with Mt. Baker and Grouse Mountain in sight. Two ranges, the Coastal Range in British Columbia and the Cascades (divided into the North and South Cascades) in Washington and Oregon, dominate. Other ranges include the impressive Olympic Mountains and Oregon Coast Range and the Blue Mountains.

The Puget/Willamette Trough separates the two major coastal mountain chains. It's made up of the Hecate Strait and the Strait of Georgia in British Columbia; Puget Sound in Washington; the Chehalis and Cowlitz River valleys in Washington; and the Willamette River in Oregon. Coastline and waterways dominate our way of life in this part of the Northwest. Lush temperate rain forests cloak the western side of the region. By contrast, the interior is a desert plateau, a basin of sometimes harsh and haunting landscape. And yet here, too, water—especially the Columbia River—has its impact.

With one side of the region very wet and one very dry, the yin and yang quality of the Northwest is underscored. Despite its extreme differences, or perhaps because of them, there is harmony, there is balance here.

OUTDOOR ACTIVITIES

If you don't bring your hiking boots to hit a trail, or plan to paddle a boat, or explore the back country of the region, you're missing the true personality of the Northwest. Skiing, snowboarding, and wind-surfing—particularly on the Columbia Gorge and Howe Sound in British Columbia—are more vigorous options that offer devotees some peak experiences. Kayaking the Cascadia MarineTrail (a 150-plus-mile route from South Puget Sound to Canada), is growing in popularity as more camping sites are established along the way. Bicycling (or moped-ing in the San Juans) is a perfect way to explore the islands here. A visit to the Kite Flying Museum at Long Beach, Washington, may draw you into a sport that attracts thousands to the Kite Flying Festival there each summer. Or you may opt for a ride in a rainbow-colored hot air balloon over the vineyards of the Northwest.

Government facilities throughout the region—state and provincial park offices, National Park Service and Forest Service offices—provide maps and valuable tips and information. If the outdoors is a new world for you, Recreational Equipment, Inc. (REI), a cooperative with stores around the country, has long been the place to get outdoor information and gear and to connect with knowledgeable people. Their impressive flagship store in Seattle, with biking trails and an indoor rock climbing facility, is an easy, one-stop way to explore outdoor options and learn of classes, programs, or tours.

And finally, there's gardening. It may be the most common out-door activity in the Northwest. Public gardens, seed and bulb growers, and terrific nurseries are scattered around the region. Victoria's Butchart Garden and the International Rose Test Garden in Portland may be the most famous, but there are many others, including estate gardens, like Lakewold in Tacoma and the Bloedell Reserve on Bain-bridge Island, that are open to the public. Large bulb-growing areas lie near Salem, Oregon, for iris, dahlia, and tulip bulbs, and near Mt. Vernon and LaConner, Washington, for tulip and daffodil bulbs. Each year in February, thousands of garden fanciers descend upon the impressive Pacific Northwest Flower and Garden Show at Seattle's Washington State Convention Center.

PRACTICAL TIPS

Nice hotel rooms in Portland, Seattle, and Vancouver average around $150 per night. Luxury hotels cost more, as do fancy B&Bs. Many B&Bs offer less expensive rooms (often with shared bath), and of course include breakfast. Choosing hotel packages or off-season times to visit can considerably reduce costs. Many chain or budget choices are well located in all three areas. Your dollar may stretch further in British Columbia as the exchange rate at publication time is about $1.40 Canadian for $1 U.S. However, in British Columbia expect to pay goods and services tax (GST), which will be reimbursed at border offices (or by mail) if you keep your receipts and submit them with a completed reimbursement form. There is no sales tax in Oregon. In Washington it's about 8.6 percent, but varies by county.

Summer camping cuts costs, and there are hostels as well, or you can choose to stay in suburban areas with chain lodging, rather than in pricier urban areas. You can also save by coming off season. Vancouver has its Entertainment Season from October to April when hotels offer better rates and Seattle has its Super Saver season about the same time. Many fine city and resort hotels have weekend packages that offer extra value. Food is available in a wide range of prices. Thai, Mexican, Japanese, and Chinese restaurants offer good value for families. Inexpensive quick meals can be had at food fairs in city shopping malls.

CLIMATE

We've agreed that it rains here. But that's only half true. In the Northwest, it rains most on the coastal, temperate side of the region, particularly in winter. Summer temperatures on the coastal side average in the 70s; very hot weather is a rarity. The interior, eastern side of the region is dry, with extremes of temperature, and most of the precipitation comes in the form of snow. Winter temperatures slip into the teens and summer highs can top 100 degrees Fahrenheit.

All the mountains and valleys combine to produce weather patterns and result in sometimes quirky and unexpected climate differences. The Hoh Rain Forest on the Olympic Peninsula is the wettest place in Washington; nearby Sequim, a popular and growing area for retirees, is the driest spot west of the mountains. It rains more in Vancouver than in Seattle and Portland.

WHEN TO GO

What's your pleasure? Summer or winter activities? The Northwest is a year-round destination. July is the busiest month for the ferry system, and with the odds high for good weather you can encounter hordes of summer travelers in the most popular haunts. July and August are the hottest months in the region's interior; consistent temperatures in the 90s are not uncommon. These are favorite months for boat charters, and the busiest in the American San Juans and Canadian Gulf Islands. It's always a good idea to check for special regional events that draw thousands of visitors to an area, like Portland's Rose Festival and Vancouver's Jazz Festival in June, and Seattle's Seafair in July and early August.

April, May, September, and October can have surprisingly good weather in many parts of the region and fewer crowds. These are particularly good times to visit the wine regions with spring barrel tastings in April, and harvest festivals in September or October.

TRANSPORTATION

There are three major international airports—Sea-Tac (halfway between Seattle and Tacoma in Washington), Portland, and Vancouver. Depending upon your objectives, there are many ways to plan your trip. Visiting just major cities? Then you can easily get around without a car, as long as you like walking and are willing to adapt to the transit systems. Amtrak's route offers a scenic tour from Portland to Vancouver, B.C. Portland has a light rail system (you ride free downtown), and Vancouver B.C. has an equivalent Sky Train. It's free to ride Seattle's bus system (Metro) downtown, and the Monorail takes you from downtown to Seattle Center. To do a city tour without a car you can fly in to Sea-Tac (Seattle-Tacoma), Portland, or Vancouver airports, then take a shuttle into the city. You can also ferry or fly (floatplane, helijet, or small plane) to Victoria.

Interstate 5 offers the quickest (though straight-as-an-arrow at times) route from the California border to the Canadian border. U.S. Highway 101 is the two-lane route along the coastline of Washington, Oregon, and British Columbia (the Sunshine Coast). It is scenic and slow as it meanders through small towns, dead-ending—or, you could say, beginning—at the tiny, picturesque village of Lund, a jumping-off point to the wilds of Desolation Sound.

FERRIES AND FLOATPLANES

The ferry and floatplane systems of Washington and British Columbia are unique in North America—both are a way to travel and a pleasurable experience in themselves.

While the Washington State Ferries and the B.C. Ferries are North America's biggest ferry fleets, there are private ferry systems (best known is the *Victoria Clipper*, with regular service between Seattle and Victoria) that offer tour services as well as transportation; they may charge more, but they also offer more conveniences—advance booking, lodging packages, connections with sightseeing cruises (like whale-watching trips), special seasonal trips, and ground transportation between ports.

You'll find that ferries come in all sizes: tiny foot ferries on Victoria Harbour and Vancouver's waterways; their somewhat larger siblings that carry 15 or so cars back and forth on short hops between small islands of the American San Juans and Canadian Gulf Islands; and the jumbo and super ferries of the B.C. Ferry System that ply the waters of the Georgia Strait and have dining rooms, gift stores, and computer stations. Ferries are a culture in themselves.

Using the ferry systems in the Northwest can make you a bit frantic, particularly if you aren't used to it. It demands you plan ahead, hurry up, then wait. And, finally, once you are aboard you must *relax*, whether you want to or not. It's best to develop a special mindset for taking the ferries.

While July is the busiest season on all runs, you can encounter a long ferry line at any time of year—on popular weekend runs, when there's a special event, or on the last run of the day. Missing a ferry after you've cut short your visit somewhere, pushed the speed limit, and gotten cranky with your kids can only double your frustration. Don't let it make you crazy. Always, always carefully check the ferry schedule (available from toll takers and at terminals). Weekday and weekend schedules often differ. Don't assume anything about the schedule, unless you are very familiar with it.

Whenever you can, plan ahead. And make reservations whenever possible. Plan to make reservations for B.C. Ferries trips to the Southern Gulf Islands, up the Inside Passage, on the new Discovery Coast passage to Bella Coola, and for cars boarding Washington State Ferries from the San Juan Islands to Sydney, British Columbia.

On the larger vessels, on all but the stormiest days, the ride is so smooth that the sound of the engines could lull you to sleep. However, if it's a gorgeous sunny day, the eye-popping scenery will keep you glued to the windows or lead you on deck into the hair-ruffling breezes.

Foot passengers and cyclists load first and have the advantage over motorists, who can get left behind at the dock when the ferry is full. Whenever possible avoid commuter runs—the busiest are between Vancouver and Swartz Bay (Vancouver Island), Seattle and Bainbridge, and north of Seattle between Edmonds and Kingston, and Mutilteo and Clinton (on Whidbey Island). Friday evening and Saturday morning traffic is heaviest westbound, and Sunday afternoon traffic is heaviest eastbound. Food service aboard varies according to the size of ship and length of run; usually shorter and faster runs have the basics— sandwiches, fruits, yogurts, and beverages. Longer runs often have full-service restaurants. If you bring pets, plan to keep them in the car, on a leash, or in carriers in outside cabin areas of Washington State Ferries. On B.C. Ferries vessels, pets must remain on the car deck.

Commuting by floatplane is one way Northwesterners get around the long ferry lines and time-consuming border crossings between Washington and British Columbia. Long a favorite way for sportsmen to reach land-locked lakes for fishing, this mode of travel has become increasingly popular in recent years. Like riding a ferry, the journey is an adventure in itself. Kenmore Air has two air harbors in Seattle, at the north end of Lake Washington and its busiest terminal at the southwest end of Lake Union. It runs daily scheduled flights to Victoria and the San Juan Islands. Harbour Air, in British Columbia, runs scheduled flights between Victoria and Vancouver. Sound Flight, whose terminal is at the south end of Lake Washington, offers specialty trips all over the Northwest. While it costs more to take a floatplane, it's like riding a magic carpet and can translate into an extra day's worth of time you won't spend to and from your destination in ferry lines.

CAMPING, LODGING, AND DINING

Remember I mentioned that the Northwest is full of choices? Well, when it comes to sleeping and eating, that goes double. My favorites are the special places that have unique qualities all their own while reflecting the region as well. When it comes to "best sleeps" they range from mountain top camps, where your mattress is heather and your fellow travelers may be marmots and eagles, to posh grand hotels with turn-down service, chocolates, and a down pillow to sink into at the end of the day.

For generations the Benson in Portland, the Olympic Four Seasons in Seattle, the Hotel Vancouver, and the Empress in Victoria have hosted the world's traveling elite and provided meeting spots for their communities' memorable moments. Thankfully, these grand hotels have been carefully updated or renovated so that much of their original glory is intact. Some of their restaurants and watering holes are legendary—the London Grill (Benson), the Georgian Room (Olympic), the Bengal Room (Empress)—and lend a sense of "occasion" to simply meeting a friend for drinks. Although new in 1989, the scale and presence of the Chateau Whistler will soon put it in this category.

There are also individualized inns and properties that have a "grand" reputation. Sooke Harbor House, west of Victoria, has been called one of the world's best B&Bs. And Salishan Lodge on the Oregon Coast wins award after award as well as the affection of a legion of guests.

I also have a great fondness for the region's genteel "secret" hotels—those stalwarts that may have dated furnishings but are always booked because generations of families return again and again appreciating the location, value, and convenience: the Mallory in Portland, the Camlin in Seattle, the Sylvia overlooking English Bay in Vancouver.

Camping options abound. There are many beautiful and amenity-rich state, national, and provincial parks with a variety of options ranging from drive-in, numbered sites with RV hookups, showers, bathrooms, and picnic tables nearby, to more spartan sites for backpackers. Some of the prettiest are along the Oregon, Washington, and British Columbia coastlines, and in the Cascade Mountains. Costs average $10 per night; reservations are often required and trail passes are required for hikers. Then, in Washington, there are the more primitive Department of Natural Resources (DNR) sites where you must pack in your water, pack out your garbage, and leave the site as if you had never been there. These offer unique remote wilderness experiences at no cost. New yurt tent camps are offered in Oregon and Washington by reservation—many at beach sites—that let you camp without taking along a lot of gear.

A very special type of camping is offered along the The Cascadia Marine Trail, an award-winning water route for kayaks, canoes, and other beachable wind- or human-powered craft. It runs from the south end of Puget Sound to the Canadian border (with plans to extend into

Canada). There are more than 40 sites along the current 140-mile route, and many are quite primitive.

WHAT TO BRING

Remember that Eddie Bauer, REI, and Nordstrom dress the Northwest. Business meetings aside, nice casual—i.e., khaki slacks, shirt, or blouse and/or sweater—will be just fine in all but the most elegant restaurants and private clubs or events, such as fancy theater, ballet, or symphony performances—although you'll see casually dressed folks even then. Jeans (or shorts) and casual shirts or T-shirts are typical knocking-around garb for most daytime activities.

Because the weather is changeable, layering is always a good strategy. A lightweight turtleneck or T-shirt, with blouse or shirt, sweater, and light jacket can handle most changes in temperature on the coastal side of the region. The layering advice is even more important if you are planning a hike or a high altitude visit (to Mt. Rainier, Whistler, or Mt. Hood). Never assume that because it's sunny and beautiful when you start out that you shouldn't take extra clothing. The reverse is true as well. Summer days can begin overcast and by midday be blistering, so don't forget your sunglasses and sunscreen. So for town touring or back country exploring, think layers . . . and appropriate footwear— hiking boots for the serious stuff and walking shoes or flat boots with ankle support to tour gardens, parks, and sometimes uneven city streets. Knapsacks, fannypacks, or backpacks are a good idea if you are comfortable wearing them.

Now a word about umbrellas. If you have a small packable one, by all means bring it. However, a rain hat or a rain coat with a hood is preferable to an umbrella if you're not used to carrying one. And if there's a real downpour, you may want to head for some shelter. If you especially want to walk in the rain—and yes, lots of us do want to— that's different. Even then, many public gardens and some hotels have umbrellas available to use during your visit.

CROSSING THE BORDER INTO CANADA

There are about a dozen border crossings into Canada from Washington state. The most active—open 24 hours—are at Blaine (Peach Arch and Pacific Highway crossings) and Sumas in western Washington, and Osoyoos in eastern Washington. If you plan to visit

Canada, keep a few things in mind before you leave home: Each adult needs proof of U.S. citizenship, (a passport, or a voter's registration card and a driver's license). Children should have picture ID or a birth certificate, and if not traveling with their legal guardians, a written authorization letter and contact number. Cats and dogs need a valid certificate indicating they've received a rabies shot within the last three years. Hand guns and weapons are not allowed. Call Canada Customs' public information line with questions, 604/666-0547.

You'll find duty-free stores at border crossings and on the Victoria Clipper and Princess Marguerite runs between Seattle and Victoria. These shops offer travelers staying longer than 48 hours savings on perfumes, liquor, and tobacco. Washington State Ferries takes U.S. cash and personal checks drawn on Washington banks; no credit cards. B.C. Ferries accepts travelers checks, U.S. and Canadian cash, Mastercard and VISA. Keep receipts of items purchased in Canada; when you return to the U.S. you can pick up a form at border crossings or duty-free shops to get a rebate of GST—a tax on most goods and services purchased during your 48-hour-plus visit.

RECOMMENDED READING

Reading is a popular Northwest pastime and bookstores are everywhere—in small towns and villages and large cities. Many shops have areas for reading and relaxing, and often coffee bars. They range from small specialty stores such as Flora & Fauna Books, a nature and garden book shop in Seattle's Pioneer Square, to renowned one-of-a-kind book worlds like Powell's in Portland. And like Powell's, certain bookstores come to mind when you think of cities: Seattle and Elliot Bay Book Company, Victoria and Munro's Books, Vancouver and Duthie's Books. There are also large chain stores like Borders, Barnes & Noble, and Chapters. Visit any one of these and you'll find plenty of books about the Northwest. Here are some suggestions of books that give you different perspectives.

Ice and volcanoes created our landscape. *Cataclysms on the Columbia*, by John Eliot Allen, Marjorie Burns, Sam C. Sargent (Timber Press, 1986), is a layman's guide to the features produced by the catastrophic Bretz Floods in the Pacific Northwest. And *Northwest Passage: The Great Columbia River*, by William Dietrich (Simon & Schuster, 1995), offers a grand tour of the many sides and forces of the Columbia River. *The Natural History of Puget Sound Country*, by Arthur R.

Kruckeberg, (University of Washington Press, 1991 and 1995), provides an understanding of the complexity of western Washington. *The Good Rain: Across Time and Terrain in the Pacific Northwest,* by Timothy Egan (Vintage Books, 1991), is a personal and political look at the environmental bounty of the Northwest. And *A Sierra Club Guide to the Natural Areas of Oregon & Washington,* by John Perry and Jane Greverus Perry (Sierra Club Books, 1983–1997), provides a practical guide for visitors.

The University of Washington Press in Seattle has published many books on the Northwest including histories and colorful pictorials, often of exhibits on Northwest native peoples (call 800/441-4115 for a catalog or to order books). Oregon State University Press, 541/737-3166, and Washington State University, 509/335-3564, also publish books on the Northwest.

A particularly impressive pictorial book that gives readers a look at a magnificent collection of art made by the Kwakiutl Indians of northern Vancouver Island is *Chiefly Feasts: The Enduring Kwakiutl Potlatch,* edited by Aldona Jonaitis (American Museum of Natural History, 1991). *Native Peoples of the Northwest: A Traveler's Guide to Land, Art, and Culture,* by Jan Halliday and Gail Chehak in cooperation with the affiliated tribes of Northwest Indians (Sasquatch Books, 1996; www.sasquatchbooks.com), is a useful and informative guide to learning about the native peoples as you travel the region. *Totem Poles,* by Canadian author Pat Kramer (Altitude Publishing Canada Ltd., 1995), is a 112-page handbook that looks at the origin, history, and symbols of totem poles.

Undaunted Courage: Meriwether Lewis, Thomas Jefferson, and the Opening of the American West, by Stephen E. Ambrose (Simon & Schuster, 1996), is a reconstruction of the journey from Meriwether Lewis' viewpoint. *Sons of the Profits,* by William C. Speidel (Nettle Creek Publishing Company, 1967), is an entertaining look at Seattle's founding fathers. *Puget's Sound,* by Murray Morgan (University of Wahsington Press, 1979), looks at the development of the southern Sound and Tacoma. And a very different and more recent pioneering journey of a different sort is told in *Dorothy Stimson Bullitt: An Uncommon Life,* by Delphine Haley (Sasquatch Books, 1995), the story of Seattle's legendary businesswoman who built and managed the king Broadcasting Company. She was dubbed "the Queen of KING" born in 1892 and died in 1989, a vigorous influence on the city till the end.

Good books to carry along to enrich your travel knowledge include *Garden Touring in the Pacific Northwest: A Guide to Gardens and*

Specialty Nurseries in Oregon, Washington and British Columbia, by Jan Kowalczewski Whitner (Alaska Northwest Books, 1993). Walking guides are helpful: like the *Footsore Books 1, 2, 3, 4: Walks and Hikes Around Puget Sound*, by Harvey and Penny Manning (The Mountaineers, 1990). *Walking Portland*, by Sybilla Avery Cook (Falcon, 1998), is a new book that looks at 30 walks that show off the historic neighborhoods and forested paths of Portland.

Golfers should check out the most recent edition of *Golf Courses of the Pacific Northwest: The Complete Regional Golf Guide*, by Jeff Shelley (Alaska Northwest Books, 1990). For fans of rustic architecture a new pictorial, *Great Lodges of the West*, by Christine Barnes (W.W. West, Inc., 1997), includes large photo sections on Paradise Lodge, Timberline Lodge, and Crater Lake Lodge.

A recent book, *The Wine Project: Washington State's Winemaking History*, by Ronald Irvine with Walter J. Clore (Sketch Publications, 1997) explores that subject. More practical pocket guides on wines and food help with dining choices, such as *Northwest Wines: A Pocket Guide to the Wines of Washington, Oregon & Idaho*, by Paul Gregutt and Jeff Prather (Sasquatch Books, 1994). The ever helpful Zagat Surveys: *Pacific Northwest Restaurants and Vancouver Restaurants* (the latest version you can get your hands on), are opinion polls by readers.

RESOURCES

Tourism Agencies
Oregon: Call Portland, Oregon, Visitors Association (POVA), 800/345-3214, for a free visitors guide. For an Oregon Travel Guide and Accommodations Guide, call 800/547-7842; or visit www.pova.com or www.traveloregon. com.
Washington: For a Washington State Lodging & Travel Guide, or to talk to a travel counselor, call 800/544-1800; or visit www.tourism.wa.gov.
British Columbia: Call 800/663-6000 for province information and lodging reservations. Visit Tourism Vancouver's Web site at www.tourismvancouver.org.

Parks
National Parks: Call National Parks and Forest Information, 800/280-2267 or 800/365-2267, for information and reservations.
State Parks Reservations: Reservations can be made up to 11 months

in advance for Washington and Oregon state parks by calling
800/452-5687.

Ferries and Tours
Washington State Ferries: The ferry system operates 10 routes in
the state, 206/464-6400 or 800/843-3779 (in Washington only).
Vehicle reservations, for international travel only, must be made at
least 24 hours prior to sailing.
British Columbia Ferries: Call 604/444-2890 for information; call
toll free in Canada, 888/724-5223, or visit at www.bcferries.bc.ca.
Grayline Tours: Call 800/426-7532, or visit www.sightseeing.com.

Culture and Entertainment
Native American information: Affiliated Tribes of Northwest Indi-
ans, 222 NW Davis, Suite 403, Portland, OR 97209; phone
503/241-0070, fax 503/241-0072.
Oregon microbreweries: For a booklet listing many Oregon microbreweries, contact Oregon Brewers Guild, 510 NW Third
Avenue, Portland, OR 97209; 503/295-1862, 800/440-2537;
www.oregonbeer.org/~beer.
Wineries: *Oregon*—Oregon Wine Advisory Board 1200 NW Naito
Parkway, Suite 400, Portland 97209; 503/228-8336 or 800/242-
2363 for free winery brochures; www.oregonwine.org.
Washington—For the Yakima Valley, call 800/258-7270; for the
Washington State Wine Center, call 206/667-9463, or visit
www.washingtonwine.org. *British Columbia*—For winery touring
information and map from Okanagan-Kelowna Info Centre, call
250/861-1515.
Bed-and-Breakfasts: *Border to Border Bed and Breakfast Directory*,
a 64-page brochure, lists 350 B&Bs (most in Oregon, some in
Washington); published by Moria Mountain Publishing,
P.O. Box 1283, Grants Pass, OR 97528; 800/841-5448;
www.moriah.com/inns. *1998 B.C. Bed and Breakfast Directory*,
published by Monday Publications, 1609 Blanshard Street,
Victoria, B.C. V8W 2J5; for information call 250/382-6188;
www.monday.com/tourism.

1

SEATTLE

Snowcapped mountain views, tangy salt air, and water, water everywhere. Add rain to the equation and you have the few things about
this virile Northwestern city that have remained constant over the last
150 years. When Seattle's forefathers arrived here in 1851 they were
reminded of another grand seaport in the east; they settled their townsite
and called it New York-Alki (adding a word that means "by-and-by" in
the native Chinook language). The name didn't stick, but today Seattle's
Fifth Avenue shops have the gloss and chic of that other Fifth Avenue.
And the city skyline is an impressive forest of skyscrapers—such as the
76-story Columbia Tower, which dwarfs the 42-story Smith Tower, the
fourth tallest building in the world when it was built in 1914.

Seattle is beginning to live like modern-day Manhattan, too.
Pricey condominiums web downtown. Dining out is a way of life for
city dwellers, restaurants are lively and varied, and new ones are crop-
ping up all the time. Richly diverse neighborhoods make up the fabric
of the city. Live theater abounds.

In the 1970s a Seattle architect Victor Steinbrueck and a group
called Allied Arts launched a vigorous effort to save historic Seattle.
Pike Place Market became the group's most visible cause. Since then,
what almost crumbled beneath a wrecking ball has become the heart
and pulse of the city. For if ever there was a poem to Seattle, to the
whole Northwest, it's here in the living and breathing daily life of Pike
Place Market, a haiku to the rich bounty of the land, the people, and
the sea that defines this region. ◼

SEATTLE

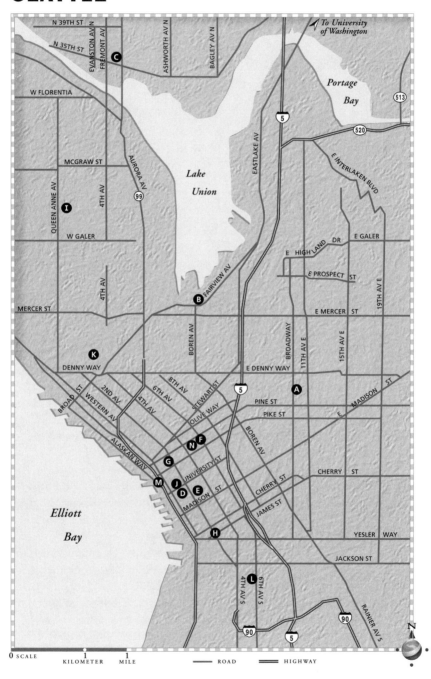

N 39TH ST
N 35TH ST
W FLORENTIA
MCGRAW ST
W GALER
MERCER ST
DENNY WAY
PINE ST
PIKE ST
UNIVERSITY ST
MADISON ST
JAMES ST
YESLER WAY
JACKSON ST

N 39TH ST N
EVANSTON AV N
FREMONT AV
ASHWORTH AV N
BAGLEY AV N
AURORA AV
QUEEN ANNE AV
4TH AV
4TH AV
BOREN AV
BROAD ST
WESTERN AV
2ND AV
4TH AV
6TH AV
8TH AV
STEWART ST
OLIVE WAY
ALASKAN WAY
BOREN AV
CHERRY ST
CHERRY ST
4TH AV S
6TH AV S
RAINIER AV S

EASTLAKE AV
FAIRVIEW AV
E HIGHLAND DR
E PROSPECT ST
E GALER
E MERCER ST
BROADWAY
11TH AV E
15TH AV E
19TH AV E
E INTERLAKEN BLVD
E DENNY WAY
E MADISON

To University of Washington

Portage Bay

Lake Union

Elliott Bay

Elliott Bay

513
520
99
5
5
5
90
90

0 SCALE   1   1
KILOMETER   MILE   ROAD ━━━ HIGHWAY ━━━

N

Sights

- **Ⓐ** Capitol Hill
- **Ⓑ** Center for Wooden Boats and Northwest Seaport
- **Ⓒ** Fremont
- **Ⓓ** Harbor Steps
- **Ⓔ** Metro Transit Tunnel
- **Ⓕ** Nordstrom
- **Ⓖ** Pike Place Market
- **Ⓗ** Pioneer Square
- **Ⓘ** Queen Anne Hill
- **Ⓙ** Seattle Art Museum
- **Ⓚ** Seattle Center
- **Ⓛ** Uwajimaya/International District
- **Ⓜ** Waterfront & Streetcar
- **Ⓝ** Westlake Center

A PERFECT DAY IN SEATTLE

Any day the sun shines is a perfect day in Seattle. Yet, rain or shine, the perfect way to begin your day in this bracing and bustling town is to start early, on foot, and head to Pike Place Market for breakfast. Soak in the action at this historic community within a city, then walk south along First Avenue to take in the Seattle Art Museum. From here amble down the Harbor Steps to the waterfront and explore. Then catch the trolley to Pioneer Square for a look at the historic business district, then on to the International District for Asian foods, goods, and herbalists. Take a Metro bus through the bus tunnel back to the center of town and get off at Westlake Center. Shop your way up the mall's four levels to the food fair and the Seattle Center Monorail. You can take this elevated train a mile north to the center, the home of the Space Needle and the Key Arena, where Seattle's Supersonics play.

If it's a wonderfully sunny day, cut your serious sightseeing in half and head to the waterfront—downtown, Lake Union, Green Lake, the Ballard Locks, or the beaches at either Alki or Golden Gardens. (Or hop a ferry to Bainbridge Island and sample the prettiest commute in the Northwest.) Laze in the sun or find a waterfront restaurant for something cold to drink, and plot your dinner destination. A half dozen restaurants along the Ship Canal from Fremont to Shilshole have outdoor view seating where you can watch the boat traffic as the sun sets.

GETTING AROUND SEATTLE

Although plans are in the works for a rapid transit system in Seattle, at present commuters who leave their cars at home rely primarily on Metro (Metropolitan Transit System) buses, 206/553-3000, to get around the city and to outlying areas.

Seattle's business district is bordered on the west by Elliott Bay. Pike Place Market District, along First Avenue, overlooks the waterfront and Highway 99 traffic on the raised Alaskan Way Viaduct. Ferries leave Seattle's waterfront (Washington State Ferries terminal is at Coleman Dock, Pier 52) to carry commuters west to Bainbridge Island and Bremerton on the Kitsap Peninsula.

Interstate 5 (running north and south) marks the east edge of downtown, separating it from Capitol Hill, First Hill, and the neighborhoods of Madison Park, Washington Park, and Leschi, which border Lake Washington. Seattle is connected to "the Eastside"—the largely upscale communities of Bellevue, Kirkland, Redmond, and Mercer Island—via two bridges: the Evergreen Point Floating Bridge (SR520) and the Mercer Island Floating Bridge (I-90). Traffic backs up during commute times (or when there's an accident) on these two bridges.

Lake Union and Queen Anne Hill lie to the North; the neighborhood of Magnolia is west of Queen Anne Hill. The waterway from Lake Washington to Puget Sound—along Montlake Cut, Portage Bay, Lake Union, and the Lake Washington Ship Canal—divides the city from the North End, which runs to the city limits.

At the south edge of the city is Pioneer Square, the International District, and the beginning of the Industrial area of town, which gets crowded during Mariners games at Safeco Stadium. Along the waterfront, south of downtown, is the Port of Seattle.

SIGHTSEEING HIGHLIGHTS

★★★★ **Bainbridge Island**—Frequent ferry runs make a visit to this island suburb a snap. Leave your car behind and you can explore antique shops, galleries, and eateries along Winslow Way and along Madison. You'll need to take your car to visit the **Bloedel Reserve,** a beautiful estate-turned-public-garden on the northwest part of the island. *Details: A half-hour ride fom Seattle's Pier 52 (Coleman Dock) puts you on the island. Reservations are required to visit Bloedel Reserve, call 206/842-7631. Admission is about $6. (5 hours)*

★★★★ **Fremont**—Crossing the bridge into Fremont from downtown, you pass a welcome sign: "The Center of the Universe, set your watch back five minutes." This is your first clue that this is a very quirky place. Your next may be the rocket poised for takeoff at the corner of 35th Street and Evanston Avenue. Stroll and check out the fun galleries, below-street hideaways, and retro shops, and soak in the sense of creative independence that is rampant here. Check out Frank & Dunya's creative furniture and Fritzi Ritzi's retro clothing, Tribes' native art and the Marvin Oliver native art gallery. The Empty Space Theater is here, as is Redhook Ales Trolleyman Pub. The district is thick with little, innovative eateries, some pricey but most not. Don't look for white linen and china but for all kinds of fun or quick meals.

Details: At the northwest end of Lake Union. A #26 bus from Fourth Avenue downtown goes to Fremont. (2 hours)

★★★★ **Hiram M. Chittenden Locks**—Also called the Ballard Locks, this is a don't-miss slice of Seattle life, especially in summer when a constant parade of pleasure boats leaves the fresh waters of Lake Washington, Lake Union, and Salmon Bay to ply the Lake Washington Ship Canal into Puget Sound. Underwater viewing windows on the south side of the locks let you watch salmon migration. Note the huge sequoia trees in the Carl English Jr. Botanical Garden on the north (entry) side of the locks. There is a visitors center here with displays on the locks. On some summer Sundays bands perform outdoor concerts.

Details: West of the Ballard business district, take Market Street west (it turns into 54th then watch for signs to the locks).The grounds are open daily 7 to 9; the visitors center is open Thursday through Monday 10 to 7 during the summer, 11 to 5 other months. Admission is free. (1–2 hours)

★★★★ **Museum of Flight**—Home to the first jet-powered *Air Force One* (a Boeing VC-137B) and many other planes, this is a visual delight and a must for anyone who loves flying. Historical exhibits are in the Red Barn, the original Boeing factory. Kids love sitting in the cockpit of an airplane; adults gravitate to the flight simulator used to train pilots. And there's a great gift shop.

Details: Located at 9404 East Marginal Way South at the southwest corner of Boeing Field. Take Exit 158 from Interstate 5. 206/764-5720; www.museumofflight.org. Open daily 10 to 5, Thursday 10 to 9. Two free tours. Admission: $8 adults (16 and over), $4 ages 6 to 15. (2 hours)

Pike Place Market PDA

The Fish Market at Pike Place Market

★★★★ **Nordstrom**—Most shoppers in the United States know of Seattle-based Nordstrom as the gem of a department store whose service philosophy brings shoppers back time after time. The Nordstrom brothers started their shoe store on Seattle's First Avenue in 1901. Now their sparkling new flagship store in downtown Seattle, between two shopping malls, Westlake Center and the new Pacific Place, has a whole floor of shoes, and a fish aquarium in the kids department.

Details: On Pine Street between Fifth and Sixth Avenues. Call 206/628-2111 (½ hour—or all day)

★★★★ **Pike Place Market**—Founded in 1907 as an experiment to bring farmers and consumers together without the middleman, Pike Place Market is one of the oldest continuously operating farmers markets in the United States. It's home to hundreds of businesses, a hundred farmers, several hundred artists (it was a favorite subject of artist Mark Tobey), and over 500 residents. Breathe deeply of the heady stew—the scent of bakeries, fresh fish, saltwater, and coffee. Midsummer crowds pack the market—go before 10 a.m. Tour the market's four levels. Look down at the names imprinted in the Market's tiles for a sense of the people who've supported the market renovation.

You could spend a lot of time here; however, a few hours will give you a sampling. The farmers' tables are in the North Arcade. Don't miss the Economhy Arcade with DeLaurenti's Italian Market, Post Alley with the Perennial Tea Room, and restaurants such as the Pink Door.

Details: Main entrance to the market is at First Avenue and Pike Street. Call 206/682-7453; www.pikeplacemarket.org. Open Monday through Saturday 9 to 6, Sunday 11 to 5, but individual shop openings vary. Check with the Pike Place Market PDA for information, you can pick up a copy of their fine dining and restaurant guides at the main entrance information booth. Park on Western Avenue in the Public Market Parking garage, and take the elevator to the North Arcade. (1–2 hours)

✯✯✯✯ **Pioneer Square**—This is the historic business district of Seattle, which lies south of present-day downtown between the waterfront and the International District. There are restaurants, galleries, and shops but the "don't miss" destinations here include the **Northwest Gallery of Fine Woodworking**, **Elliott Bay Books**, and the **Klondike Gold Rush National Park** facility at 117 South Main. The much photographed landmark **pergola** is at First Avenue and Yesler Way in Pioneer Park Place near the entrance to Doc Maynard's Public House and **Bill Speidel's Underground Tour**, a fun and unique look at the city's history (206/682-4646).

Details: (2 hours for the square, 2 hours for the Underground Tour)

✯✯✯✯ **Seattle Art Museum**—Architect Robert Venturi designed this uplifting space. The large stone camels on the steps of the gallery were longtime guardians outside the entrance to the original Seattle Art Museum, now the Seattle Asian Art Museum on Capitol Hill (see below). There are changing special exhibits and a wonderful Northwest native arts collection. You can join in an authentic tea ceremony in an authentic Japanese teahouse.

Details: 100 University Street between First and Second Avenues. The museum store offers a huge collection of art books (specialties) and gifts. The café offers light meals. Admission is $6 for adults (the ticket is good for admission to the Seattle Asian Art Museum if used within a week). (1–3 hours)

✯✯✯✯ **Seattle Center**—The site of the 1962 World's Fair. Seattle Center is now home to the **Space Needle**, **Pacific Science Center**—an interactive experience—Key Arena, Pacific Northwest Ballet, Seattle Repertory Theater, Intiman Theater, Seattle Children's Theater, and

Children's Museum. The grounds here offer a pleasant stroll, and you can take the elevator to the top of the Space Needle for incredible views. The **Fun Forest Amusement Park** draws kids of all ages. The center celebrates the beginning of summer with the Northwest Folklife Festival over Memorial Day weekend and marks the end with the Bumbershoot Arts Festival during Labor Day weekend.

Details: A mile north of downtown Seattle, the center is open year-round. Call 206/684-7200 for upcoming events. (3 hours)

★★★★ **Waterfront & Streetcar**—Seattle's waterfront experienced a revitalization in the 1990s, and it bustles. Here the **Seattle Aquarium** and **Omnidome Film Experience** are fun family destinations. There are plenty of restaurants on the waterfront. Try Ivar's Acres of Clams, a waterfront tradition for fish and chips. There are also luxury condominiums, an international trade center, the terminus for Washington State Ferries (regular ferries to Bainbridge Island and Bremerton on the Kitsap Peninsula leave from here). The terminal for the *Victoria Clipper* is also here. Explore by foot or take the Waterfront Streetcar, which runs from Myrtle Edwards Park at the north end to the south end of the waterfront, and continues to Pioneer Square and the International District, ending at Fifth Avenue and Jackson Street.

Details: Fares and schedules are posted at trolley stops. Seattle's only waterfront hotel, the Edgewater, is located here. (3 hours)

★★★★ **Woodland Park Zoo**—North of downtown, near Green Lake, the zoo features natural settings with few barriers for the animals residing here. Exhibits on 92 acres include an elephant forest, a butterfly exhibit, a tropical rain forest, and the Northern Trail that covers six acres of dramatic landscape and focuses on animals who live in the cold regions of the Far North—brown bears, river otters, bald eagles, and the snowy owl. There's also a food court (bring cash or traveler's checks to eat here).

Details: From I-5 take NE 50th Exit (#169), go west on 50th Avenue about a mile to Fremont Avenue, and the zoo's south gate; 206/684-4800; www.zoo.org. Open daily, including holidays, March 15 through October 14 9:30 to 6; 9:30 to 4 the remainder of the year. Admission is $8 for adults, $7.25 for seniors and students with ID. (2–3 hours)

★★★ **Ballard**—The Ballard area northwest of downtown is the heart of the Scandinavian community, strongly involved in the fishing industry. West of the Ballard Bridge is Fisherman's Terminal, home to Puget Sound's fishing fleet. **Market Street** is Ballard's main street and has Scandinavian specialty shops. **Shilshole Marina** and **Golden Gardens**, a stretch of beach with walking paths, picnic areas, and wetlands are well worth exploring. The **Nordic Heritage Museum** has displays showing the Scandinavian influence on Northwest life, as well as contemporary exhibits of art.

Details: Take 15th Avenue West northwest from downtown (off 15th Avenue west at the Emerson/Nickerson Exit); continue north across Ballard Bridge and turn left at Market Street. Follow it to the Ballard Locks. The museum is north of the locks at 3014 NW 67th Street, 206/789-5707. Open Tuesday through Saturday 10 to 4 and Sunday noon to 4. Admission $4. (4–6 hours for the whole area, 1–2 hours for the museum)

★★★ **Blake Island**—This whole island is a marine park that features **Tillicum Village Northwest Coast Indian Cultural Center**. They serve alder-smoked salmon dinners and showcase a native dance exhibition. A scenic boat crossing makes this a special day trip from Seattle's waterfront. Go in the morning, take a picnic, hike the three-mile trail around the island, and catch a late afternoon or evening boat back.

Details: Tours leave Piers 55 and 56 daily May 1 through mid-October and weekends throughout the year; 206/443-1244. Cost is about $50, including boat ride and meal; $24 per person passenger only. (4–6 hours)

★★★ **Center for Wooden Boats and Northwest Seaport**—These two stops make up the three-acre Maritime Heritage Center park on Lake Union. The center displays wooden vessels, and you can rent a classic wooden rowboat or a sailboat here (or take a course in building a boat). At Northwest Seaport you can tour the schooner *Wawona* and the tugboat *Arthur Foss*.

Details: At the south end of the lake near the Burger King; the center is at 1010 Valley, Seattle; 206/382-2628. Docks are open for viewing boats from 10 to 5 daily except Tuesday. Rentals from 11 to 7; costs vary depending on size, but start with $8 for a rowboat. $5 charge for checking out larger boats. The Northwest Seaport at 1002 Valley. Admission to the center is free, to the seaport by donation. (1–2 hours)

★★★ **Green Lake**—The "sole" of Seattle is Green Lake's 2.8-mile paved path around the lake, where Seattleites routinely walk, jog, inline-skate, and bicycle. During warm months paddle boats and canoes can be

GREATER SEATTLE

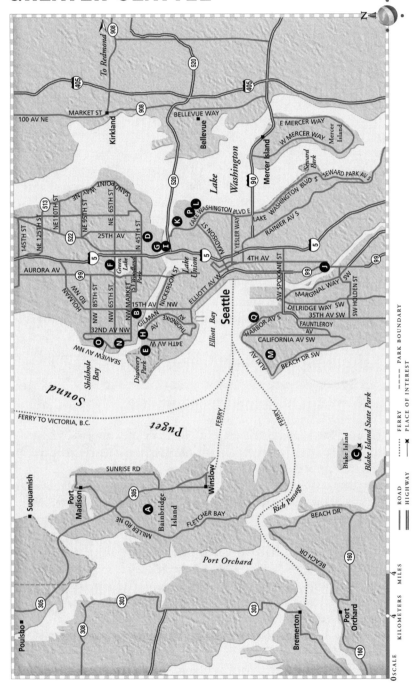

N

To Redmond

908

520

405

405

100 AV NE

MARKET ST

908

BELLEVUE WAY

E MERCER WAY

Kirkland

Bellevue

W MERCER WAY

Mercer Island

Lake
Washington

Mercer Island

Seward Park

90

SEWARD PARK AV S

513

SAND POINT WAY NE

NE 65TH ST

LAKE WASHINGTON BLVD E

LAKE WASHINGTON BLVD S

145TH ST

NE 125TH ST

NE 110TH ST

NE 95TH ST

522

25TH AV

NE 45TH ST

N 45TH ST

P L

K

RAINIER AV S

5

5

D

G I

MADISON ST

YESLER WAY

LAKE WASHINGTON BLVD E

AURORA AV

99

F

Green Lake

Woodland Park

Lake Union

NICKERSON ST

5

4TH AV

SW SPOKANE ST

99

J

99

HOLMAN RD NW

85TH ST

65TH ST

NW MARKET ST

15TH AV NW

GILMAN AV

B

THORNDIKE AV

ELLIOTT AV W

Seattle

MARGINAL WAY SW

SW HOLDEN ST

DELRIDGE WAY SW

35TH AV SW

32ND AV NW

SEAVIEW AV NW

O

N

H

E

34TH AV W

Elliott Bay

Q

HARBOR AV S

FAUNTLEROY AV

CALIFORNIA AV SW

M

ALKI AV

BEACH DR SW

Discovery Park

Shilshole Bay

Puget Sound

FERRY TO VICTORIA, B.C.

Blake Island

C

Blake Island State Park

FERRY

FERRY

FERRY

Rich Passage

Winslow

SUNRISE RD

Suquamish

Port Madison

305

A

Bainbridge Island

FLETCHER BAY

MILLER RD NE

BEACH DR

Port Orchard

BEACH DR

160

305

303

303

160

308

Poulsbo

Bremerton

Port Orchard

····· ROAD
═══ HIGHWAY
······· FERRY
✕ PLACE OF INTEREST
----- PARK BOUNDARY

0 SCALE

4 KILOMETERS

4 MILES

Sights

A Bainbridge Island

B Ballard

C Blake Island

D Burke Museum of Natural History and Culture

E Discovery Park

F Green Lake

G Henry Art Gallery

H Hiram M. Chittenden Locks

I Museum of History and Industry

J Museum of Flight

K Woodland Park Zoo

L Washington Park Arboretum

M West Seattle

Food

F Duke's Green Lake Chowder House

N Pescatore Fish Cafe

O Ray's Boathouse

P Rover's

Q Salty's on Alki

R Six Degrees

Note: Items with the same letter are located in the same town or area.

rented at the recreation center, and there are swimming beaches. The Bathhouse Theatre is on the west side of the lake. There are eateries and coffeeshops, particularly around the north end of the lake.

Details: Go north on Aurora Avenue and watch for signs to Green Lake at about 50th Street. You can rent bicycles and inline skates at Gregg's Green Lake Cycle, east of the lake. 206/523-1822. (1 hour to "walk the lake")

★★★ **Harbor Steps**—Seattle's newest downtown neighborhood has sprung up around the Harbor Steps that descend west at the end of University Street to Western Avenue, a block from Seattle's waterfront. Water features, plantings, and an outdoor sculpture are tucked between modern highrise apartment buildings. This is a favorite sunny-day lunch spot for downtown office employees. This new neighborhood is the location of Wolfgang Puck's Cafe, his second eatery in Seattle (his first is Obachine on Sixth Avenue). The Inn at Harbor Steps is an elegant, well-located hideaway here.

Details: The top of the steps is across from the Seattle Art Museum at First Avenue and University Street. (15 minutes)

★★★ **Queen Anne Hill**—Queen Anne Hill, one of Seattle's oldest neighborhoods just five minutes from downtown, rises to about 460 feet and is the highest spot in Seattle, offering expansive vistas. It's divided into two shopping districts: Lower Queen Anne, around busy Seattle Center, and Upper Queen Anne, on top of the hill that feels like a small town's main street with coffee shops, bistros, and a wide variety of restaurants. For a mini morning or afternoon getaway, spend a few hours and get to the top of Queen Anne. Check out Homing Instincts, a home and accessories shop with a hidden courtyard, Ravenna Gardens Accessories and garden shop, and Nelly Stallion and Annie Cruz for high-style clothing. Pasta & Co. is a fun stop for food fans and gourmets. And the Queen Anne Thriftway started the city's trend of grocery shopping as entertainment.

Details: Seattle Center is at the heart of Lower Queen Anne; Upper Queen Anne, a six-block stretch of Queen Anne Avenue North from Galer to McGraw. (2 hours)

★★★ **Uwajimaya/International District**—This large Asian market with its shiny blue–tile room, shopping (giftwares are upstairs), and busy parking lot, draws people in. The variety of seafoods and foods is a treat to see, and the cafeteria and Japanese deli offer tasty options for refueling. Uwajimaya has plans to expand, so don't be surprised if construction is underway when you arrive.

Details: 519 Sixth Avenue S., Seattle, a block from the Bus Tunnel's south terminal; 206/624-6248; www.uwajimaya.com. No admission. (1 hour)

★★★ **Washington Park Arboretum**—This was Seattle's first park. Though it's beautiful year-round, spring is especially nice in this 200-acre park with cherry trees, rhododendrons, and azaleas in their glory. The arboretum is south of the University of Washington adjacent to the neighborhood of Washington Park. A walled Japanese garden has a teahouse and monthly tea ceremony demonstrations.

Details: Located off Madison Street on Lake Washington Blvd. E. (which runs through the arboretum); 206/543-8800. Free tours are offered on weekends from the Graham Visitor Center, 1502 Lake Washington Blvd., open daily 10 to 4. The Japanese Garden is open March through November; 206/684-4725. Admission is $2.50 for adults. Park open daily 8 to sunset. (2 hours)

✩✩✩ **West Seattle**—Seattle's founders landed on Alki Beach in West Seattle. Visit the **Log House Museum** for exhibits and displays on the history of Seattle and the Duwamish people who first lived here. Alki Beach is a popular destination for summer sunbathers, volleyball fans, and inline skaters. The Mediterranean-style Phoenecia at Alki restaurant views the action.
Details: The museum is at 3003 61st Avenue SW just off Alki Avenue; 206/938-5293. Phoenecia, 206/935-6550. (1 hour)

✩✩ **Burke Museum of Natural History and Culture**—This museum on the University of Washington campus is known for its Native American art collection. There's also an expanding dinosaur collection.
Details: 17th Avenue NE entrance to the UW campus; 206/543-5590 (recorded info) or 543-7907; www.washington.edu/burkemuseum. Open daily 10 to 5, until 8 on Thursday. Admission is $5.50. (1–2 hours)

✩✩ **Capitol Hill**—A widely diverse neighborhood, east of downtown. The northwest crest of the hill is home to some of the city's most beautiful old homes and mansions. The main shopping district lies along Broadway Avenue, a lively shopping street and gathering place for counterculture groups and conservatives alike. **Volunteer Park**, home of the **Seattle Asian Art Museum**, is at the north end of the hill.
Details: From downtown follow Pike Street to E. Pike and Broadway and go north. The entrance to Volunteer Park is on 14th E. Prospect between Broadway and 15th Avenue E. The museum is open Tuesday through Sunday, 10 to 5 and Thursday 10 to 9; closed Monday; 206/654-3100. Admission: $6 for adults (price covers a visit to the Seattle Art Museum if used within one week).

✩✩ **Discovery Park**—This 500-plus-acre park features the Daybreak Star Indian Cultural Center, a lighthouse, and plenty of trails and a beach to walk that look west over Puget Sound.
Details: northwest of downtown in the Magnolia neighborhood; 206/386-4236. (2 hours)

✩✩ **Henry Art Gallery**—This gallery on the University of Washington campus, noted for its contemporary art collection, was recently expanded to almost three times its original size, and the new facility includes a café. It's a block from "the Ave," the University District's ecletic main business street.

Details: NE 41st and NE 15th, Seattle; 206/543-2280 (recorded message) or 543-2281; www.henryart.org; open 11 to 5 Tuesday through Sunday, until 8 on Thursday. Admission is $5. (1 hour)

★★ **Metro Transit Tunnel ("Bus Tunnel")**—Completed in 1990, this is a 1.3-mile underground bus-only roadway beneath downtown Seattle, linking Westlake Center with the International District. Access to the tunnel, at the south end, is a half block from Uwajimaya, an Asian market, and next to Union Station.

Details: No fares are charged in the downtown 7- by 20-block Ride Free Zone.

★★ **Museum of History and Industry**—Their exhibits on early Seattle history include historic rooms, an exhibit on the Great Seattle Fire, a cable car, and a miniatures collection. Combine a visit here with a stroll; the Washington Park Arboretum's Foster Island walking trail starts east of the museum's parking lot.

Details: South of Husky Stadium, 2700 24th Avenue East, Seattle; 206/324-1125; www.historymus-nw.org. Admission: $5.50 suggested donation. (1 hour)

★★ **Westlake Center**—This four-story vertical mall in the heart of Seattle's downtown shopping district contains over 80 shops and eateries. Here you'll find a wide variety of clothing stores and shops such as the Disney Store, Garden Botanika, Natural Wonders, and Brentano's Books. The Plaza in front of the center on Pine is a lively gathering spot.

Details: On Pine Street between Fourth and Fifth Avenues, between the Bon Marché and Nordstrom, connected to the Mayflower Hotel and close to the Westin Hotel. A Ticketmaster booth located at the Information/Concierge desk sells tickets on a cash-only basis. For information, call 206/467-1600. (1 hour)

KIDS' STUFF

The Seattle Aquarium on the waterfront, Woodland Park Zoo, and the Seattle Center are especially fun for kids. At the Center, the Fun Forest amusement park, the Children's Theater and Children's Museum, and the Pacific Science Center offer plenty to keep kids in all age ranges busy for hours. The wading pool and the paddle boats at Green Lake please different ages. A ferry ride across Puget Sound on a sunny day is always appealing.

FITNESS AND RECREATION

Walk, jog, or bicycle along the waterfront at **Myrtle Edwards Park**. Seattle's newest golf facility, a nine-hole executive course at **Interbay**, has a two-level driving range and putting facility. Kite flying at **Gasworks Park** north of Lake Union is fun to do or fun to watch. The **Burke-Gilman Trail** runs through Gasworks Park from Ballard in Northwest Seattle—you can bike or walk part of the 30-plus-mile trail from North Seattle to the east side of Lake Washington. Drive north about a half hour to Everett and you can take an all-day whalewatching tour with the **Mosquito Fleet**, 800/325-6722.

There are three classic Seattle viewpoints: from **Kerry Park** on Queen Anne Hill (West Highland Drive and Third Avenue West), perhaps the most photographed view of Seattle's skyline; from **Volunteer Park** in front of the Seattle Asian Art Museum; and from West Seattle's **Admiral District Park**.

Chateau Ste. Michelle, 425/488-3300, the largest winery in the state, is in Woodinville, a half-hour's drive from Seattle. Tours are offered from 10 to 4:30. Summer concerts feature a variety of performers. Nearby is Redhook Ale's largest brew facility and pub, and Columbia Winery. This is the destination of the *Spirit of Washington*, 206/227-7245, a vintage dinner train that leaves from Renton, at the southeast end of Lake Washington.

SHOPPING

The main shopping destinations in downtown Seattle are **Westlake Center; City Centre** at Fifth Avenue and Pike Street; **Rainier Square** (on Fifth between Union and University Streets); and the sparkling new **Pacific Place, Nordstrom,** and the **Bon Marché** department stores along Pine Street between Second and Sixth Avenues). **Nike Town** and **Planet Hollywood** are nearby. Away from downtown, east of the University District, is **University Village** with shops such as Sundance and Eddie Bauer, and some good restaurants. An even longer drive from downtown, **Northgate** and **Southcenter malls** and **Bellevue Square** are popular shopping destinations.

SPECTATOR SPORTS

"The wave" was born in Seattle, and this is a city that definitely loves its sports. Professional teams are the **Mariners** (baseball), the **Seahawks** (football), the **Supersonics** (men's basketball), the **Thunderbirds** (hockey), and the **Sounders** (soccer). Individual tickets can be purchased through Ticketmaster (206/622-4487). The hottest ticket in town (unless a team makes the playoffs) is a football game at the University of Washington Husky Stadium with the excitement of 70,000-plus fans doing the "wave" to cheer on the **Huskies**, views of Lake Washington and the Cascades, and tailgating in automobiles and in boats. That's right. A whole contingent of fans arrive by boat (some families have done so for decades) to moor behind the stadium. And you can arrive by boat, too! Brunch-and-boat packages are available through several restaurants. Call **Argosy Cruises**, 206/623-1445, or **Power Tours**, 206/682-8864, for boat schedules and departure spots. Power Tours has packages that include tickets (pricey but good to know if you're keen to go and don't have game tickets). Also, other UW Huskies' teams serve up many men's and women's spectator events and are always in the hunt for one championship or another. Call 206/543-8463 (recorded message) or 206/543-2210 for events, schedules, and ticket information.

FOOD

Coffee bars—**Starbucks, Tully's, Seattle's Best Coffee,** and many more—are almost as thick as rain and many offer cozy chairs for relaxing. Oyster bars (they serve other seafood as well) are Seattle specialties—popular downtown area haunts are **Anthony's Bell Street Diner**, 206/448-6688 on the waterfront at the foot of Bell Street; the **Brooklyn Seafood-Steak & Oyster House**, 1212 Second Avenue, 206/224-7000; **Elliott's Oyster House**, on Pier 56, 206/623-4340; **McCormick's**, 722 Fourth Avenue, 206/682-3900; and **Shuckers**, (in the Four Seasons Hotel), 206/621-1984. **Emmet Watson's Oyster Bar**, 206/448-7721, in Pike Place Market, is the most casual of the lot.

The "best" when it comes to restaurants is a crowded list. At the top of the favorites list is **Rover's**, 206/325-7442, tucked away in the Madison Park neighborhood east of downtown. Known for consistent, beautifully prepared food, especially seafood, they offer fairly pricey five-course meals. Another favorite, **Wild Ginger**, 1400

Western Avenue, 206/623-4450, offers a la carte Pan-Asian meals for a competitive Seattle-restaurant price, located below the Market. And yes, the food at both restaurants is wonderful. Tom Douglas' restaurants—**Dahlia Lounge**, 206/682-4143; **Etta's Seafood**, 206/443-6000; and the **Palace Kitchen**, 206/448-2001—in the Belltown and Pike Place Market areas, also get high marks. The Dahlia and Etta's are smaller and more intimate; Palace Kitchen is the most unusual. Check out Douglas' Website: www.tomdouglas.com. **Flying Fish**, 2234 First Avenue, 206/728-8595, is chef Christine Keff's popular eatery, also in the Belltown area at the northeast edge of the Market.

There are notable hotel restaurants, too. For a special occasion or splurge, dress up to go to **Fullers**, in the Sheraton, 206/447-5544; the **Georgian Room**, in the Four Seasons, 206/621-7889; and the **Hunt Club**, 900 Madison Street, in the Sorrento Hotel, 206/343-6156. Expect fine food, top service, soothingly elegant settings (and a tab to match). A little more relaxed, **Tulio's**, in the Hotel Vintage Park, 1100 Fifth Avenue, 206/624-5500, specializes in Italian food and **Andaluca**, in the Mayflower Park Hotel, 206/382-6999, is a romantic, gem-toned hideaway with tapas style dishes.

The **Canlis Restaurant**, 206/283-3313, north of downtown on Aurora Avenue, a Seattle tradition for generations, still has the cachet of being a "luxe" place to go to have a Canlis salad (like a caesar) and grilled steak or scampi for that special-event dinner. Recently updated (by Bill Gate's architect, Jim Cutler) it still offers its signature piano and a breathtaking view of Lake Union.

The **El Gaucho**, 2505 First Avenue, 206/728-1337—a long time favorite Seattle steak house, gone for a while and resurrected in recent years—is known for its cigar room. **Oliver's**, 206/382-6995, in the Mayflower Hotel makes award-winning martinis.

Food stalls for quick take-away meals and many wonderful eateries are hidden away in **Pike Place Market** (request their restaurant guide and map and their fine dining guide brochure by calling 206/682-7453). Lunch on the outdoor terrace of the **Pink Door**, 206/443-3241, with its romantic arbor and view of Elliott Bay, is a real treat. **Campagne**, 206/728-2800, across from the Inn at the Market, is another at the top of the "Bests" lists (its bistro on the lower level is *the* place for a chic and tasty breakfast—try a French-style omelet). **El Puerco Lloron**, 206/624-0541, serves budget Mexican food in a lively setting behind the Market off Western Avenue.

On Queen Anne Hill the fun diner-style **5 Spot**, 1502 Queen

SEATTLE

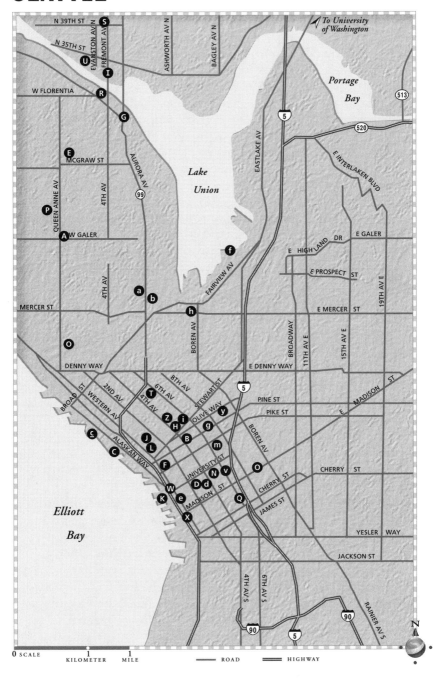

To University of Washington

Portage Bay

N 39TH ST
N 35TH ST
EVANSTON AV N
FREMONT AV
ASHWORTH AV N
BAGLEY AV N

S
U
I
R
G
E
McGRAW ST
P
A W GALER
O

W FLORENTIA

AURORA AV
99

QUEEN ANNE AV
4TH AV
4TH AV

Lake
Union

EASTLAKE AV

513
520

E INTERLAKEN BLVD

E GALER
E HIGHLAND DR
E PROSPECT ST
E MERCER ST

FAIRVIEW AV
BOREN AV

f

a b
h
MERCER ST

DENNY WAY

BROADWAY
11TH AV E
15TH AV E
19TH AV E

E DENNY WAY

5

BROAD ST
WESTERN AV
2ND AV
ALASKAN WAY

8TH AV
6TH AV
4TH AV
STEWART ST
OLIVE WAY

PINE ST
PIKE ST

E MADISON ST

T
Z H i
J B
L
F
C
K W
X
e
D d
MADISON ST
UNIVERSITY ST

y
g
m
N V
Q

O

BOREN AV

CHERRY ST
CHERRY ST
JAMES ST
YESLER WAY
JACKSON ST

Elliott
Bay

4TH AV S
6TH AV S

RAINIER AV S

90
5
90

N

0 SCALE
1 KILOMETER
1 MILE
ROAD
HIGHWAY

Food

- **A** 5 Spot
- **B** Andaluca
- **C** Anthony's Bell Street Diner
- **D** Brooklyn Seafood-Steak & Oyster House
- **E** Buongusto
- **F** Campagne
- **G** Canlis Restaurant
- **H** Dahlia Lounge
- **I** El Camino
- **J** El Gaucho
- **B** El Puerco Lloron
- **K** Elliott's Oyster House
- **G** Emmet Watson's Oyster Bar
- **G** Etta's Seafood
- **L** Flying Fish
- **I** Fremont Noodle House
- **M** Fullers
- **N** Georgian Room (Four Seasons Olympic)
- **O** The Hunt Club
- **P** Longshoreman's Daughter
- **Q** McCormick's
- **B** Oliver's
- **R** Ponti Seafood Grill
- **N** Shuckers
- **S** Swingside Cafe
- **T** The Palace Kitchen
- **G** Pike Place Market
- **G** The Pink Door

Food (continued)

- **U** Trolleyman's Pub
- **V** Tulio's
- **R** Ventana
- **W** Wild Ginger
- **E** Wild Hare

Lodging

- **X** Alexis
- **Y** Camlin Hotel
- **Z** Claremont
- **N** Four Seasons Olympic
- **a** Hampton Inn/Seattle Center
- **b** Holiday Inn Express/Seattle Center
- **c** Hotel Edgewater
- **e** Hotel Monaco
- **W** Hotel Vintage Park
- **e** Inn at Harbor Steps
- **O** Inn at the Market
- **O** International Hostel
- **O** Pensione Nichols
- **f** M.V. Challenger
- **B** Mayflower Park
- **g** Paramount Hotel
- **h** Residence Inn by Marriott/Lake Union
- **M** Sheraton Seattle
- **O** Sorrento
- **i** Westin Hotel

Note: Items with the same letter are located in the same town or area.

Anne Avenue North, 206/285-SPOT, is always packed for weekend breakfasts. **Buongusto**, 206/284-9040, serves Italian food. Also on Queen Anne Avenue North, the **Hilltop Ale House**, 206/285-3877, and **Paragon Bar & Grill**, 206/283-4548, with entertainment—jazz, blues, reggae—are lively night spots. The **Wild Hare**, 206/285-3360, in a romantic old house, specializes in wild game entrees. **Kaspar's**, 19 West Harrison, 206/298-0123, on Lower Queen Anne Hill, is an elegant spot with European-style food.

In Fremont you'll find fun and funky neighborhood hangouts. At the **Fremont Noodle House**, 3411 Fremont Avenue North, 206/547-1550, try the roast duck and noodle soup with a bottle of Bangkok Beer—and finish with a bowl of coconut ice cream. Redhook Ale's **Trolleyman's Pub**, 3400 Phinney North, 206/548-8000, offers microbrews, sandwiches and soups. Though the walls are pale pink at **El Camino**, 607 North 35th Street, 206/632-7303, the weekend atmosphere in this Mexican-style restaurant is as boisterous as the riotously colorful tablecloths. Try the **Longshoreman's Daughter**, 3508 Fremont Place North, 206/633-5169, for breakfast or lunch, serving classics with a twist, like macaroni and cheese with béchamel sauce. **Ventana**, 4401 Fremont Avenue North, 206/632-6825, and the **Swingside Cafe**, 4212 Fremont North, 206/633-4057, offer "downtown" food at better prices in more modest settings.

If you want to play hooky from sightseeing on a beautiful, sunny afternoon, visit the restaurants along the Lake Washington Ship Canal: **Ponti Seafood Grill**, 3014 Third Avenue North, 206/284-3000, near Fremont, **Pescatore Fish Cafe**, 5300 34th Avenue NW, 206/784-1733, overlooking the Ballard locks; at Shilshole Bay, **Ray's Boathouse**, 6049 Seaview Avenue North, 206/789-3770, another Seattle institution; and **Anthony's** next door, 6135 Seaview Avenue North, 206/783-0780, all offer decks or terraces with great views of the boat traffic. At Green Lake you'll have water views from **Six Degrees**, 7900 East Green Lake Drive, 206/523-1600, and **Duke's Green Lake Chowder House**, 7850 North Green Lake Drive, 206/ 522-4908. And in West Seattle, **Salty's on Alki**, 1936 Harbor Avenue SW, 206/937-1600, offers a panorama of the water and Seattle's skyline along with seafood.

LODGING

There's a wide range of lodging types and prices in Seattle. To get the most out of your visit, plan to stay in or near downtown.

You have several quite different choices in or near Pike Place Market. At the high end there's the charming English country–style hideaway, **Inn at the Market**, 86 Pine Street, 206/443-3600, with Campagne Restaurant across the courtyard. The **Pensione Nichols**, 1923 First Avenue, 206/441-7125 or 800/440-7125, with a wide range of room rates, offers a continental breakfast, comfortably updated rooms—some with a shared bath—and views. A little more expensive is the **Claremont**, 2000 Fourth Avenue, 206/448-8600 or 800/448-8601, with updated units in an older hotel building.

At the very basic and thrifty end of the spectrum is the **Hostel International of Seattle**, 84 Union Street, 206/622-5443, at the south end of the Market off Western Avenue. Also at the south edge of the Market, but much harder on the wallet, is the **Inn at Harbor Steps**, 1211 First Avenue, 206/748-0973 or 888/728-8910, a sophisticated hideaway, kitty corner from the Seattle Art Museum. **Hotel Edgewater**, 2411 Alaskan Way, 206/728-7000 or 800/624-0670, is Seattle's only waterfront hotel.

The city's grande dame is the **Four Seasons Olympic**, 411 University Street, 206/621-1700 or 800/821-8106. Smaller luxury hotels include the **Alexis**, 1007 First Avenue, 206/624-4844 or 800/426-7033, not far from the Seattle Art Museum, **Hotel Vintage Park**, 1100 Fifth Avenue, 206/624-8000 or 800/624-4433; the **Hotel Monaco**, 1011 Fourth Avenue, 206/621-1770 or 800/945-2240, in downtown; and the **Sorrento**, 900 Madison Street, 206/622-6400 or 800/426-1265, on First Hill's Madison Street with palm trees out front, is one of the town's most romantic hotels. **Mayflower Park Hotel**, 405 Olive Way, 206/623-8700 or 800/426-5100, is a small European-style hotel that offers a central downtown location and access directly into Westlake Center. All of these have delightful restaurants on site.

The **Paramount Hotel**, 724 Pine Street, 206/292-9500, new in 1997, is within a block or so of the Washington Convention Center and competitively priced given that Seattle is an expensive city. The slightly less expensive **Camlin Hotel**, 1619 Ninth Avenue, 206/682-0100, a long-time favorite older hotel is also near the Washington Convention Center. Also close is the **Sheraton Seattle**, 1400 Sixth Avenue, 206/621-9000 or 800/204-6100, with a terrific glass collection in Fuller's Restaurant. The **Westin Hotel**, 1900 Sixth Avenue, 06/728-1000 or 800/228-3000, is at the north end of the business district (Seattle is their international headquarters).

Unique and affordable lodging (some roomy with great views, some in tight quarters) can be had on Lake Union aboard the **M.V. Challenger** tugboat, 206/340-1201, or in yachts moored nearby.

There are several chain accommodations around Seattle Center and the South end of Lake Union, some are good choices for families. There's a new **Hampton Inn**, 700 Fifth Avenue North, 206/282-7700 or 800/426-7866, and a **Holiday Inn**, 226 Aurora Avenue North, 206/441-7222 or 800/465-4329, near Seattle Center. At the southwest end of Lake Union is a **Residence Inn by Marriott**, 800 Fairview Avenue North, 206/624-6000 or 800/331-3131.

Seattle's **Super Saver** program, with downtown hotel savings up to fifty percent, runs November 7 through March 31; reservation lines open October 31. A **Hotel Hotline** operates from April to October offering peak-season travelers the lowest room rates at hotels in downtown Seattle, Sea-Tac airport area, the University District or Bellevue. Call 206/461-5882 or 800/535-7071 (U.S. only).

NIGHTLIFE

Seattle is one of the biggest theater towns in the country, with diverse offerings to please every taste. Check schedules for the **Seattle Repertory Theater**, **ACT**, and **Intiman**, **Empty Space**. The **Paramount** and the **Fifth Avenue** are two visually fabulous restored theaters that book popular shows and entertainment.

Dimitrou's Jazz Alley in Denny Regrade area not far from the Westin Hotel is one of the best jazz venues on the coast. And nearby, the offbeat **Crocodile Cafe** packs in crowds. For lively late night jazz and blues in bars and coffee hangouts, try **Pioneer Square**, south of downtown, or **Ballard Avenue**, the northwest end of town. **Broadway Avenue** on Capitol Hill is also a lively evening gathering spot.

There are several movie theaters downtown and entertainment complexes in **Pacific Place** and **City Centre**.

HELPFUL HINTS

Parking prices vary widely in downtown; some garages and lots can be outrageous. Those lots with good locations and more reasonable rates include the new parking garage in Pacific Place and the Public Market Parking Garage, 1531 Western Avenue.

Some good bus or boat tours offer quick and fun orientations of the city. A complete city tour is offered by **Grayline Tours**, 206/624-6349, or **Seattle Tours** (smaller coach, fewer pick-up stops), 206/660-TOUR. **Argosy Tours,** 206/623-4252, has boat tours (including speedboat tours) of the harbor, Ballard Locks, and Lake Washington.

SIDETRIP: SNOHOMISH ANTIQUES

The small riverfront community of Snohomish, 35 miles and a half hour north of Seattle, was settled in the gold rush days of the mid-1800s and thrived as a pioneering logging town in the 1880s. For decades, though, it's been known less for timber and more for antique furniture and accessories; it's home to more than 350 antique dealers and considered the antiques capital of the Northwest.

To reach Snohomish, take Interstate 5 north from Seattle; at Everett take Highway 2 east (Exit 194) and follow the signs. **Star Center Mall,** 829 Second Street, houses 165 dealers. Park in the large lot, then explore three packed levels of antiques that include everything from Civil War memorabilia to antique comic books. Stroll south to the four-block stretch of First Street where smaller enclaves such as **River City Antiques** and **Victoria Village** are packed with Victorian furniture. Avenues A through E, west of the business district, comprise the historic part of town. The area is dotted with old Victorian homes, many accented with gingerbread trim. The **Blackman House,** 118 Avenue B, built by pioneer logger Hyrcanus Blackman in 1878, is now a museum operated by the Snohomish Historical Society. Stop by their office, next door, for a self-guided walking map of historic homes. Snohomish has a number of restaurants, coffeeshops, saloons, and bakeries. Try the boisterous family-style **Cabbage Patch,** 111 Avenue A, for an omelet breakfast or brunch, and **Collector's Choice** (Star Center Mall) for pasta. For an old-time lodging experience, check out the 1914 **Grand Hotel,** a comfortably updated inn on First Street with antique-filled rooms; some share a bath. For more information, call the Snohomish Chamber of Commerce at 360/568-2526.

Scenic Route: Whidbey and Fidalgo Islands and the Skagit Delta

Whidbey Island has been called Paradise, a Garden of Eden. In 1792, Joseph Whidbey charted the 40-mile-long island—the longest in the contiguous United States—at the entrance to Puget Sound. Today it is home to some of the oldest farms in Washington, the nation's first historical reserve, beachfront parks, a thriving arts community, and a naval station. At its north end, Whidbey is connected to Fidalgo Island and the mainland by Deception Pass bridge, one of the state's most photographed attractions, and then onward to the Skagit Delta. The route takes you to picturesque waterfront villages. Though the loop is an easy day trip from Seattle, it's much better to make it an overnight or longer.

The Mukilteo ferry terminal is 30 minutes north of downtown Seattle via Interstate 5; watch for exit signs south of Everett. A 20-minute ferry ride puts you at Clinton on the south end of the island. From here Highway 525 goes up the island.

Take the South Langley Road to the **Whidbey Island Winery**, 5237 S. Langley Road, 360/221-2040, where you can sample wines made from Siegerrebe and Madeleine Angevine grapes. Continue north to Langley, a waterfront village of galleries, restaurants,

WHIDBEY/SKAGIT LOOP

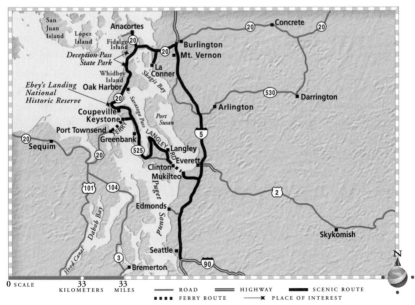

antiques shops, and a performing arts center. An arts and crafts festival held here in July and a county fair in August draw crowds. On First, the stylish and contemporary **Inn at Langley**, 360/221-3033, offers views of Saratoga Passage from jetted tubs in each room and is renowned for its five-course dinners on weekends (by reservation). Get back on 525 and continue north to **Greenbank**. The picturesque red and white barn at **Greenbank Farm**, on Wonn Road off Highway 525, was once a dairy. Now it houses a tasting room for Ste. Michelle Winery, open daily from 10 a.m. to 5 p.m., 360/678-7700.

SR 525 becomes SR 20 at the intersection, west, to the Keystone Ferry. This takes you to Port Townsend and the Olympic Peninsula, and offers an extension to the loop.

As you approach Coupeville, on Highway 20, you're driving through **Ebey's Landing National Historical Reserve**, a 17,400-acre national park that encompasses prairies, woodlands, and uplands, a western coastal strip along Admiralty Inlet, Penn Cove, and **Coupeville**, the state's second oldest town. Here the **Coupeville Arts Center** draws artists and instructors from all over the world to participate in workshops on needlework, photography, and painting. With its wharf, clapboard storefronts, and Victorian-style homes—many built by sea captains—the town looks much as it did in the 1800s. Stop by the **Island County Historical Museum** at the west end of Front Street for a self-guided walking tour map of the historical buildings in town. Later take winding Madrona Way west of Coupeville. You'll spot the rafts of Penn Cove mussel farm, famous for the succulent shellfish grown there. **Toby's Tavern** in Coupeville sells the most Penn Cove mussels on the island, yet having steamed mussels in the cozy old bar at the **Captain Whidbey Inn**, overlooking Penn Cove, is a real treat. The inn is a separate annex of rooms and several cottages spread on 12 acres, 360/678-4097 or 800/366-4097.

Continuing north on 20 you'll reach Oak Harbor, the island's largest community. A marina, motels, and other services are here. North of here is the Whidbey Island Naval Air Station; you'll likely see and hear planes soaring overhead. As you near Deception Pass watch for signs for **Dugwalla Bay Farms'** roadside stand. During summer berry season fresh sauces are made daily, and you can buy an ice-cream cone topped with warm berry sauce. You'll soon see signs for **Deception Pass State Park**, 4,128 acres that flank the northern tip of Whidbey Island and the southern tip of Fidalgo Island. You'll find camping, picnic spots, and lakes and shoreline to explore. Parking areas on either side of the bridge let you stop and walk across.

Once you cross the bridge, you're on **Fidalgo Island**. The Washington State Ferry terminal, at the outskirts of **Anacortes,** is the jumping-off spot to the San Juan Islands. Old Town Anacortes has a maritime heritage that goes back more than a hundred years. Take Commercial Street through the dozen blocks of historic downtown and you'll see signs of revitalization—spruced-up shops, eateries, a brewpub, art galleries. Don't miss **Marine Supply and Hardware**—the oldest marine hardware store on the West Coast (on the National Register of Historic Places). Its interior is packed with wooden ships' wheels, portholes, oil lamps, and Greek fishermen's hats, for starters. Drive north a few blocks to the viewpoint at the top of **Cap Sante** for ringside views of the pleasure boat traffic in the Port of Anacortes Marina. Along the marina, visit the 1919 drydocked sternwheeler the *W. T. Preston*, open weekends, 11 to 5. Children love the Anacortes Railway train and can get tickets and board here. The grand old **Majestic Hotel**, 800-588-4780, on Commercial, is worth a stop. Guest rooms are decorated with antiques; there's a garden, and a restaurant and pub serving up plenty of seafood.

The Skagit Delta, a gorgeous green wedge of alluvial plain, lies between Fidalgo Island and the freeway. In spring it is blanketed with blooming tulips and droves of visitors there to see the flowers. The delta is also an artistic home, for here is where the painters who became known as "the Northwest School" thrived. The storefronts along this picturesque fishing, farming, and arts village of **La Conner** look much as they did in the late 1800s. It's the crowds of people who look different, and the gift shops and restaurants that diverge from fishing and farming activities that dominated it years ago. Don't miss the **Museum of Northwest Art, Gaches Mansion**, the **Tillinghast Seed Company**, the **Quilt Museum**, and the shops and galleries on First Street. The **Channel Lodge**, La Conner, 360/466-1500, is a 40-unit Craftsman-style inn that clings to the Swinomish Channel offering views of the boat traffic. **Viking Cruises** 360/466-2639, offers whalewatching trips and tours of Deception Pass from here.

Continue along Highway 20 toward Mt. Vernon and watch for signs for Padilla Bay. A **National Estuarine Research Reserve and Interpretive Center** is here, and you can learn about the hawks and waterfowl, such as trumpeter swans, that make stopovers on the delta. ◼

2

OLYMPIC PENINSULA

Mists, mystery, moss, and music—that's what comes to mind when I think of the Olympic Peninsula. Mists are easy to explain. You'll find them on beaches, in the mermaid-green rain forest, and curling around the tips of the majestic Olympic Mountains. The mystery aspect is more complex and has at its heart the Native American culture, the legends of the settlers, and the moody atmosphere created by the towering and ancient cedar and fir trees.

In the center of Olympic National Park is 7,965-foot Mt. Olympus. Snowcapped year-round, the base is the wettest spot in the lower 48 states, it receives 200 inches of precipitation a year; the three rain forest valleys—the Quinault, Queets, and Hoh—each receive between 141 and 161 inches per year. The moss hangs like curtains from tree limbs in the forest, especially along the Hall of Mosses Trail in the Hoh Valley. You'll likely hear the legend of the Iron Man of the Hoh, John Huelsdonk, an early settler who carried an iron stove on his back for miles through the rain forest.

You can sit on a hay bale or sprawl on a blanket in a meadow and listen to the Chamber Musicians play Mozart and Bach at the Olympic Music Festival's "Concerts in the Barn," performed each summer near Port Ludlow. For blues and fiddle music, Fort Worden's summer festival near Port Townsend provides those and more. And, of course, there's the rhythm of the rain—drip, drip, dripping in the rain forest. ◣

OLYMPIC PENINSULA

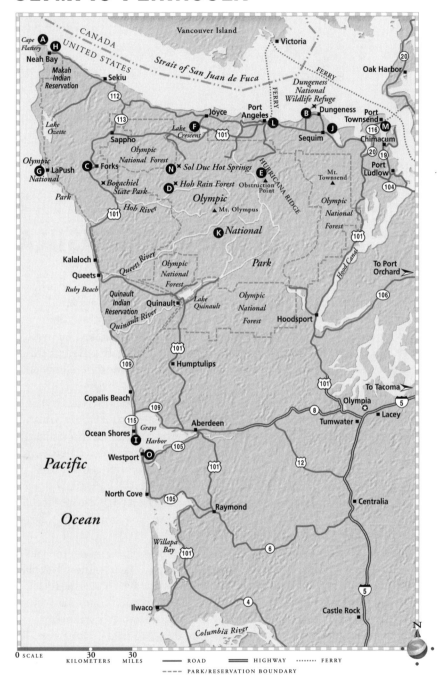

Cape Flattery
A
H
Neah Bay

CANADA
UNITED STATES

Vancouver Island

Strait of San Juan de Fuca

Victoria

FERRY

Oak Harbor
20

Makah Indian Reservation

Sekiu

112

FERRY

Dungeness National Wildlife Refuge

Lake Ozette

113

Joyce

Lake Crescent
F

Port Angeles
L

101

B
Dungeness

Sequim
J

Port Townsend

M
116
Chimacum

Sappho

Olympic National Forest

20
19

Port Ludlow

Olympic
G
National
LaPush

C
Forks

N
Sol Duc Hot Springs

Hoh Rain Forest
D

HURRICANA RIDGE

Obstruction Point
E

Mt. Townsend

104

Park

Bogachiel State Park

Olympic

Olympic National Forest

101

Hoh River

Mt. Olympus

K
National

Kalaloch

Queets River

Olympic National Forest

Queets

Ruby Beach

Quinault Indian Reservation

Quinault

Quinault River

Lake Quinault

Park

Olympic National Forest

Hood Canal

To Port Orchard

106

Hoodsport

101

Humptulips

109

101

To Tacoma

Olympia
5

Copalis Beach

109

Ocean Shores
115

I

Grays
Harbor

Aberdeen

105

8
Tumwater

Lacey

Westport
O

101

12

Pacific

North Cove
105

Raymond

Centralia

Ocean

Willapa Bay
101

6

5

Ilwaco

4

Castle Rock

Columbia River

N

0 SCALE
30 KILOMETERS
30 MILES
ROAD   HIGHWAY   .... FERRY
- - - - PARK/RESERVATION BOUNDARY

Sights

- **Ⓐ** Cape Flattery
- **Ⓑ** Dungeness Spit
- **Ⓒ** Forks
- **Ⓓ** Hoh Rain Forest
- **Ⓔ** Hurricane Ridge
- **Ⓕ** Lake Crescent
- **Ⓖ** LaPush
- **Ⓗ** Makah Cultural and Research Center

- **Ⓘ** Ocean Shores
- **Ⓙ** Olympic Game Farm
- **Ⓚ** Olympic National Park
- **Ⓛ** Port Angeles
- **Ⓜ** Port Townsend
- **Ⓙ** Sequim
- **Ⓝ** Sol Duc Hot Springs
- **Ⓞ** Westport

Note: Items with the same letter are located in the same town or area.

A PERFECT DAY ON THE OLYMPIC PENINSULA

The eastern portion of the peninsula is easily reached on a day trip, but it's more fun to overnight. A perfect day would begin early with breakfast at an inn or B&B around Port Ludlow (for golfers), Port Townsend (for history fans), or Sequim (to guarantee your best weather); it would include a meander along Port Townsend's Waterfront, a picnic lunch listening to classical music (Concerts in the Barn), and a splurge on dinner at Heron Beach Inn.

A perfect day on the west side of the peninsula includes a thoughtfully reflective walk in the rain forest or along a primitive beach—such as Cape Alava—and ends after dinner at a classic old lodge like Lake Quinault or Kalaloch.

SIGHTSEEING HIGHLIGHTS

☆☆☆☆ **Cape Flattery**—There's a spectacular view of Tatoosh Island and lighthouse from the cliffs where the Pacific Ocean meets the Straits at the far northwest corner of the peninsula. Little known is that it's the site of a Civil War naval battle between the CSS *Shenandoah* and the USS *Abigail*.

Details: *Going west from Port Angeles, follow SR 112. (half day)*

✵✵✵✵ **Hurricane Ridge**—A 17-mile drive along a steep winding road from Port Angeles brings you to over 5,200 feet above sea level with magnificent views of the glacier-covered peaks, subalpine tundra, and deeply carved river valleys of the Olympic Mountains. You can downhill and cross-country ski and snowshoe the trails in winter. During the summer, park naturalists lead meadow walks.

Details: From U.S. 101 in Port Angeles, take the Race Street Exit . Obstruction Point Road, a steep 8.4-mile road east of the ridge, offers the best views of Mt. Olympus; open mid-summer to early fall. For general road conditions call the park visitors center, 360/452-0330. (3 hours)

✵✵✵✵ **Ocean Shores**—There's plenty of action at this sprawling fifties-style beach community on the southwest Olympic Peninsula. On a beautiful day the six miles of flat sandy beach turn into a highway for horseback riders, mopeds, cars, kite flyers, and strollers. Away from the beach there's plenty of activity, too—bicycling, bumper cars, boating, gambling, golf—enough to keep all family members happy.

Details: Ocean Shores is about 120 miles south of Forks, 70 miles west of Olympia. For details and lodging information, call the chamber at 360/289-2451 or 800/76-BEACH.

✵✵✵✵ **Olympic National Park**—Presidents Theodore and Franklin Roosevelt both were instrumental in setting aside over a million acres of wilderness that comprises Olympic National Park, one of the nation's most beautiful parks. You'll find a rare rain forest, wildlife—it is home to the country's largest herd of Roosevelt elk—and 600 miles of hiking trails. There are 57 miles of primitive coastline. The park is surrounded by the reservations of several Native American tribes including the Chehalis, Hoh, Quileute, Quinault, and Makah.

Details: Olympic National Park visitors center is in Port Angeles; 360/452-0330. (1 day minimum)

✵✵✵✵ **Port Townsend**—A National Historic Landmark, 70 buildings in this Victorian-style seaport town of 7,000 are on the National Register of Historic Places; many of the historic homes are B&Bs. Nearby Fort Worden guarded Admiralty Inlet during World War II and is the site of a popular arts and music festival. The Keystone Ferry leaves from here to Whidbey Island.

Details: Contact the Port Townsend Chamber of Commerce Visitor Center for tour information, 2437 East Sims Way, 360/385-2722. (3 hours)

★★★ **Forks**—A town of 5,000, Forks is synonymous with the logging industry and the spotted owl controversy. Here you'll find the Forks Timber Museum and Loggers Memorial. The area is also known for fast-running rivers with steelhead and salmon.
Details: Forks Chamber of Commerce, 360/374-2531 or 800/443-6757. (1 hour)

★★★ **Hoh Rain Forest**—The magical heart of the forest is in the moss-draped trees. The **Hall of Mosses Trail** is less than a mile long and offers a close-up look at the flora of the rain forest ecosystem.
Details: Exit off U.S. 101 about 13 miles south of Forks and follow road 19 miles to visitors center, 360/374-6925. Open summers 9 to 6:30, remainder of year 9 to 5. (1–2 hours)

★★★ **Lake Crescent**—This is an impressive 12-mile-long, glacier-carved freshwater fishing lake west of Port Angeles known for its Beardslee trout and gem-like setting. The lodge on its shores was visited by Franklin Roosevelt. A short mile-long trail leads to 90-foot Marymere Falls.
Details: 17 miles west of Port Angeles on U.S. 101. (2 hours)

★★★ **LaPush**—This coastal community is home to the Quileute Indian Nation, whose square-mile reservation is located at the mouth of the Quileute River. Beach hiking and osprey and seal watching are tops here. Try First Beach, a mile-long crescent beach with resident opreys at the south end.
Details: Watch for exit onto SR 110 2 miles north of Forks. (half day)

★★★ **Makah Cultural and Research Center**—The impressive $3 million facility in Neah Bay at the tip of the peninsula contains the artifacts from the Ozette Village ruins, a 2,000-year-old site at Cape Alava. Buried about 500 years ago in a mudslide, the site was excavated in the 1970s. It is sealed, but the artifacts, including harpoons, an old fishing net, carved figures, and household items, are on display at the center. Combine a stop here with a hike at Cape Flattery.
Details: On SR 112 at Neah Bay; 360/645-2711. Summer hours 10 to 5 daily, Wednesday to Sunday remainder of year. Admission about $4. (2 hours)

★★★ **Westport**—You can fish from boats or from shore in the town of Westport on Washington's southwestern coast. Deep-sea fishing charters run year-round. There's surf fishing here, a breakwater area, and jetties to fish from as well; you can go crabbing in season in the inner harbor off any of the floats or docks. Whalewatching season is March through May; you can join a charter boat excursion or view from city viewing tower. The Westport Maritime Museum has whaling exhibits.

Details: 22 miles southwest of Aberdeen. For details and lodging info— there are numerous motels here—call 800/345-6223. Crab rings and bait are available at the Hungry Whale Grocery on Montesano Avenue, 360/268-0136, the town's main street, and at Neptune Charters, 360/268-0124, across from Float 14. (half day or overnight)

★★ **Dungeness Spit**—This is a narrow, nearly six-mile-long finger of land that hooks out into the Strait of Juan de Fuca, near Sequim. It's thought to be the longest natural sandspit in the world. A wildlife refuge, its inner shores are rich with grasses and shorebirds. A lighthouse is located at its tip.

Details: About 7 miles northwest of Sequim, U.S. 101, turn north on Kitchen Dick Road; 360/457-8451. Open dawn to dusk daily. Admission $2 per family. (2–4 hours)

★★ **Olympic Game Farm**—You can drive or take guided walks through buffalo, elk, and zebra habitats where many other wild animals roam. Predators like lions, tigers, leopards, wolves, and cougars are in enclosures. There's a petting zoo for smaller children. A fishing pond is open during the summer.

Details: 1423 Ward Road, Sequim, 800/778-4295; www.north olympic.com/gamefarm. Open daily at 9 a.m.; closing times vary. Admission about $6 adults, free for kids 4 and under. (1 hour)

★★ **Port Angeles**—The bustling commercial hub and largest town of the northern peninsula, Port Angeles has a population of about 18,000. It has a five-mile waterfront trail and the Arthur D. Feiro Marine Lab that offers hands-on orientation to sea creatures. Black Ball ferry leaves from here to Victoria. Hurricane Ridge is a 40-minute drive from here. The Olympic National Park visitors center is here.

Details: Visitor Information Center is at 121 East Railroad Avenue; 360/452-2363. (1–2 hours)

★★ **Sequim**—The town of Sequim (pronounced "squim"), population about 4,000, is the driest spot in western Washington with an annual rainfall of approximately 16 inches (a perfect example of how Northwest weather can differ dramatically in short distances). Growing numbers of active retirees who play its golf courses, boat, and like easy access to Victoria from nearby Port Angeles, are locating here. Sequim hosts the oldest festival in the state, the Irrigation Festival; a Lavendar and Jazz Festival; and a Salmon Bake in August. The Olympic Game Farm, wineries, a flower farm, and Dungeness Golf Club are nearby.

Details: Sequim Visitors Information Center, U.S. 101 East, P.O. Box 907, Sequim, WA 98382; 360/683-6197. (1 hour)

✰✰ **Sol Duc Hot Springs**—These hot mineral springs with hot and cool pool facilities sit amidst the moss-draped forest. This is a popular spot and can be crowded in summer. There is some cabin-style lodging and a campground.

Details: 30 miles west of Port Angeles on U.S. 101 to the turnoff to the hot springs, then another 12 miles or so, and takes a about an hour; 360/327-3583. (2 hours or longer)

FITNESS AND RECREATION

Fishing, hiking, river rafting, birdwatching, horseback or llama trekking—these are just some of the activities to pursue on the Olympic Peninsula. Hundreds of trails in the Olympic National Park include rugged beaches, rain forest, and mountain hikes. The **Concerts in the Barn** run June through September, in an old dairy barn on a 40-acre farm, 10 miles west of the Hood Canal Bridge. For performance and ticket information, contact the Philadelphia String Quartet, P.O. Box 45776, Seattle, WA 98145-0776; 206/527-8839.

Sea kayaking is a favorite of water hounds. Sailors and would-be sailors can try *The Adventuress,* a 101-foot gaff-rigged tall ship often moored in Port Townsend. Mates teach about the marine environment, navigation, and history. You can sign aboard for day sails (about $30 per person) or longer cruises. Be prepared to hoist or lower sails and to join in singing rousing sea shanties. No experience necessary, sailings run April through October. For schedule and reservations, call Sound Experience, 360/379-0438.

The **Dungeness Golf & Country Club**, 1965 Woodcock Road, outside Sequim, has a crab-shaped sand trap. It's open to the public and year-round golf packages are available; call 800/447-6826. Boaters will want to check out the John Wayne Marina in Sequim. East of town is **7 Cedars Casino,** with a native arts store, operated by the Jamestown S'Klallam tribe. Also around Sequim are several wineries to tour, including **Lost Mountain** and **Neuharth.**

Ruby and **Kalaloch Beaches** are two of the most accessible beach areas. A half dozen short paths off U.S. 101 lead to these driftwood rich spots. Ruby Beach is a wilderness beach with sea arches and tiny islands. Kalaloch, to the south, has a campground. Tide pool walks are offered by the National Park Service (listed in the park's newspaper).

Olympic Park Institute offers a wide variety of field-oriented classes covering the arts and natural and cultural history of the peninsula while staying in their historic Lake Crescent site. Elderhostel and school programs are also offered. Call 800/775-3720 for a free catalog; or check the Web: www.olympus.net/opi.

FOOD

Try the dining room at the **Heron Beach Inn,** 360/437-0411, for fine food in a stylish, romantic atmosphere. Port Townsend's **Lonny's Restaurant**, 360/385-0700, is a popular destination for a special meal. The menu offers rich and delicious seafood dishes among other interesting items. **Khu Larb Thai**, 360/385-5023, in Port Townsend, makes a good stop if you're in the mood for curries and spicy Thai food. In Port Angeles it's **C'est Si Bon**, 360/452-8888, for French food and fine dining. Crab is what you come for at the **Three Crabs Restaurant**, 360/683-4264, an un-fancy café and local hangout overlooking the beach in Dungeness, near Sequim; their pies are worth the stop, too. You'll sometimes see the crab pots steaming outside, and there's a crab shack with retail seafood. The park-lodge-style dining rooms at **Kalaloch Lodge** and at **Lake Quinault Lodge** make good evening meal destinations, with traditional American food and Northwest seafood offerings.

LODGING

Heron Beach Inn (formerly called the Inn at Port Ludlow) is a posh eastern peninsula destination a few miles north of the Hood Canal Bridge, on its own peninsula on Port Ludlow Bay. It has more than 30 rooms with fireplaces and water views. Port Townsend's many historic B&Bs are a favorite destination of couples; some favorites are the **James House,** 1238 Washington Street, 360/385-1238 or 800/385-3205 and the **Ann Starrett Mansion**, 744 Clay Street, 360/385-3205 or 800/321-0644. With a swimming pool and a pet policy (pets accepted with some restrictions), the **Best Western**, 360/683-0691 or 800/238-7234, on Sequim Bay makes a good stopover for families; ask for family rates. **Red Ranch Inn**, 830 West Washington Street, Sequim, 800/777-4195, is a motel on the main thoroughfare of Sequim that's good for families and golfers. (They often have golf packages with the Dungeness Golf Club.) Some units have kitchens. **Groveland Cottage**, 360/683-3565, is a turn-of-the-century clapboard home in the village of Dungeness. **Domaine Madeleine**, 360/457-4174, a B&B between Sequim and Port Angeles, has dramatic views overlooking the Strait of Juan de Fuca toward Vancouver Island. **Miller Tree Inn B&B**, 654 East Division Street, 360/374-6806, www.northolympic.com/millertre, or e-mail: milltree@ptinet.net, is a rambling and comfortable two-story house on a spacious lot in Forks that's a favorite with fishermen. There are two rooms that accommodate up to four people. **Eagle Point Inn** is a spacious log lodge tucked away in the woods by a river near Forks, 360/327-3236, built by owner hosts Dan and Chris Christiansen. And there are several classical, old lodge-style destinations: **Lake Crescent Lodge**, 21 miles west of Port Angeles, 360/928-3211, has five rooms with shared bath in the main lodge that was built in 1916; 30 modern guest rooms and 17 cottages, four built in the 1930s, are rustic and have fireplaces. Open April through late October. There's a dining room, rowboat rental, and gift shop. For generations, beach lovers have found their way to **Kalaloch Lodge**, about 35 miles south of Forks on U.S. Highway 101, 360/962-2271, to hole up in a rustic cabin above the beach and wish for a storm. There are wide driftwood beaches to explore. Well-known Ruby Beach is six miles north. Kalaloch Lodge has 40 cabins, including eight original bluff cabins (these have a view), a restaurant, and motel rooms. **Lake Quinault Lodge**, 360/288-2900 or 800/562-6672, a rustic and beloved timber structure on the south shore of Lake Quinault, has been enchanting visitors since 1926. A spacious lobby with fireplace has a gift shop with Native American art. More than 70 rooms include guest rooms, lakeside rooms, and rooms with a fireplace.

Most of the fifties-style motels in Ocean Shores on the southwest peninsula have been upgraded over the years, and there's newer beach-front lodging such as the affordable **Best Western Lighthouse Suites Inn**, 800/757-7873, at the north end of town. The $14 million **Shilo Inn** with its huge saltwater fish tank, 800/222-2244, is also a good

OLYMPIC PENINSULA

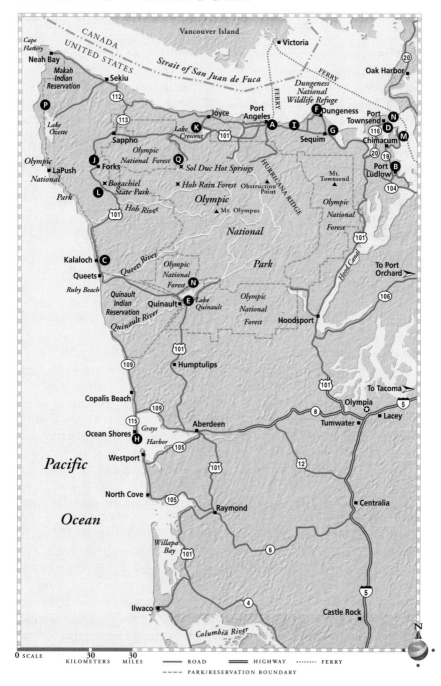

Food

- **A** C'est Si Bon
- **B** Heron Beach Inn
- **C** Kalaloch Lodge
- **D** Khu Larb Thai
- **E** Lake Quinault Lodge
- **D** Lonny's Restaurant
- **F** Three Crabs Restaurant

Lodging

- **D** Ann Starrett Mansion
- **G** Best Western
- **H** Best Western Lighthouse Suites Inn
- **I** Domaine Madeleine
- **J** Eagle Point Inn
- **F** Groveland Cottage

Lodging (continued)

- **B** Heron Beach Inn
- **D** James House
- **C** Kalaloch Lodge
- **K** Lake Crescent Lodge
- **E** Lake Quinault Lodge
- **J** Miller Tree Inn B&B
- **F** Red Ranch Inn
- **H** Shilo Inn

Camping

- **L** Bogachiel State Park
- **M** Fort Flagler State Park
- **N** Fort Worden State Park
- **O** July Creek
- **P** Lake Ozette Trails Triangle
- **Q** Sol Duc

Note: Items with the same letter are located in the same town or area.

value. For a lodging and activities list, call the Ocean Shores Chamber of Commerce, 360/289-2451 or 800/76-BEACH.

CAMPING

There are almost 1,000 campsites within **Olympic National Park**, 360/452-0330, including a wide variety of camping options for hikers and car and RV campers; be sure to pack waterproof gear and rain clothes. **Sol Duc** campground, 27 miles west of Port Angeles, then 12 miles into the camp, is a popular campground close to Sol Duc Hot Springs facility. It also has facilities for the handicapped. **July Creek** is a walk-in campsite for hikers on the north shore of Lake Quinault. Its

29 tent sites are situated where the creek empties into the lake. Turn off Highway 101 two miles north of the community of Amanda Park. No reservations are accepeted. For information call Olympic National Park, 360/452-0330.

Another walk-in experience is beach camping at **Lake Ozette Trails Triangle**. It's a bit of a hike, but for a beautiful wilderness beach experience, this Olympic Peninsula gem is the best. From SR 112 near Seikiu take the well-marked turnoff Road 21 to the ranger station, where the road deadends. It's a little over three miles along a board-walk to Cape Alava (the most westerly point in the continental United States), three miles south on a beautiful sandy beach, and three miles back to the ranger station via another boardwalk. The loop takes about six hours or you can camp overnight. Deer are common, and racoons especially like this beach. If you camp, hang your food high in the trees so you don't lose it. Make reservations (there's a quota system), 360/452-0300, up to 30 days in advance of your trip.

State parks on the peninsula include **Fort Flagler State Park** on Marrowstone Island, eight miles northeast of Port Hadlock; **Fort Worden State Park** in Port Townsend; and **Bogachiel State Park**, six miles south of Forks. For reservations call 800/452-5687.

HELPFUL HINTS

The website for the **Olympic Peninsula Visitor's Association** is www.northolympic.com. For more B&B options, contact the **Olympic Peninsula Bed & Breakfast Association**, 360/374-6806.

TACOMA AND MT. RAINIER

In the past, Tacoma was thought of as Seattle's rowdy sibling—a mill town, a port town, and a railroad town on south Puget Sound. But this city is through with that image. A steady revitalization is drawing more and more visitors to what is increasingly becoming an international arts and cultural destination. The Broadway Center for the Performing Arts, including the restored 1918 Pantages and Rialto Theaters and the modern and colorful Theater on the Square, form the heart of a performing arts district that draws people from all over. The renovated Union Station and its neighbor, the impressive new Washington State History Museum, also draw visitors.

Hometown of internationally known glass artist Dale Chihuly, the city will boast a new International Glass Museum at the turn of the century, with working furnaces and resident artists. A Glass Bridge will connect the waterfront to the museum. Nearby will be the new Tacoma Art Museum with more glass exhibits. More than a hundred years ago, Tacoma was dubbed the "City of Destiny," because it was the railroad terminus on the Puget Sound. Then the tracks moved to Seattle and at times Tacoma's destiny has been hazy. Now it's as clear as glass.

The city has plentiful scenic attractions, too. Point Defiance Park with its zoo and aquarium offer wraparound views of both the freighter traffic on Commencement Bay and ferry and pleasure boaters on south Puget Sound. Tacoma has also been the city most closely connected to Mt. Rainier. The historic Mountain Highway leads from the city to Paradise Lodge atop the mountain. ◣

TACOMA

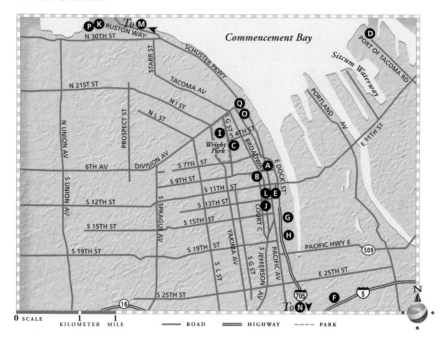

Sights

- **A** Broadway Center for the Performing Arts
- **B** Children's Museum of Tacoma
- **C** Karpeles Manuscript Museum
- **D** Port of Tacoma
- **E** Tacoma Art Museum
- **F** Tacoma Dome
- **G** Union Station
- **H** Washington State History Museum
- **I** W.W. Seymour Botanical Conservatory

Food

- **J** Altezzo
- **K** Harbor Lights
- **L** Fujiya
- **M** Lobster Shop
- **N** Stanley & Seafort's

Lodging

- **O** Chinaberry B&B
- **P** Commencement Bay B&B
- **U** Sheraton Tacoma Hotel
- **Q** The Villa B&B

Note: Items with the same letter are located in the same town or area.

A PERFECT DAY IN TACOMA

For a perfect day in Tacoma, visit Point Defiance Park and see the gardens and aquarium. Enjoy a leisurely lunch in the park at the new Anthony's Home Port and get great water views with your steaming bowl of clam chowder. Spend time in the Washington State History Museum. Then move on to Union Station to marvel at the play of light through the pieces of Chihuly glass on exhibit there; the Tacoma Art Museum also displays Chihuly. Have dinner at a restaurant with a view, such as Altezzo or Stanley & Seaforts, and plan your next day—a trip to Mt. Rainier.

SIGHTSEEING HIGHLIGHTS

✩✩✩✩ **Point Defiance Park and Point Defiance Zoo and Aquarium**—Within this nearly 700-acre park surrounded on three sides by Puget Sound are an excellent zoo and aquarium, a replica of Fort Nisqually, a Hudson's Bay Company fur trading post (circa 1855), a logging museum, and Never Never Land—a children's fantasy world filled with sculpted storybook characters. There are seven different gardens, including a Japanese, rhododendron, dahlia trial garden, and herb garden. In addition, fourteen miles of hiking trails offer dramatic views over the water to the Olympic Mountains. Take the ferry to Vashon Island.

Details: From I-5, take Exit 132 to Highway 16 and take Sixth Avenue Exit and turn left. Take the next right onto Pearl Street and follow signs to Point Defiance Park; signs will direct you to the zoo. Point Defiance Zoo and Aquarium, 253/591-5335 (recorded message with hours and directions) or 253/591-5337. Open year-round, 10 to 7 during summer. Admission is $7, seniors $6.55, kids 4–13 $5.30, 3 and under free. (2–3 hours)

✩✩✩✩ **Washington State History Museum**—This impressive building echoes the design of its neighbor, Union Station; walk in and you feel like you're entering a train station—explore and feel as if you're on a journey into Washington's past. The 106,000-square-foot facility cost $40.8 million to build in 1996. There are permanent exhibits on the fishing, fruit, timber, and wheat industries of Washington and special changing exhibits. Their geological display gives an excellent visual overview of the formation of the Northwest. The extensive gift shop here sells Washington wines.

Details: 1911 Pacific Avenue, Tacoma; 888/238-4373. Open Tuesday through Saturday 10 to 5, Thursday until 8, Sunday 11 to 5. Admission is $7, seniors $6, students $5, ages 6–12 $4. (2–3 hours)

★★★ **Broadway Center for the Performing Arts**—The renovations of the Pantages Theater is at the heart of the cultural arts center along Broadway. Built as a Vaudeville house in 1918 by Alexander Pantages, it is a striking example of early 20th century Greco-Roman design. The Rialto, also built in 1918, has a Beaux Arts decor. These historic venues, as well as Theatre on the Square, showcase regular live theater and musical performances.

Details: Ticket office at 901 Broadway open Monday through Friday from 11:30 to 5:30. Tickets may be purcahsed in person or by calling 253/531-5894.

★★★ **Karpeles Manuscript Museum**—A surprise of a museum showcases historical original handwritten drafts, letters, and documents of famous people like Napoleon and Thomas Jefferson; they host special exhibits, too. Across the street from the W. W. Seymour Botanical Conservatory.

Details: At 407 South G Street; 253/383-2575. Open 10 to 4 Tuesday through Sunday. Admission is free. (1 hour)

★★★ **Lakewold Gardens**—Beautiful former private gardens designed by noted landscape architect Thomas Church, mix Northwest and classic styles combining one of the largest Japanese maple and rhododendron collections in the Northwest. This 10-acre estate is considered one of the best gardens in America. A treat for gardeners and non-gardeners alike.

Details: South of Tacoma at 12317 Gravelly Lake Drive SW; 253/584-3360; open Thursdays through Mondays 9 to 4. Admission $6, seniors and kids under 12 $5. (2 hours)

★★★ **Nisqually National Wildlife Refuge**—One of the few remaining untouched river deltas in the United States, the refuge covers nearly 3,000 acres of salt marsh, forested swamp, and wetland meadows. Boaters, canoers, and kayakers can explore by water. Walking loops from ½ to 5.6 miles long take you through wildlife viewing areas. And it's a scenic drive past the refuge on I-5.

Details: On the Pierce-Thurston county line west of I-5, take Exit 114.

Open daily during daylight hours, information office open 7:30 to 4. Admission $2 per family. (1–2 hours)

★★★ **Northwest Trek Wildlife Park, Eatonville**—You can take an hour-long tram tour of this 625-acre sanctuary with its herds of free-roaming bison, caribou, and big-horned sheep. And you'll see wolves and grizzly bears and birds of prey in contained natural habitats. There are five miles of walking trails.

Details: The park lies about 17 miles east of Tacoma off SR 161 near Eatonville; call 360/832-6117 for directions; visit www.nwtrek.org for more information. Open at 9:30 daily. Admission is $8.25 for adults, $7.75 for seniors, $5.75 for kids 5–17, $3.75 for kids 3 and 4, free for 2 and under. (2–3 hours)

★★★ **Steilacoom**—Washington's oldest incorporated town lies west of Tacoma. The whole town of Steilacoom is on the National Register of Historic Places and includes the oldest standing church in the state. Bair Drug & Hardware Museum with a delightful 1906 soda fountain is a café as well and serves up old-fashioned ice-cream sodas, sasparillas, and sundaes.

Details: Maps of a self-guided walking tour are available at Steilacoom Historical Museum at 112 Main Street in the lower level of the town hall. Bair Drug, 1617 Lafayette Street, serves breakfast and lunch; open daily year-round, 9 to 4. (1–2 hours)

★★ **Children's Museum of Tacoma**—Hands-on arts and science exhibits, a play village, lots of colorful fish, activities, and much more keep children entertained.

Details: 936 Broadway, Tacoma; 253/627-6031. Open Tuesday through Saturday 10 to 5, Sunday noon to 5. Admission is $4.25 per person, seniors $3.25, under 2 free. Every Friday night is free from 5 to 9.

★★ **Port of Tacoma**—Sixth largest container port in North America, the Port of Tacoma lies north of the city. A 24-hour observation tower, with interpretive information, views Sitcum Waterway and the port activities.

Details: One Sitcum Plaza; 253/383-5481. From I-5 take the City Center Exit (#133), follow signs for 705 north to the "A" Street Exit. From A street take a right onto 11th street and follow it to SeaLand Drive. Free admission. Open 24 hours. (1 hour)

★★ **Puyallup**—Since 1900 Puyallup (pronounced "pew-AL-up") has hosted the Western Washington State Fair, which now draws 1.5 million visitors annually. It is also known for its spring fields of daffodil and other bulb flowers. Seventeen-room Ezra Meeker Mansion, built by Puyallup's founder in 1890, is open for touring.

    Details: Meeker Mansion, 253/848-1770; open April through December, Wednesday through Sunday afternoons. Admission is $4 adults, $3 students and seniors. (45 minutes)

★★ **Tacoma Art Museum**—You'll find sculptured glass by Dale Chihuly and the works of other Northwest artists, as well as classics by Renoir, Chagall, and Dali at this museum.

    Details: 12th and Pacific Avenue, Tacoma; 253/272-4258. Open 10 to 5 Tuesday through Saturday, noon to 5 Sunday. Admission charged. (1 hour)

★★ **Union Station**—Built in 1911 by Northern Pacific Railroad, this landmark domed brick building was a railway station until 1983. Now it's a federal courthouse with a public rotunda that exhibits Chihuly glass. It's well worth a quick look before you head into the Washington State History Museum, next door.

    Details: 1717 Pacific Avenue, Tacoma; 253/931-7884. (15 minutes)

★★ **Rhododendron Species Botanical Garden**—One of the largest collections of species rhododendrons in the world, this garden includes 24 acres of rhododendrons from one-inch Chinese dwarfs to 100-foot Himalayan giants. It's on the Weyerhaeuser Company campus in Federal Way.

    Details: 33660 Weyerhaeuser Way S., Federal Way; 253/661-9377. Open March to May daily 10 to 4, closed Thursday. Call for additional hours information. Admission $3.50. (2 hours)

★★ **W. W. Seymour Botanical Conservatory**—This Victorian-style conservatory, built in 1908, in Wright Park contains over 200 species of exotic and tropical plants including ornamental figs, bird-of-paradise, and bromeliads. It's on the State and National Historic Registers, and is located across from Karpeles Museum.

    Details: From I-5 take Exit 133 to City Center, follow signs for 705 North, take Stadium Way Exit, right on Stadium Way, left on 4th Street, and follow to "G" Street. 316 South G Street, Tacoma, 253/591-5330. Open daily 10 to 4:30. Admission free. (½ hour)

FITNESS AND RECREATION

Jogging or walking **Ruston Way**'s two-mile waterfront promenade offers great views of Commencement Bay; more views can be had exploring Point Defiance Park and Zoo.

The Proctor District is a historic village-like enclave in the North End known for fine shopping. With no large department stores in downtown Tacoma, the best draw here for those born to shop is browsing **Antique Row**. Located in the city's historic district, its antique and memorabilia shops offer a wide range of deluxe junk and some fine antiques. The **Tacoma Farmer's Market** is held on Antique Row from June to September every Thursday from 10 to 3.

SPECTATOR SPORTS

The **Tacoma Dome**, the largest wooden dome in the nation, is the venue for sports, entertainment, and trade shows. The city's hockey team, the Tacoma Sabercats, plays here as well. For event information and tickets, call 253/272-6817. Tacoma has a professional baseball team, the Tacoma Rainiers, who play class-AAA Pacific Coast League baseball at Cheney Stadium; 800/281-3834.

FOOD

Ruston Way is known as "Restaurant Row." You'll find **Harbor Lights,** 2761 Ruston Way, 253/752-8600, with waterfront views of Commencement Bay. For decades it's offered delightful classics like steamed clams. Two **Lobster Shop** restaurants offer nice dining options with simply prepared seafood and great views of Commencement Bay. The newer location is at 4013 Ruston Way, 253/759-2165, in a modern setting; and the original, 253/927-1513, across the bay at 6912 Sound View Drive NE off Dash Point Road, a 15-minute drive from downtown Tacoma, is worth it if you prefer the ambiance and charm of a restaurant in an old house. **Fujiya** at 1125 Court "C", 253/627-5319, near the Broadway Theater district and the Sheraton Hotel, has great sushi and Japanese food at reasonable prices. Go to **Stanley & Seaforts**, 115 East 34th Street, 253/473-7300, for a seafood and salad lunch and a great view of Commencement Bay. Also, an incredible view can be had from **Altezzo**, 253/572-3200, along with the Northern Italian–style food served at the top of the

TACOMA AND MT. RAINIER REGION.

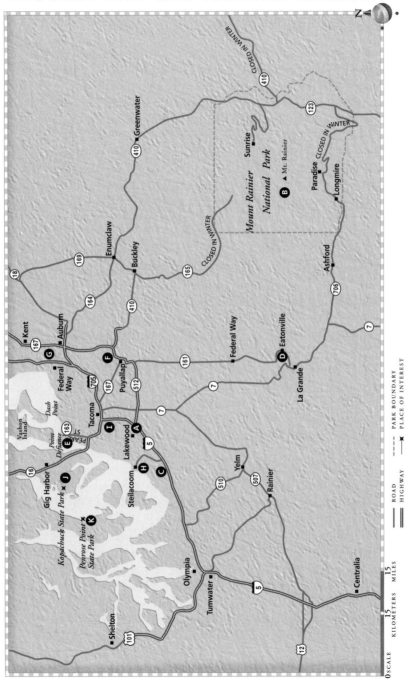

Sights

Ⓐ Lakewold Gardens

Ⓑ Mt. Rainier National Park

Ⓒ Nisqually National Wildlife
Refuge

Ⓓ Northwest Trek Wildlife Park

Ⓔ Point Defiance Park and Point
Defiance Zoo and Aquarium

Ⓕ Puyallup

Ⓖ Rhododendron Species
Botanical Garden

Ⓗ Steilacoom

Food

Ⓔ Anthony's Home Port

Ⓗ E.R. Rogers Restaurant

Ⓘ Mama Stortini's

Camping

Ⓙ Kopachuck State Park

Ⓚ Penrose Point State Park

Note: Items with the same letter are located in the same town or area.

Sheraton Tacoma Hotel. **Mama Stortini's** at 3715 Bridgeport Way, 253/566-1976, serves up family-style Italian food. The orders are big; request a full order of spaghetti and you'll probably take half home.

Or A great family stop for lunch or dinner is the new **Anthony's Home Port**, 5910 N. Waterfront Drive, 253/752-9700, located on pilings over the water next to the Vashon Ferry terminal at the base of Point Defiance Zoo and Aquarium. The **E.R. Rogers Restaurant**, 1702 Commercial Street, 253/582-0280, in Steilacoom south of Tacoma offers views of the Tacoma Narrows bridge, along with salmon dishes and other classics (Sunday brunch and dinners only), in a historic 1891 mansion that's been decorated in the Victorian style.

Or plan to eat at one of the lodges in Mt. Rainier National Park. **Paradise Inn** has a rustic, open-beamed dining room that seats 200. Sunday brunch ($15 per person) is a special event with gourmet touches like crepes and omelets made to order. In Longmire, on the approach to Paradise, the **National Park Inn**'s restaurant offers soups, sandwiches, daily specials, and yummy desserts.

LODGING

Located in the heart of downtown and visible from I-5 is the **Sheraton Tacoma Hotel**, 1320 Broadway, 206/572-3200. There are several popular B&Bs, including **Commencement Bay B&B**, **The Villa**, and **Chinaberry**. For more information on these and others, contact the **Greater Tacoma B&B** reservation service, 253/759-4088 and 800/406-4088 or www.bestinns.net/usa/wa/gtbbr.html; or the **B&B Association of Tacoma and Mt. Rainier**, 253/593-6098 or 888/593-6098 or www.tribnet.com/bb/tacomainns. There are also plentiful motel lodgings off I-5 south of Tacoma and along the Mountain Highway, just east of the city; contact the visitors bureau, 800/272-2662.

CAMPING

Kopachuck State Park, 360/265-3606, is on Henderson Bay, north of Tacoma. Go north on Interstate 5. There are more than 40 campsites for tents and self-contained motor homes up to 35 feet. There's a beach area for exploring. No reservations. Another waterfront camping spot is **Penrose Point State Park**, also northwest of Tacoma, over-looking Carr Inlet on Puget Sound, 253/884-2514. No reservations. Mt. Rainier National Park offers five campgrounds (including the popular area of Ohanapecosh at the park's southeast edge) with tent sites; none have R.V. hookups. Most sites are open from Memorial Day to mid-October. For details, call 360/569-2211.

NIGHTLIFE

Sometimes you'll have to stand in line to get into **Drakes**, 734 Pacific Ave., 253/572-4144, a popular downtown hot spot. **Jillian's**, 1114 Broadway, 253/572-0300, offers billiards and entertainment. There's evening entertainment at the new **Harmon Brewery**, 1948 Pacific Avenue, 253/383-2739, across from the museum. At **The Swiss**, 1904 South Jefferson, 253/572-2821, the entertainment includes a Sunday Polka Dance. Evenings are lively at the **Spar Tavern**, 2121 North 30th, 253/627-8215 a fixture in Tacoma for over a century and a fun place to peruse the walls covered with turn-of-the-century photos. For an evening at the theater, tickets for **Tacoma Actors Guild** (TAG) performances are available at their ticket office at 915 Broadway, near the Theatre on the Square Broadway Street entrance, or by calling 253/272-2145.

HELPFUL HINTS

For a visitor information packet, contact the **Tacoma-Pierce County Visitor & Convention Bureau**, 906 Broadway (P.O. Box 1754), Tacoma, WA 98401; 800/272-2662; www.tpctourism.org.

SIDE TRIP: MT. RAINIER

Mt. Rainier, "the mountain" of the Northwest, is about a 90-minute drive from Tacoma along the Mountain Highway. En route, you'll pass the visitors center at Longmire, near the National Park Inn (past the western entrance to the park). Stop here or at the Jackson Visitors Center at Paradise to peruse maps, books, videos, and wildflower and wildlife exhibits. A good book on wildflowers will enrich your visit.

Summer afternoon temperatures at Paradise average in the mid-60s with nighttime temperatures in the lower 40s. Hikers should carry extra clothing, raingear, map and compass, extra food, and keep altitude in mind (Mt. Rainier peaks at 14,411 feet), taking rest breaks as needed; hiking boots are recommended. Hiking staffs and bear bells are available for sale in the gift shops at Paradise Inn, at the visitors center, and at Longmire. Check with the ranger on snow conditions before venturing on the high trails. Peak bloom time when there is the greatest flower variety and abundance is July. To reach Mt. Rainier from Interstate 5, take Exit 134, just south of Tacoma. This is Highway 7 (and connects to State Route 706), the most direct route, and is also the route known as the Mountain Highway. For park information and maps, contact Mt. Rainier National Park, 360/569-2211. Park admission is $10. Gray Line of Seattle offers daily escorted bus tours to the mountain; call 800/426-7532.

It's easy to combine a trip to Mt. Rainier with an overnight visit, and there are some terrific options, like a stay at **Paradise Inn.** While not luxurious, the old lodge is cozy, and it's on a spectacular site. The original guest rooms on the second floor of the main building are not soundproof, so expect creaking floors and thin walls. In keeping with the original building, there are no telephones or televisions. If you want to be awakened early, alert the desk and you'll receive a wake-up knock on the door. There is no elevator; some rooms are handicapped accessible. **National Park Inn** (Longmire) has 25 rooms; two on the ground floor are handicapped accessible. Built in 1989—similar to the log inn James Longmire built here in 1884—this lodge has an older feel and modern amenities. Rooms are light and cheery, decorated with twig furniture; all have forest views. Rooms fronting the lodge and road have mountain views. For reservations at Paradise Inn and Longmire's National Park Inn, contact Mount Rainier Guest Services, P.O. Box 108, Ashford, WA 98304; 360/569-2275, fax 360/569-2770. **Alexander's Country Inn,** 800/654-7615, one mile west of the Nisqually entrance (on State Route 706) in the small town of Ashford, is another historic lodging. Built in 1912 and renovated over time, it is a comfortable blend of old and new. There are no elevators, phones, televisions, or air conditioning; and no smoking.

Scenic Route: Kitsap Peninsula

This "back door" route to Tacoma takes you on several ferries and gives you a flavor of the Kitsap Peninsula and Vashon Island. You'll have expansive views of the Cascade and Olympic Mountains on the ferry from Seattle's waterfront to Bainbridge Island (35-minute crossing). The ferry landing is north of the town of Bainbridge (formerly called Winslow), which has antique shops, galleries, and restaurants. If you stay on Highway 305, you'll pass **Bainbridge Island Winery**, 682 State Highway 305, 206/842-WINE, which has a tasting room. Continue northwest to the Scandinavian town of Poulsbo. Even at first glance, its marina filled with boats, skyline dominated by the steeple of the First Lutheran Church, and historic district fit snugly along fjord-like Liberty Bay look like a Scandinavian fishing village. Known as "Little Norway," the town was settled in 1892 by farmers, fishers, and loggers from Norway who saw similarities to their native land; the Nordic character of the community has remained strong. Plan to spend time strolling Front Street's variety of arts, crafts, bakery, and antique stores. In **Verksted Gallery**, 1882 Front street, 360/697-4470, an artists' cooperative that showcases

KITSAP PENINSULA AND HOOD CANAL

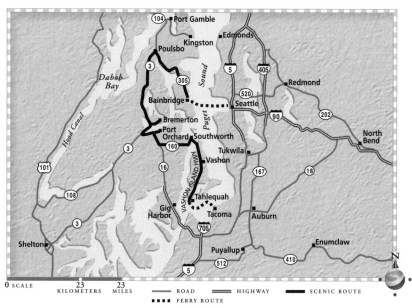

Nordic crafts, you'll see dolls dressed in *bunads* (folk costumes) reflecting authentic designs from different villages and districts of Scandinavia. The **Marine Science Center**, 18743 Front Street NE, 360/779-5549, is a great place for kids to get the "feel" of touch tanks and see educational exhibits.

From Poulsbo, take Highway 3 south to the city of Bremerton. This is the largest city on the peninsula and home to the **Bremerton Naval Museum**, 360/479-7447, and **Puget Sound Naval Shipyard**. A rejuvenated downtown is coming alive with art galleries, restaurants, museums, and many new shops. The city is looking to the future with its **Sinclair Landing** project, to be complete by the turn of the century. It will feature an outdoor amphitheater, the *Kalakala* (the only "art deco" ferry ever built), more good quality restaurants, and high-end speciality shops. You can take a harbor tour of the Navy's mothball fleet for $8.50, **Kitsap Harbor Tours**, 360/377-8924, and visit the most decorated ship in World War II, the USS *Turner Joy* (**Bremerton Historic Ships Association**, 360/792-2457).

From Bremerton, take the 10-mile loop around the west end of Sinclair Inlet to Port Orchard, where antique shopping awaits, and continue east on Highway 166 to Southworth. Take the ferry to Vashon Island, which in recent years has become a bedroom community to Seattle and Tacoma. It is a quiet place that is best explored on bicycle. So, if you plan to spend time here, bring your bikes and dress accordingly. Roads are bike-friendly and you can get a pretty good workout exploring them.

Travel south on Vashon Island to the town of Tahlequah and take the ferry to the **Point Defiance Zoo** in Tacoma. ◼

VICTORIA

Rudyard Kipling came to Victoria in 1908 as a journalist covering the opening of the Empress Hotel. He described the city this way:

> *"To realize Victoria you must take all the eye admires in Bournemouth, Torquay, The Isle of Wight, the happy valley at Hong Kong, the Doon, Sorrento, and Camp's Bay—add reminiscences of the Thousand Islands and arrange the whole around the Bay of Naples with some Himalayas in the background."*

Got that picture? Add another observation that it was "San Francisco on the Solent," and you'll get a complete sense of this elegant but lusty, civilized but exciting, Western frontier boomtown at the turn of the century.

The Hudson's Bay Company built Fort Victoria on the Inner Harbour in 1843 and the town was a thoroughfare for boats bringing miners from all over the world. Victoria provisioners outfitted these dream-seekers heading to the gold fields of the Frasier and Cariboo. Fortunes were made and society was splendid. The architecture of the homes and public buildings—especially those designed in the 1890s by Victoria's renowned architect Francis M. Rattenbury—proclaims the wealth of the city's forefathers. One of Canada's best known artists, Emily Carr, was born here in 1871 and raised in an elegant home in the historic James Bay neighborhood. A talented and eccentric woman, she painted totems and the wilderness of the Northwest with a genius that is arresting to this day.

VICTORIA

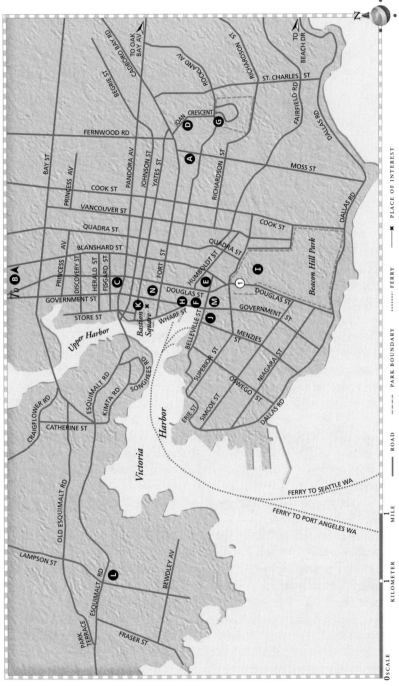

Sights

- **A** Art Gallery of Greater Victoria
- **B** Butchart Gardens
- **C** Chinatown
- **D** Craigdarroch Castle
- **E** Crystal Garden
- **F** Empress Hotel
- **G** Government House Gardens
- **H** Inner Harbour
- **I** James Bay and Beacon Hill Park
- **J** Legislative Buildings
- **K** Maritime Museum of B.C.
- **L** Olde England Inn
- **M** Royal British Columbia Museum
- **N** Victoria Eaton Centre

While Greater Victoria now encompasses a busy city of nearly 400,000 at the south end of the Saanich Peninsula, downtown Victoria is a village at its soul, made for walkers and accented with gardens and the lush hanging flower baskets for which the city is renowned. Travelers making the 2½ hour trip from Seattle on the *Victoria Clipper* arrive in Victoria's Inner Harbour within walking distance from many don't-miss sights, with plenty of food and lodging choices.

A PERFECT DAY IN VICTORIA

A perfect day in Victoria includes tea, history, gardens, and shopping—all of which abound. Start with a quick "cuppa" at Murchie's Tea & Coffee, Ltd. on Government Street or a more leisurely breakfast at Kipling's in the Empress. Walk off your breakfast exploring Victoria's Inner Harbour. Small wooden foot ferries ply the waters. Catch a ride on one to spots on the harbor and walk back along the promenade. Spend time in the Royal British Columbia Museum and strolling Government Street. Have afternoon tea at the Empress or Butchart Gardens, and if at all possible, manage to be in the gardens on a summer Saturday evening for the exciting fireworks show.

TRANSPORTATION

Getting to Vancouver Island depends on your travel plans and preferences, whether you're on foot, have a car, are pressed for time, or have all the time in the world. Foot passengers can reach Victoria from Seattle by taking the *Victoria Clipper* from Seattle's Pier 69, the *Princess Marguerite* car and passenger ferry, 206/448-5000 or 800/888-2535, offers daily direct passenger and vehicle service between Seattle and Victoria, mid-May to mid-October. **Black Ball Transport**, 360/457-4491, www.north olympic.com/coho, offers two sailings a day from Port Angeles on the Olympic Peninsula. The **Washington State Ferry** from Anacortes sails to Sidney (at the northeast end of the Saanich Peninsula). The most frequent ferry service is from **B.C. Ferries'** Tsawwassen terminal (about a half hour south of Vancouver) on large super-ferries; for schedule information, call 250/386-3431, www.bcferries.bc.ca/ferries. If you're driving to Victoria from Washington give yourself an extra hour for the border crossing.

Going by air saves time, and there are plenty of regularly scheduled flights. **Kenmore Air,** 206/364-6990 or 800/543-9595, has eight floatplane flights a day from their Lake Union air harbor in Seattle. **Harbour Air**, 250/385-2203, has 10 flights a day, high season, from Vancouver; **West Coast Air,** 800/347-2222, has 12 flights daily. Also, **Helijet Airways,** 250/382-6222 or 800/665-4354 offers flights from Seattle's Boeing Field to Victoria, and from Vancouver to Victoria. **Horizon Air**, 800/547-9308, provides service between Seattle and Victoria airports.

SIGHTSEEING HIGHLIGHTS

★★★★ **Butchart Gardens**—Each season offers a new kind of beauty in 50-acre Butchart Gardens. The famous Sunken Garden (an old limestone quarry) is filled with thousands of bulbs in spring; the Rose and Italian Gardens are in romantic bloom in summer; and firework displays enchant visitors on summer Saturday evenings. In autumn, dahlias and chrysanthemums offer vibrant contrast to the garnet leaves of maples in the Japanese Garden. In winter the holly, heathers, Christmas lights, and decorations transform the gardens.

Details: 800 Benvenuto Drive, about 13 miles north of downtown Victoria; 250/652-5256 (recorded information); email: butchartgardens.bc.ca; www.butchartgardens.bc.ca/butchart/. Wheelchair accessible. The gardens open daily (including holidays) at 9 a.m.; closing time varies according to time of year. Tea is served in the dining room from noon to 4; reservations recommended; 250/652-8222. There are several other restaurants on site. Admission to the gardens is seasonal, about $6–$12 (U.S.). (2–3 hours)

★★★★ **Empress Hotel**—A grand stone chateau whose image defines the city, the Empress was named for Queen Victoria, the Empress of India. It's one of the most beloved institutions in North America. The guest list here includes luminaries of the century: Rudyard Kipling, Charles Lindbergh, Shirley Temple, Rita Hayworth, the King and Queen of Siam, John Travolta, Barbra Streisand, and Mel Gibson are but a few. The British Royal Family are frequent visitors. Designed by Francis M. Rattenbury and open in 1908, its stately Edwardian charm had aged and faded by the mid-1960s when "Operation Teacup" was launched. Since then Canadian Pacific Hotels has invested more than $50 million to return the grand lady to her former glory. Stay here if you can afford it, or come to view, shop, or eat. The Canadian Pacific store has archival art-quality posters for around $20 that make great souvenirs. And a dinner in the rich, wood-paneled Empress Room with its massive chateau fireplace, Tudor arches, and stained glass window panels (not to mention the food) is a mental souvenir you won't soon forget.

Details: 721 Government Street (you can't miss it), 250/384-8111 or 800/441-1414.

★★★★ **Inner Harbour**—The site of Fort Victoria, built by the Hudson's Bay Company in 1843, it's a gathering spot for street artists and musicians, sailing vessels, and visitors. Foot ferries take you all over the harbor. Fishing and sightseeing cruises leave from here. Stop by the information office at the north edge of the harbor for maps, brochures, and other information, including tips for fishing and whalewatching.

Details: Visitor Info Centre, 812 Wharf Street; 250/953-2033. (½ –2 hours)

★★★★ **Royal British Columbia Museum**—A fixture in Victoria for over a hundred years, this is a very special museum. Exhibits on the fishing industry and whaling history of British Columbia are fascinating, but it's the displays on aboriginal culture that the museum is known for. Outside the museum in Thunderbird Park are huge totem poles and ceremonial houses. Inside are more totems and extensive displays. April through October the museum runs nearly 50 ecotours in British Columbia, ranging from guided field trips to sailing excursions. Check out their new National Geographic IMAX Theater, which offers films featuring the museums' exhibits.

Details: 675 Belleville Street, south of the Empress. General 250/387-3701 or 800/661-5411; 250/387-5745 for ecotour information; www.rbcm1.rbcm.gov.bc.ca; open daily 9 to 5. Admission is $5 for adults, $2.50 seniors, $1.50 children (U.S.). Wheelchair accessible. (2 hours or more)

✯✯✯ **Art Gallery of Greater Victoria**—You'll find the work of Emily Carr here, as well as a permanent collection of Canada's finest Japanese art that includes 10,000 works. In the garden is the only Shinto shrine outside Japan. It's located in Victoria's historic Rockland district near Craigdarroch Castle and Government House.
Details: 1040 Moss Street, Victoria; 250/384-4101. Open Monday through Saturday 10 to 5, Thursday 10 to 9, and Sunday 1 to 5. Admission is $5; free general admission on Monday. (2 hours)

✯✯✯ **Chinatown**—Before World War I, when Victoria was a major port of entry on the West Coast, this was the largest Chinatown in Canada. It is marked by the colorful Gate of Harmonious Interest. Don't miss mysterious Fan Tan Alley, a narrow interior street and the legendary location of gambling dens and opium houses.
Details: The gates mark the main entry on Government and Fisgard Streets. (1 hour)

✯✯✯ **Craigdarroch Castle**—Robert Dunsmuir, a prosperous British Columbia Coal baron, died months before this majestic mansion was completed in 1889. His wife, Joan, lived there for the next 18 years, managing the business left to her. Their fortune is reflected in the unique architecture, the sweeping staircases, the exquisite woodwork, and the stained glass throughout. Rooms and furnishings have been restored to their Victorian-era beauty.
Details: 1050 Joan Crescent off Fort Street; open daily; 250/592-5323. Admission about #5 (U.S.) (1 hour)

✯✯✯ **James Bay and Beacon Hill Park**—The historic James Bay neighborhood is the oldest residential district in the city. Take a walking, bicycling, or carriage tour to best explore. You can visit Emily Carr's birthplace, a Victorian gingerbread heritage house at 207 Government Street.
Details: The southwest portion of the city surrounded by water on the north, west, and south sides and Beacon Hill Park to the east. You'll see horse-drawn carriages near the Empress and Parliament Buildings; bicycle

Jeff Barber—Craigdarroch Castle

Craigdarroch Castle

tours can be arranged through Pacific Rim Bicycle Tours, 250/881-0585. (2 hours)

☆☆☆ **Legislative Buildings**—Designed in the 1890s by Victoria's renowned architect Francis Rattenbury, when he was still in his twenties, these grand buildings are the second structures you notice when sailing into the harbor (the Empress is the first). The grounds are always beautifully planted with flowers. Enjoy them as you stroll the harbor. Don't miss the Legislative Buildings at night, outlined in sparkling white lights and looking like fairyland.

Details: *Call 250/387-3046 for tour and special event information. Guided tours are offered Monday through Friday. (½ to 1 hour)*

☆☆☆ **Maritime Museum of B.C.**—Explore historic Bastion Square, then take in maritime history through a vast collection of models and sailing ship displays. You can imagine "Rumpole of the Bailey" in the newly refurbished Vice-Admiralty Courtroom on the third floor, which can be reached via a large open-cage elevator. The museum underwent a renovation in 1998 that added 12 new galleries.

Details: Bastion Square, 250/385-4222. Open daily 9:30 to 5:30. Wheelchair accessible. Adults $5, seniors $4. (1–2 hours)

★★★ **Olde England Inn**—This inn is part of a village that contains a replica of the home where William Shakespeare was born and of Anne Hathaway's thatched cottage, furnished with sixteenth-century antiques.

Details: 425 Lampson Street, 250/388-4355 Guided tours include a look at the Shakespearean lifestyle. Summer season 9 to 8, otherwise 10 to 4. Admission about $5 (U.S.). (2 hours)

★★ **Crystal Garden**—This historic glass-roofed building behind the Empress, designed by Francis Rattenbury and P. L. James, housed the largest indoor saltwater swimming pool in the British Empire. Now it contains thousands of exotic plants, tropical birds, and tiny monkeys.

Details: 713 Douglas Street; 250/381-1213. Open daily. Admission is $7 for adults, $6 seniors, $4 children (Canadian). (1 hour)

★★ **Government House Gardens**—Queen Elizabeth visited these lovely restored gardens on the lieutenant governor's residence grounds, which were restored in the mid-1990s. You can take a self-guided tour of the nearly 15-acre grounds.

Details: 1401 Rockland Avenue, Victoria. Open from sunrise to sunset. Admission is free. (1 hour)

★★ **Victoria Eaton Centre**—This vertical mall's 100-plus shops include Marks & Spencer, Purdy's Chocolates, Eaton's department store, and dozens of others. Not only for shoppers, it's worth a visit to see the massive British Empire clock that hangs from the ceiling of its 85-foot atrium. The food circus on the fourth floor is a good place for a fast food stop.

Details: Corner of Government and Fort Streets, Victoria; 250/389-2228. Call for hours information. (1 hour)

KIDS' STUFF

Kids love the **Royal British Columbia Museum**, the monkeys at the **Crystal Palace**, riding on the foot ferries, and carriage rides in the horse-drawn buggies that queue up near the Legislative Buildings. **Beacon Hill Park** has a petting zoo, and the **Butterfly Gardens** near

Butchart Gardens (20 minutes from Victoria) is also a hit. And what can beat cuddling a cockroach at the **Bug Zoo** at 1107 Wharf Street, 250/384-2847; or seeing iguanas or boa constrictors at the **Reptile Zoo**, 1420 Quadra Street, 250/885-9451. **Willows Beach** in Oak Bay offers calm waters for swimming and plenty of sand for castle building.

FITNESS AND RECREATION

In Victoria salmon fishing and whalewatching are close at hand and fun for all members of the family. You can leave from the Inner Harbour, Sooke Harbour, or Oak Bay. I caught my first chinook salmon (a thrilling experience) on an outing with **Gordy's Guides**, 250/642-4998, one of a number of services that operate out of Sooke Harbour. From the Oak Bay Beach Hotel you are close to the departure point for whalewatching cruises on the **M.V.** *Pride of Victoria*, a 45-foot catamaran. Cruising to see orcas (killer whales) is a popular event; call 250/592-3474 or 800/668-7758. Victoria's 150-acre **Beacon Hill Park** is only a five-minute walk south from downtown along Douglas Street and contains a rose garden, wild bird sanctuary, a century-old cricket pitch, and a children's petting zoo.

FOOD

Afternoon tea in Victoria is a classic experience. Two of the best, albeit most expensive, tea services are at the **Palm Court** and **Tea Lobby** of the **Empress Hotel**, 250/384-8111. The dining room of the historic main house at **Butchart Gardens**, 250/652-8222; also serves a wonderful tea. Reservations are a must for either of these in high season. Other options are the **Oak Bay Beach Hotel**, 1175 Beach Drive, 250/598-4556, and the **Windsor House Tea Room & Restaurant** in Oak Bay, 250/595-3135. For fine dining in elegant settings, try the **Empress Dining Room** (see above) or the **Victorian Restaurant** at the Ocean Pointe Resort, 250/360-2999. Excellent food can be found in more casual eateries. The **Herald Street Caffe**, 546 Herald Street, 250/381-1444, is famous for its lighter-than-air crab cakes in cilantro-lime pesto. The real fantasy builder is the Shaker lemon pie. **Cafe Brio** opened in 1998 by the creator of the Herald Street Caffee, with a menu featuring organic vegetables grown from special seeds. It's a chic destination along Antiques Row on Fort Street, with a mini courtyard, terra-cotta colored exterior, and lively paintings on the walls. Crowded, noisy, and

VICTORIA

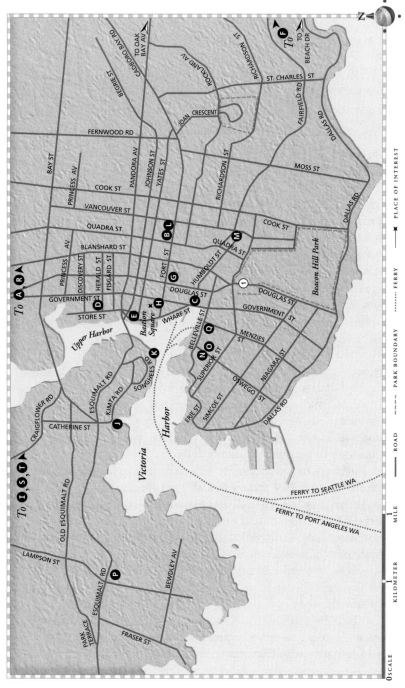

Food

- Ⓐ Butchart Gardens
- Ⓑ Cafe Brio
- Ⓒ Empress Dining Room
- Ⓓ Herald Street Caffe
- Ⓔ Il Terrazo
- Ⓕ Oak Bay Beach Hotel
- Ⓖ Pagliacci's
- Ⓒ Palm Court
- Ⓗ Re-Bar Modern Food
- Ⓘ Sooke Harbor House Restaurant
- Ⓙ Spinnakers Brew Pub Restaurant
- Ⓒ Tea Lobby
- Ⓚ Victorian Restaurant
- Ⓕ Windsor House Tea Room & Restaurant
- Ⓛ Wonton Noodle House

Lodging

- Ⓜ Beaconsfield Inn
- Ⓝ Best Western
- Ⓞ Days Inn
- Ⓒ Empress Hotel
- Ⓕ Oak Bay Beach Hotel
- Ⓚ Ocean Pointe Resort Hotel & Spa
- Ⓟ Olde England Inn
- Ⓠ Quality Inn
- Ⓘ Sooke Harbor House
- Ⓙ Spinnakers Guest House

Camping

- Ⓡ Island View Beach RV/Tent Park
- Ⓢ Goldstream Provincial Park
- Ⓣ Thetis Lake Campground

Note: Items with the same letter are located in the same town or area.

fun, **Pagliacci's**, 1011 Broad Street, 250/386-1662, serves Italian food reasonably priced in a high energy atmosphere near Eaton Centre. You'll find Italian specialties in a quieter setting at **Il Terrazo**, 555 Johnson Street, 250/361-0028. It's hidden away off Waddington Alley and has outside dining in a walled courtyard where umbrellas ward off the sun and outdoor heaters warm the evening making for cozy, romantic dining. The un-fancy **Wonton Noodle House** on Fort Street, 250/383-0680, is known for its yummy noodle dishes and good prices. **Re-Bar Modern Food,** 50 Bastion Square, 250/361-9223, offers healthy, vegetarian cuisine and a juice bar that serves up refreshing fruit smoothies. The Re-Bar is popular for weekend brunch, and you'll often see the line of people waiting to be seated extending out the door.

Spinnakers Brew Pub Restaurant, 308 Catherine Street, 250/386-2739, on the Inner Harbour waterfront, is Canada's oldest brewpub. It offers great waterfront views and a wide variety of traditional ales and lagers brewed on the premises. **Sooke Harbor House Restaurant,** 250/642-3421, is the place for connoiseurs seeking Canadian regional cuisine.

LODGING

It doesn't matter where the traveler is from, the Northwest or New York, if you bring up Victoria, two very different lodgings, each reflecting the essence and culture of the region, are usually mentioned: the Empress and Sooke Harbor House. The Beaconsfield Inn is a third one that also comes up. The **Empress Hotel,** 250/384-8111 or 800/441-1414, www.com/empress, is one of the most beloved of the vast and impressive chain of chateau-style hotels that Canadian Pacific runs across Canada. Afternoon tea here is legendary. If you're going to splurge on a grand hotel stay, this is it. Surprisingly, it's a kid-friendly place with a welcoming bag of playtime goodies for young folks. There are 475 rooms, a pool and spa, and an Entrée Gold option with breakfast included. **Sooke Harbor House,** 1528 Whiffen Spit Road, 250/642-3421, www.sookenet.com/shh, has a well-deserved reputation for excellence—for its location, artful rooms, food, and vigorous attention to detail by owners Sinclair and Frederica Philip. The romantic clapboard inn overlooking Sooke Harbor is a 40-minute drive west of Victoria. The on-site restaurant is known for seafood cuisine with regional, fresh, and organic ingredients (many grown on the premises). The food is pricey but worth it. A new addition in 1998 brings the room count to more than 20. The **Beaconsfield Inn,** 998 Humboldt Street, 250/384-4044, www .islandnet.com/beaconsfield/, is tucked away in a residential community about four blocks southeast of the Empress. Named after a luxurious hotel in London frequented by King Edward VII, it has an English country house atmosphere; nine rooms are individually decorated with antiques. Non-smoking and not suitable for children under 18.

The **Olde England Inn,** 429 Lampson Street, 250/388-4353, is part of a small re-created village that includes Anne Hathaway's Cottage; a stay here let's you indulge in an English fantasy. Rooms are individually decorated with antiques and canopy beds and some have fireplaces. It lies across the harbor from downtown Victoria. The **Oak Bay Beach Hotel,** 1175 Beach Drive, 250/592-3474 or 250/598-4556, is located "behind the tweed curtain" in the thoroughly English village of Oak Bay, a 10-minute drive from downtown; it's on the water and adjacent to a marina. You can take a whalewatching cruise nearby, or enjoy lazing in the hotel's waterfront garden. The **Ocean Pointe Resort Hotel & Spa,** 45 Songhees Road, 800/667-4677, www .oprhotel.com, is a modern and elegant chateau-like hotel with 250 rooms at the entry to the harbor; a full-service spa and excellent water-front-view restaurant make this a sybaritic choice. **Spinnakers Guest House,** 308 Catherine Street, 250/386-2739, with five rooms (queen beds), is adjacent to Spinnakers Brew Pub, on the Inner Harbour. It is ideal for an adult getaway. Breakfast included at the pub.

There are also numerous international chain hotels on the Inner Harbour. The **Best Western,** 800/528-1234; **Days Inn,** 800/329-7466; and **Quality Inn,** 800/228-5151, are near the *Victoria Clipper* terminal.

Call Tourism Victoria's reservation line, 800/663-3883, to make reservations at any hotel in the city.

CAMPING

Though tent camping wouldn't be my first choice for accommodations when visiting Victoria—I camped here in the rain as an impoverished student—there are over a dozen campgrounds and RV parks in the Greater Victoria area. Good bets are **Island View Beach RV/Tent Park,** 250/652-0548, close to Butchart Gardens; **Goldstream Provincial Park,** 250/391-2300, in heart of old growth forest, 12 miles north of Victoria, and **Thetis Lake Campground,** 250/478-3845, six miles north of the city center.

SHOPPING

Shoppers can get plenty of exercise walking Government Street, with its wide array of china, woolens, Irish and Scottish clothing shops, and specialty shops, like long-time favorites **Munro's Books, Rogers Chocolates,** and **Murchie's Tea.** Check out Cowichan sweaters (a thick fisherman knit–like garment) at **Cowichan Trading, Ltd.** and **Sasquatch Trading, Ltd.** On **Bastion Square,** across from the Maritime Museum, you'll find **Dig This,** a gardening store that carries a video on how to create Victoria's hanging baskets. If you love fabrics and interior furnishings, head to **Chintz & Company;** for samples of the country's furniture and accessory designs browse through **Canadian Heritage**

Designs. Both stores are a little off the beaten path on Store Street.

Chinatown's Fan Tan Alley is fun to explore; and **Market Square** is a colorful two-level shopping area in restored buildings. **Antique Row** on Fort Street is a favorite destination for those who crave vintage English-style furniture and accessories. You will also see masks, drums, carvings, and more aboriginal art in places throughout the city. **Alcheringa Gallery** (on Fort Street) focuses on Canadian Northwest coast art.

Warm air from the Pacific keeps Victoria's climate moderate and the precipitation light compared to other mainland communities, so you may be pleasantly surprised by good weather here even during winter months. Christmas is a wonderful time to visit this city. There are British feasts and celebrations at Craigdarroch Castle, the Empress, the Oak Bay Hotel, and the Olde England Inn. After-Christmas Boxing Day sales on Government Street offer bargains on china, Scottish sweaters, English tweeds, and more. In Feburary, the **Victoria Symphony Society's Pacific Northwest Wine Festival**, which takes place at the Empress, features wines of the whole Northwest region in seminars and tastings and is reason enough to visit Victoria. Call the Empress for details.

NIGHTLIFE

There's plenty of music and nightlife pubs and clubs. **Millenium Jazz Club**, 1605 Store Street, 250/360-9098, is an elegant spot beneath **Swans Pub** on Store Street. The **Sticky Wickett Pub**, 919 Douglas Street, 250/383-7137, is a city tradition and its four floors offer plenty of options from quieter pub food rooms to lively pool and darts rooms. **Legends**, entrance adjacent to the Sticky Wicket, is the largest nightclub in town and has a state-of-the-art sound system where all ages come to dance to rock and roll, rhythm and blues, and jazz. Listen to jazz in the Empress's **Bengal Lounge** on Thursday and Friday nights. Pacific Opera Victoria opens its season each fall in the **McPherson Playhouse**, and there are summer plays here as well.

HELPFUL HINTS

Tourism Victoria provides a wide variety of information; 250/953-2033, travel.victoria.bc.ca. Also, Tourism Vancouver Island's Web site provides information on Victoria and other destinations on the island, www.islands.bc.ca.

5

COWICHAN VALLEY AND UP-ISLAND

The Cowichan Valley, 45 minutes northwest of Victoria by car, is known for its dairies, logging, and increasingly for its wines and arts. It's also known for Cowichan sweaters—rustic fisherman-style sweaters made from the wool of local sheep and crafted in distinctive patterns of cream, brown, and gray tones by Cowichan native peoples who learned how to knit from British settlers in the mid-1800s. A sweater-knitting demonstration is among many excellent exhibits at the Cowichan Native Village in Duncan. Chemainus, at the north end of the valley, was once a dismal mill town on the skids. Now it's a vibrant mural town rich in the history of the area and a center for the arts. Attractions around South Cowichan Valley communities such as Cobble Hill, Cowichan Bay, and Shawnigan Lake include provincial parks, small wineries, and a cidery.

Further up-island, the city of Nanaimo is one of the fastest growing in Canada. One look at the harbor and coastline tells you why. You can take a ferry from here to explore Gabriola, one of the Gulf Islands. Parksville and Qualicum Beach north of Nanaimo offer a playground for sunseekers, and since a new stretch of Highway 1 has circled around these communities, they have become off-the-beaten-path destinations. Rathtrevor Provincial Park is a beautiful spot claiming wide stretches of sandy beach that have more in common with the Oregon coast than the rocky shores that dominate Washington's coast. ◣

COWICHAN VALLEY

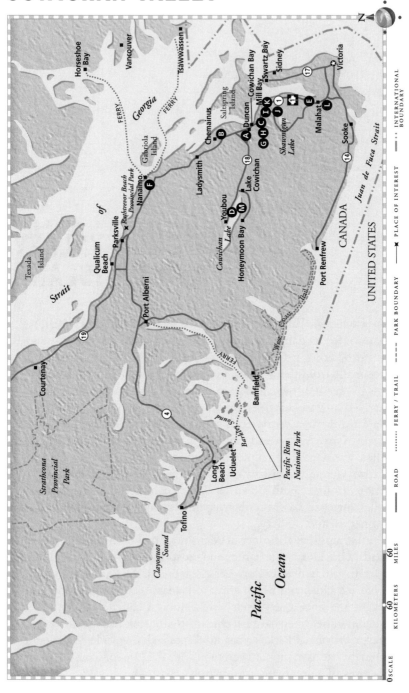

Sights

- Ⓐ B.C. Forest Museum
- Ⓑ Chemainus
- Ⓒ Cowichan Bay
- Ⓐ Cowichan Native Village
- Ⓐ Duncan Totems
- Ⓓ Lake Cowichan
- Ⓔ Malahat Summit
- Ⓕ Nanaimo

Food

- Ⓔ The Aerie
- Ⓖ The Bistro
- Ⓗ Cobble Hill
- Ⓘ Merridale Cider Works
- Ⓐ Starbucks
- Ⓐ Sahtlam Lodge
- Ⓗ Verturi-Schulze

Lodging

- Ⓔ The Aerie
- Ⓐ Best Western Cowichan Valley Inn
- Ⓑ Bird Song Cottage B&B
- Ⓐ Fairburn Farm
- Ⓒ Old Farm Bed & Breakfast
- Ⓐ Sahtlam Lodge
- Ⓙ Whistlestop B&B

Camping

- Ⓚ Bamberton Provincial Park
- Ⓛ Goldstream Provincial Park
- Ⓜ Gordon Bay Provincial Park
- Ⓕ Newcastle Island Provincial Park

Note: Items with the same letter are located in the same town or area.

A PERFECT DAY IN THE COWICHAN VALLEY

Drive up-island on a clear day and stop at the look-out at Malahat Pass. Visit a winery or two around Cobble Hill. Stop in Duncan to spend time in the Cowichan Native Village and take a look at the town's totems. The mural town of Chemainus provides a rich cultural experience and has plenty to explore. Then check into Fairburn Farm; plan dinner at Sahtlam Lodge and enjoy river, bird, and night sounds—the perfect romantic way to end the day. (Reservations suggested.)

SIGHTSEEING HIGHLIGHTS

★★★★ **Chemainus**—More than 30 outdoor murals depict the early settlement and history of this waterfront lumber-town-turned-arts-community. Learn from educational and interpretive programs and walking tours, horse-drawn carriage tours, live theater, artists and crafts shops, (including a fall artist's open house).

Details: North of Duncan. Contact the Arts and Business Council of Chemainus, 250/246-4701. (2–3 hours)

★★★★ **Cowichan Native Village**—Features a traditional Big House and a gallery of West Coast art, carvings, a display of Cowichan sweaters, demonstrations on knitting, beading moccasins, and other crafts. Restaurant, coffee shop, gift shop, and book shop.

Details: 200 Cowichan Way, Duncan; 250/746-8119. Open mid-May to mid-September 9:30 to 5, otherwise 10 to 4:30. Wheelchair accessible; plenty of parking. Admission $8. (2 hours)

★★★★ **Nanaimo**—A Hudson's Bay Company fort was built here in 1850 to protect coal miners brought from England and Scotland. Now the logging industry, a deep-sea harbor, and a pleasant climate are among the reasons this is one of the fastest growing cities in Canada. It is the up-island terminus for Tsawwassen and Horseshoe Bay on the mainland; the new B.C. Ferry terminal at Duke Point is about two miles south of town. A small ferry from downtown Nanaimo goes to **Gabriola Island**. South of town in **Petroglyph Provincial Park** are prehistoric rock carvings that represent humans, birds, wolves, lizards, and sea monsters. Each July, the town hosts the International Bathtub Race where powered bathtubs and other bizarre craft navigate the Strait of Georgia.

Details: The city can be reached by car from Victoria, or ferry from Tsawwassen or Horseshoe Bay terminals near Vancouver. Tourism Nanaimo, 2290 Bowen Road; 250/756-0106 or 800/663-7337. (4–6 hours)

★★★ **B.C. Forest Museum**—Steam locomotives, a sawmill, smithy, hand-pump cars, logging industry exhibits, and more commemorate the 100-plus years of British Columbia's logging history. A steam train carries passengers over the museum's 100 acres.

Details: 2892 Drinkwater Road, Duncan, B.C. 250/715-1113. Open daily May through September 9:30 to 6. Admission $7, over 65 and ages 13–18 $6. (2 hours)

★★★ **Cowichan Bay**—Europeans settled here in 1862 to farm and fish and by the turn of the century it was a tourist destination. This waterfront town offers fishing and sightseeing charters on sailing boats from the harbor, restaurants, and galleries to explore.

Details: Southeast of Duncan. For more information, contact Cowichan Tourism, 250/715-0709. (2–4 hours)

★★★ **Duncan Totems**—Duncan has over 30 totem poles that represent a blending of traditions of native cultures of the Northwest coast, but most are the carvings of the Cowichan band who, beginning in 1985, worked with the city to celebrate the renaissance of the art form. You can see carvers at work at the Cowichan Native Village (see above).

Details: Stop by the Chamber of Commerce Travel Infocentre for a self-guided tour map; 250/746-4636. (1 hour)

★★ **Lake Cowichan**—West of Duncan, Lake Cowichan is a year-round source of giant cutthroat and rainbow trout. The most dense stands of fir on Vancouver Island are in Gordon Bay Provincial Park on the south shore of the lake. Back roads lead from here to the wild west coast and Bamfield in the Pacific Rim National Park.

Details: About 20 miles west of Duncan on Highway 18.

★★ **Malahat Summit**—The Trans Canada Highway leads northwest from Victoria via Malahat Pass. A stop at the viewpoint gives you a panoramic view over Saanich Inlet northwest up the Strait of Georgia.

Details: About 30 miles northwest of Victoria on Trans Canada Highway (1). (15 minutes)

FITNESS AND RECREATION

Hike the Cowichan River Trail. Ride on a sailboat out of Cowichan Bay with **Great Northwestern Adventure Company, Ltd.**, 800/665-7374. The Cowichan Bay Regatta is held here the first weekend in August, the second largest on Canada's west coast.

The museum shop at the Cowichan Native Village in Duncan offers good shopping, as do the galleries and shops in town, in Chemainus, and in Cowichan Bay. The **Judy Hill Gallery,** 250/746-6663, features Northwest coast native art; and **Hill's Indian Crafts,** about a mile south of Duncan in Koksilah, 250/746-6731, in business since 1946, has carvings, artwork, and original Cowichan sweaters. Play on the beaches at Parksville and at Rathtrevor Park.

Golf courses to watch for are the **Arbutus Ridge Golf & Country Club,** 250/743-5000, in Cobble Hill; the **Cowichan Golf and Country Club,** 250/746-5333, south of Duncan; and **Duncan Meadows Golf Course,** 250/746-8993, west of Duncan off Highway 18.

FOOD

The Aerie near Malahat, 250/743-7115, has a terrific view of Saanich Inlet, and offers fine dining. There's a **Starbucks** in Duncan, 15-350 Trunk Road, 250/746-9394, for easy breakfasts and quick snacks. The dining room at **Sahtlam Lodge**, 5720 Riverbottom Road, 250/748-7738, is a gourmet experience in a romantic country-woods-by-the-river setting west of Duncan. You can make reservations to stay in one of the cabins at the lodge, but dinner alone is worth the drive (you'll need directions). **The Bistro** at Vigneti Zanatta Vineyard is a special countryside experience; call 250/748-2338 for reservations.

Other wineries offering tasting are **Venturi-Schulze** and **Cobble Hill**. For cider tasting try the Old Scrumpy at **Merridale Cider Works,** 1230 Merridale Road, 250/743-4290.

LODGING

As you drive up-island you'll see signs for **The Aerie,** 250/743-7115, a luxury destination with fabulous views of the Saanich Inlet from the treetops of Malahat. **Whistlestop B&B,** 250/743-4896, is a small waterfront lodge with luxuriously appointed rooms or suites on Shawnigan Lake. Near Duncan is **Fairburn Farm,** 250/746-4637, a working farm on several hundred acres. Reminiscent of the English countryside, it has walking trails through the fields. Also near Duncan, along the Cowichan River, is **Sahtlam Lodge,** 250/748-7738, sahtlam@islandnet.com., with cabins to rent and a wonderful restaurant. **Best Western Cowichan Valley Inn**, north of Duncan on Trans Canada Highway, 250/748-2722 or 800/528-1234, has a swimming pool and restaurant and is a good family stop. In Chemainus, try **Bird Song Cottage B&B,** 250/246-9910, within walking distance of the beach and restaurants. In Cowichan Bay, **Old Farm Bed & Breakfast,** 888/240-1482 or 250/748-6410, is a heritage home on an estuary.

CAMPING

Several provincial parks along Highway 1 as you travel up-island offer camping facilities. Most are on a first-come, first-served basis. However, reservations are permitted at some campsites; contact B.C. Parks district office, 250/391-2300. There is a fee for camping that is sometimes paid through a self-registration system, so it's a good idea to carry money in small denominations. Mid-June through early September is the busiest time. **Goldstream Provincial Park**, on the Goldstream River near Victoria as you head up-island, has beautiful hiking trails that meander through 600-year-old Douglas fir and western red cedar forests. There are numerous special events—nature hikes, bald eagle viewing, and programs for children that can be arranged through the visitors center; call 250/478-9414. **Bamberton Provincial Park**, near Mill Bay, fronts on the Saanich Inlet with views of the water, Saanich Peninsula, the Gulf Islands, and Mt. Baker. **Gordon Bay Provincial Park** is on the south shore of Cowichan Lake, where you can fish for Dolly Varden trout or swim in warm lake waters. **Newcastle Island Provincial Park**, situated in Nanaimo Harbour and reached by passenger ferry, offers camping, swimming, boating, and picnicking.

HELPFUL HINTS

VIA Rail's E&N (Esquimalt and Nanaimo) Line has a once-daily trip from Victoria (the station is at 450 Pandora Avenue, Victoria; 250/383-4324 or 800/561-3949 from the U.S.) to Courtenay, near Campbell River. It leaves Victoria early in the morning and returns about dinner time. It stops at Chemainus about 10 a.m. on the way up-island and stops back in Chemainus about 4 p.m. on its return, making for a convenient and fun day trip. It also stops at Duncan.

Information and trip planning assistance is available from **Tourism Vancouver Island**, 250/382-3551, fax 250/382-3523; e-mail: tavi@islands .bc.ca; and Web site: www.islands.bc.ca. Or, for lodging reservations, call West Coast Trail reservations, 800/663-6000 or to receive a travel kit, call **Super Natural British Columbia** at 800/663-6000.

SIDE TRIP: PACIFIC RIM NATIONAL PARK

There are three parts to this park, which was established in 1970: Long Beach (the Tofino area), the West Coast Trail, and the Broken Group

Islands. The easiest to access is Long Beach, about 16 miles of surf and sandy beach. The West Coast Trail, 77 kilometers, goes through dense coastal rain forest of cedar, hemlock, spruce, and fir. You must make reservations to hike part or all of the trail; call 800/663-6000.

This route takes you from north of Nanimo into Pacific Rim National Park, along Provincial Highway 4. **Port Alberni**, at the northern end of Alberni Inlet, is the jumping-off spot for boat connections into Barkley Sound.

Eagle Nook Ocean Wilderness Resort, 800/760-2777 or 604/723-9842 (open May to October), is located on Barkley Sound a short cruise away from the Broken Group Islands. Only reached by boat or floatplane, this hideaway offers hiking, sea kayaking, whale-watching, and sport fishing in a comfortably, unexpectedly civilized setting on its own 70-acre peninsula.

You can drive to the Long Beach area. Just north of Nanaimo, go west on Highway 4 from the Island Highway. While the roads are generous and well maintained from Port Alberni, the route beyond narrows and has more twists and turns. Persevere—this journey puts you in the heart of the national park, with lakes, inlets, mountains and beaches all around. The 46-room **Wickaninnish Inn**, 800/333-4604, www .island.net/~wick, is on Chesterman Beach near Tofino. A stone fireplace, hand-adzed cedar posts, and Northwest art grace the lobby of the $8.5 million structure. This world-class resort was built to be the best place in North America to watch storms. There are fireplaces, soaker tubs, balconies, and views of the ocean from the rooms. It's pricey, but well worth it; packages are available. The **Pointe Restaurant** at the inn features a signature potlatch stew—a succulent combination that includes salmon, prawns, and scallops—served in a copper pot.

Tofino is home to a long house gallery that houses carvings and modern art of well-known native artist Roy Henry Vickers. Storm-watching season lasts from November through very early March. *Note*: It is about five degrees warmer here than in the rest of the province. April through October you can fly from Vancouver or Victoria to Tofino, 800/228-6608, and also floatplane from Vancouver via Harbour Air in peak season, 250/278-3478.

The park is 200 miles northwest of Victoria on Highway 4; contact Pacific Rim National Park Reserve, Box 280, Ucluelet, B.C. V0R 3A0; 250/726-7721. Long Beach Park is open year-round, the West Coast Trail is open April to October, and the Broken Group Islands May through September.

Scenic Ferry Circle: Strait of Georgia

The Strait of Georgia separates Vancouver Island from mainland British Columbia. Like Puget Sound, it is dotted with forested islands and rich with mountain scenery. It's a favorite destination of boaters, and the first leg of the water journey for cruise ships leaving Vancouver and heading up the Inside Passage to Alaska. Ferries crisscross the strait. In the height of summer, at least 16 sailings a day carry travelers each way between Tsawwassen and Swartz Bay on Vancouver Island. It's the system's most popular run and a good starting point for exploring the Strait of Georgia's coastal communities by car. Buy a **Sunshine Coast CirclePac** ticket (good for six months) at your first ferry stop and save 15 percent off your fare to circle the strait (call B.C. Ferries for details, 250/386-3431 or www.bcferries.bc.ca). You'll have spectacular scenery, a variety of ferry, touring, and recreation options, and get a crash course in British Columbia's history and culture.

You can start from **Tsawwassen.** Large super-ferries ply the waters of the strait through the gem-like **Southern Gulf Islands**—Galiano, Mayne, Pender, and Salt Spring—to **Swartz Bay**. From

STRAIT OF GEORGIA

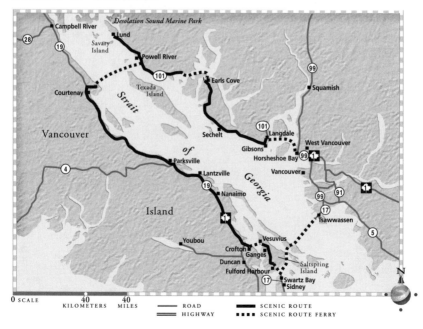

0 SCALE   40 KILOMETERS   40 MILES

━━━ ROAD   ━━━ SCENIC ROUTE
═══ HIGHWAY   ■■■■ SCENIC ROUTE FERRY

here a half-hour drive down the **Saanich Peninsula** takes you to **Victoria.** Or catch the small ferry *Brentwood Bay* that carries you up-island to **Mill Bay**, in the **Cowichan Valley**. You can explore here (see Cowichan Valley chapter) or drive up-island. **Nanaimo** is the up-island terminus for travel from Tsawwassen (a two-hour ferry ride) and Horseshoe Bay. Ferries from Tsawwassen land at Duke Point, about two miles south of town. Ferries from Horseshoe Bay land at Departure Bay, north of downtown. North of Nanaimo, the creamy sand shoreline of **Rathtrevor Beach Provincial Park** and the beach communities of **Parksville** and **Qualicum Beach** draw crowds. Summer sun fans also love Denman and Hornby Islands, secluded spots favored by '60s-style dropouts.

Continue northwest along Highway 1 to Comox and **Campbell River**, renowned as a salmon fishing destination. From Comox, a ferry crosses the strait to **Powell River** on B.C.'s "Sunshine Coast"—the warmest and driest area in the province. The impressive, snowy coast mountains rise up before you on a clear day. They isolate the coast from interior communities creating a low-key feeling that pervades the area. Crossing takes 1.25 hours.

There's plenty of fishing, camping, and boating along the coast and on Powell Lake. **Lund**, the small town north of Powell River, at the end of Highway 101, is a jumping-off spot for trips to **Desolation Sound**. Meander south and two more ferries—Saltery Bay to Earls Cove, Langdale to Horseshoe Bay—put you in West Vancouver, completing your circle. ◼

6

WHISTLER

Princes Charles, William, and Harry skied here in 1998 and drew the international spotlight on Whistler. For years, though, ski magazines have rated it the top ski resort in North America, an amazing achievement considering Whistler Village was built in 1980 and the ski facility had only been operating since the mid-1960s. But more amazing still—Whistler isn't just a downhill skier's paradise. This two mountain complex—Whistler and Blackcomb Mountains—and the village areas at their base offer an all-season recreational cornucopia. You can have great fun here and never snap on a ski. Hike, bike, play tennis, and golf top courses. Shop designer stores, galleries, and boutiques. Have a full-service spa getaway, or throw moderation out the window, eat wonderful food, and kick up your heels. If you love a snow-laden landscape, the exhilaration of crisp mountain air, and the feeling that you've stumbled upon a chic alpine hamlet filled with endless possibilities, Whistler is the place to be.

What's almost as good as time spent at Whistler is the time spent getting there along Highway 99. The route from West Vancouver is called the Sea to Sky Highway, which offers expansive views of glacially sculpted Howe Sound and the Coast Mountain Range. Squamish is a logging town at the north end of the sound in the heart of hiking, climbing, and rafting country. The main entrance to Garibaldi Provincial Park is nearby, as is the village of Brackendale, known for the amazing number of eagles that gather here each January. ◼

WHISTLER REGION

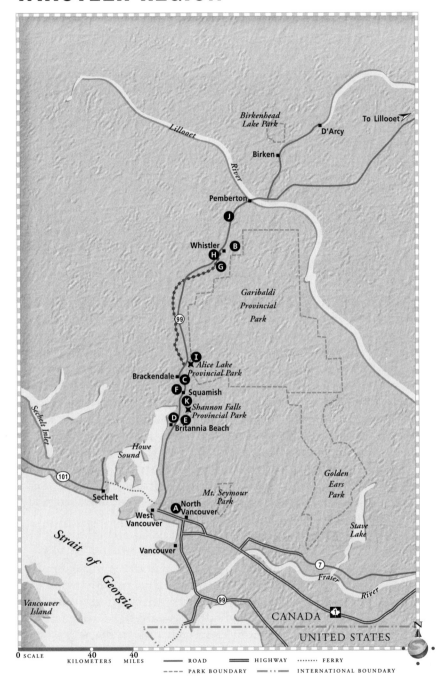

Birkenhead
Lake Park

D'Arcy

To Lillooet

Lillooet

River

Birken

Pemberton

J

Whistler **B**
H
G

*Garibaldi
Provincial
Park*

99

I
★ *Alice Lake
Provincial Park*

Brackendale **C**
F
Squamish
K
*Shannon Falls
Provincial Park*
D
E
Britannia Beach

Sechelt Inlet

*Howe
Sound*

*Golden
Ears
Park*

101

Sechelt

*Mt. Seymour
Park*
North **A**
Vancouver
West
Vancouver

Vancouver

*Stave
Lake*

7

Fraser

River

Strait

of

Georgia

99

CANADA **1**

*Vancouver
Island*

UNITED STATES

N

0 SCALE   40   40
KILOMETERS   MILES   ROAD   HIGHWAY   ········ FERRY
──── PARK BOUNDARY   ▬▬▬ INTERNATIONAL BOUNDARY

Sights

Ⓐ B.C. Rail's Cariboo Prospector

Ⓑ Blackcomb Mountain

Ⓒ Brackendale

Ⓓ British Columbia Museum of Mining

Ⓔ Shannon Falls Provincial Park

Ⓕ Squamish

Ⓖ Whistler Mountain

Ⓗ Whistler Village

Food

Ⓑ Joel's at Nicklaus North

Camping

Ⓘ Alice Lake Provincial Park

Ⓙ Nairn Falls

Ⓚ Stawamus Chief Provincial Park

Ⓑ Whistler Campground

Note: Items with the same letter are located in the same town or area.

A PERFECT DAY AROUND WHISTLER

A perfect summer day starts with breakfast at Durlocher Hof B&B, then a ride up the Whistler Mountain gondola (watching the mountain bikers come down the mountain roads as the gondola goes up). Stop at the new Roundhouse Lodge to pick up a sandwich and to take in the view from the outside deck. Then hike to Harmony Lake, stopping beside the trail to eat the sandwich and enjoy the views. Back down the mountain, some shopping and dinner at Bear Foot Bistro while a torchy lounge singer performs. In winter, if you're a skier, a perfect day in Whistler has sunshine and is spent on the slopes. And evening ends at one of the lively restaurant or nightclub hot spots.

SIGHTSEEING HIGHLIGHTS

★★★★ **B.C. Rail's Cariboo Prospector**—B.C. Rail's scheduled train from North Vancouver station meanders through shorefront communities along Burrard Inlet and Howe Sound, hugging the coastline as it goes and offering ever more spectacular water and mountain views. Then it leaves the water and continues north through Cheakamus Canyon to Whistler. You can do it as a day trip or combine it with the full route, which continues on to Pemberton, Lillooet, and points north as far as Prince George on its 463-mile route through B.C.'s Cariboo gold country.

Details: For reservations, call 800/663-8238. One round-trip daily between North Vancouver and Whistler leaves North Vancouver at 7 and returns at 6:10; round-trip package rate about $50 U.S. (includes breakfast and dinner). Departures from North Vancouver to Prince George are on Sunday, Wednesday, and Friday. (2 1/2 hours one way to Whistler)

✮✮✮✮ **Whistler Mountain**—You can quickly orient yourself to the layout of Whistler by taking a ride on the **Whistler Gondola.** Twenty scenic minutes put you at tree line—the top station is at 6,030 feet—where you'll not only get eye-popping views of Whistler and Blackcomb Villages, but also your choice of more than half a dozen hiking trails to meadows, small lakes, or granite ridges offering even more spectacular wraparound views. Also here is the Roundhouse Lodge, where you can get a bite to eat or a sandwich-style picnic for the slopes. In July the snows melt, baring Whistler Mountain's rocky bone structure, high alpine trails, and early wildflowers. It's a good time for a hike. Access to the **Harmony Lake Trail and Loop** is not far from the gondola station at the top of the mountain. The route is steep and somewhat challenging, winding down about 400 feet through sparse alpine forest. There are lots of spots along the way to rest or enjoy a sandwich while you take in views of the tiny glacial lake chain. Another very different hike takes you up a moonscape-like terrain to **Little Whistler Peak,** where you'll have stunning views of Black Tusk Peak and glacial green Cheakamus Lake. A less arduous way to scale this is on horseback.

Details: Gondola rates are $18 (Canadian) including tax. Kids 13 to 18 and 65 and over, are $15. Children 12 and under free. Open daily 10 to 5. Inside the Roundhouse Lodge (at the gondola's top station) pick up a trail map or sign up for free guided nature walks, rent snowshoes if the snow has lingered, or get information about horseback trail rides. Be sure to wear sturdy shoes or hiking boots and take a jacket, hat, sunscreen, and water. We encountered mosquitoes around Harmony Lakes; repellant would be handy. It takes about 1½ hours to do the Harmony Lake Trail. Be sure to watch your time; the last gondola goes down the mountain at 5. Advanced hikers can take the full day for the Musical Bumps Trail to Singing Pass from the Harmony area. For more information on this extended hike, call Whistler Resort Guest Services at 604/932-3434. (2–4 hours)

★★★★ **Whistler Village**—At the heart of the resort is Whistler Village, a European-style pedestrian enclave with rambling gabled-roof buildings and lanes that meander past lodgings, galleries, shops, restaurants, and ski lifts. At the north end of the village, just steps away, is Whistler Village Center, a complex of shops and restaurants. The Upper Village (Blackcomb lifts) is a five-minute stroll away.

Details: The Whistler Village Resort Association office in the Conference Center provides information on activities. (1 hour)

★★★ **Blackcomb Mountain**—Though quieter up top in summer, there are hikes and mountain-biking trails to enjoy. The heaviest wildflower bloom—with heathers, arnica, and Indian paintbrush—comes in August.

Details: Blackcomb is accessed from lifts in the North Village, near the Chateau Whistler. You can pick up a map at the Wizard Chair, a 10-minute walk from the Whistler Gondola. (1–2 hours)

★★★ **Brackendale**—Each winter, from November through February, eagles are drawn to the Squamish Valley because of an abundance of spawning salmon in a largely undisturbed habitat. The small village of Brackendale, north of Squamish, is known for the Brackendale Winter Eagles Festival. The **Brackendale Art Gallery,** a combination restaurant and gallery, is a popular gathering spot for eagle fans. Owner Thor Froslev created the festival in the mid-1980s. In 1997 the government established a 1,300-acre reserve to protect the eagles. In summer there are outdoor activities and river-running in the area.

Details: North of Squamish. For details on the festival, call the gallery, 604/898-3333. (1 hour to visit, longer for eagle viewing)

★★★ **British Columbia Museum of Mining**—In the 1930s the mines around Britannia Beach, south of Squamish, were the largest producers of copper in the British Empire. Now defunct as a mining community, Britannia Beach is the home of a mining museum where visitors put on hard hats to explore the underground mines on guided tours. The mines are more recently famous as the site where an *X-Files* episode was filmed.

Details: At Britannia Beach, about 30 miles from West Vancouver, just off Highway 99, 604/688-8735 or 604/896-2235. Call for hours. Admission $7 (U.S.). (2 hours)

★★★ **Shannon Falls Provincial Park**—You'll see signs for this park about a mile before you reach the town of Squamish. A viewing platform at the base of Shannon Falls, a short walk from the parking lot, offers a dramatic view of the 1,099-foot waterfall. There is picnicking and hiking on the grounds as well.

Details: On Highway 99 watch for signs for this park about a mile before you reach the town of Squamish. (½ hour)

★★★ **Squamish**—At the north end of Howe Sound, Squamish's industry is logging. Huge log booms are assembled here for towing to southern mills. Squamish Loggers Day is an international logging competition held each August. There's plenty of recreation here—rafting trips, sport fishing, golfing, mountain biking. There's the **Railway Heritage Park** to explore, and this is also the destination of the **Royal Hudson Steam Train/M.V. Britannia** tour from North Vancouver. Stop long enough to take a long look at the rock face of **Stawamus Chief Mountain**, referred to as "the Chief." It's a favorite of rock climbers and photographers. There are shops, restaurants, and services in town.

Details: Squamish and Howe Sound Chamber of Commerce, Visitor Info Centre, 37950 Cleveland Avenue; 604/892-9244. (1 hour)

KIDS' STUFF

Whistler/Blackcomb Mountain Ski School program offers classes for kids as well as after-ski care. There's a summer trapeze and instruction at the Upper Village near the Blackcomb lifts. The Chateau Whistler has a kids' club with crafts and activities arranged through the health club.

FITNESS AND RECREATION

Whistler is a mecca for fitness, recreation, and special events. First of all, the ski season lasts until the end of April; there's glacier skiing on Blackcomb from May to August. At 5,020 feet, Whistler has the second-highest vertical rise of any North American ski mountain. Between the two mountains there are over 7,000 acres of skiable terrain; Whistler alone has 100 marked trails. They are hosts of the Men's World Cup Downhill race. Day lift ticket prices that offer access to both mountains are $57 (Canadian) for adults, $48 for youth and seniors, and $28 for children.

There are three lakes in the main Whistler area: **Alta, Green,** and **Lost** Lakes. **Green Lake** has a park at its north end. **Alta Lake** has trails, boat launches, and picnic park areas. In winter you can snowshoe or set your own cross-country trails. The **Lost Lake** trail system, just northwest of the upper village, is a favorite for set-track cross-country skiing (day rates are $10 per person; at night it's well lit and free after 8).

There's summer hiking and mountain biking on both mountains. Be aware that you might encounter black bear. Make a lot of noise or wear bear bells.

At village level there's plenty to do as well. Golf is top-notch—try the **Whistler Golf Club**, 604/932-4544 or 800/376-1777; **Chateau Whistler Golf Club**, 604/938-2092; **Nicklaus North Golf Course**, 604/938-9898; or **Sky Golf and Country Club**, 604/894-6106 or 800/668-7900. Bicycling trails proliferate. Another way to get away from the ski area into snowy back country is to take a snowmobile ride with one of the outfitters that provides a warm snowsuit, protective headgear, and lunch off the beaten path. Sleigh riding, winter fishing, and flightseeing trips can also be arranged through the resort.

The **Whistler Activity and Information Centre**, 604/932-2394, provides complete information on tour operators, maps, and a list of equipment rental outlets. (Many of the hotels have their own equipment rental shops.) Sleigh riding, dog sledding, winter fishing, and flightseeing trips can also be arranged through the center. The CP Hotel's **Chateau Whistler** (in the upper village) offers comprehensive spa packages. The **Delta Mountain Inn** (in Whistler Village) has dome-covered tennis courts, and there is a tennis center north of the village. At the **Meadow Park Sports Centre,** a five-minute drive north of the village, you can ice skate, swim, work out with weights, or play squash.

FOOD

World class cuisine and fine dining choices abound in Whistler. **Araxi**, 4222 Village Square, 604/932-4540, in the heart of the village, has a definite European ambiance. The **Bear Foot Bistro**, 1121 Village Green, 604/932-1133, also in the village, not only offers creative food in a Italian country–style setting, but the restaurant has been collecting Dom Perignon to have plenty for celebrating as the century ends. **Val d'Isère**, 4433 Sundial Place, 604/932-4666, upstairs on a village side street, serves impressive, memorable food. **Chef Bernard's** (Bernard Cassavant, formerly chef of Wildfower at the Chateau Whistler), 4573

WHISTLER

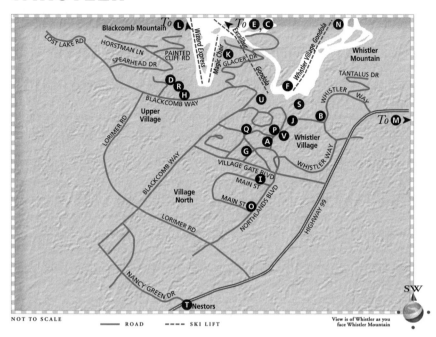

NOT TO SCALE ——— ROAD ---- SKI LIFT

View is of Whistler as you
face Whistler Mountain

SW

Food

- **A** Araxi
- **B** Bear Foot Bistro
- **C** The Bite
- **D** Chef Bernard's
- **E** Christine's Restaurant
- **F** Garibaldi Lift Company Bar and Grill
- **G** Glacier Lodge Restaurant
- **G** Hard Rock Café
- **H** La Rua
- **I** Moe's Deli & Bar
- **J** Old Spaghetti Factory
- **K** Quattro at Pinnacle
- **L** Rendezvous
- **M** Rim Rock Cafe and Oyster Bar

Food (continued)

- **C** River Rock Grill
- **N** Roundhouse Lodge
- **O** Splitz Grill
- **P** Trattoria de Umberto
- **Q** Val d'Isère
- **R** Wildflower

Lodging

- **R** Chateau Whistler
- **S** Delta Hotel
- **T** Durlacher Hof
- **U** Pan Pacific Lodge Whistler
- **V** Whiski Jack Condos

Note: Items with the same letter are located in the same town or area.

Chateau Boulevard, 604/932-7051, offers takeout food and is a good place for breakfast or lunch. **La Rua**, (in Le Chamois hotel in the Upper Village), 4557 Blackcomb Way, 604/932-5011, offers high-end Mediterranean food and has a consistent and excellent reputation. Nearby in the Chateau Whistler, **Wildflower**, 4599 Chateau Boulevard, 604/938-2033, serves Northwest produce Canadian Pacific–style in a lively, colorful, and comfortable restaurant that views toward the slopes. **Quattro at Pinnacle**, 4319 Main Street, 604/905-4844, is an "in" place for skiers to gather for dinner; year round it serves excellent pasta, and if you can't make up your mind, you can order a sampling of five types. The **Rim Rock Cafe and Oyster Bar**, 2117 Whistler Road, 604/932-5565, in the Creekside area, is packed with folks craving seafood. **Joel's Restaurant at Nicklaus North**, 8080 Nicklaus Boulevard North, 604/932-1240, overlooks the golf course, and is a several-mile-drive north of Whistler. It's owned by well-known Whistler restauranteur and welcoming host Joel Thibault.

    Trattoria de Umberto on Sundial Place, 604/932-5858, has outdoor tables and is a good lunch destination. You'll have fun choosing your special-order hamburger at tiny **Splitz Grill**, 4369 Main Street, 604/938-9300. Good breakfast hotel spots are the Delta and Chateau Whistler. **Moe's Deli & Bar**, 604/905-7772, in the new Delta Village Suites, has a kids' menu—one of the reasons it's a good family spot. The **Hard Rock Café**, 4295 Blackcomb Way, 604/938-9922, and The **Old Spaghetti Factory**, 4154 Village Green, 604/938-1081, are good family eateries.

    And there are plenty of restaurants on the mountains: You can take the high-speed quad chair lift to the **Rendezvous** day lodge complex on Blackcomb to nosh on takeout. Enjoy panoramic views of the village, sip fine wines, and dine off linen at **Christine's Restaurant**, 4545 Blackcomb Way, reservations recommended, 604/938-7437. Blackcomb Mountain's multimillion-dollar **Glacier Lodge Restaurant** can be reached only on skis, offers ethnic and West Coast cuisine at the **River Rock Grill** and bistro-style counter service at **The Bite**. Atop Whistler, **The Roundhouse Lodge**, 604/932-3434, offers great views down into the village, along with burgers, soups and sandwiches. Or you can stop for a post-mountain pizza at the **Garibaldi Lift Company Bar and Grill**, 604/905-2220, at the gondola base station at the foot of Whistler Mountain—fairly pricey but fun and lively.

    Each November Whistler Resort hosts the **Cornucopia Food &**

Wine Celebration, a three-day event that features tastings, seminars, cooking demonstrations, hands-on workshops, gourmet dining, and special events. Packages start from about $260 U.S., call 800/944-7853 for details.

LODGING

Accommodations at Whistler range from intimate B&B rooms to suites in grand hotels. For instance, you'll be immersed in an authentic Austrian atmosphere at eight-room **Durlacher Hof** inn, where you'll doff your shoes and don cozy wool slippers to sit by the *kachelofen* (tile oven) fireplace and be pampered by hosts Erika and Peter Durlacher. At the baronial-style 558-plus-room **Chateau Whistler,** you can relax in front of the massive limestone fireplace in the great hall and experience the full services and amenities of a grand hotel. With a total of over 4,400 rooms in the Whistler area, you can also pick and choose from anything in between, including a wide variety of condominium rentals through **Whiski Jack Resort**. Specify if location adjacent to the lifts is important. There's also the impressive new **Pan Pacific Lodge** and the ever popular **Delta Whistler Resort,** steps from the Whistler gondola. Call 800/944-7853 in the United States and Canada for brochures, reservations, and information.

CAMPING

Whistler Campground opened late summer of 1998. It's a private facility just five minutes north of the village on Highway 99. Call the Whistler Activities Center for details. **Nairn Falls** lies 20 minutes north and is closer to Pemberton. **Alice Lake Provincial Park** and **Stawamus Chief Provincial Park** are south of Whistler, near Squamish. For information about these and other parks in the area, call B.C. Parks, Garibaldi-Sunshine District, 604/898-3678.

NIGHTLIFE

Whistler's night spots are packed Thursday, Friday, and Saturday nights during ski season. In the village center **Buffalo Bill's**, below the stairs under the Timberline Lodge, and **Garfinkels**, in Town Plaza, often have live bands and appeal to thirty-somethings. The **Savage Beagle** has a cigar lounge and downstairs is a nightclub. **Maxx Fish,** with its new techno music and trendy interior and **Tommy Africa's,** 604/932-6090, both cater to a younger crowd.

HELPFUL HINTS

Whistler is 75 miles north of Vancouver on Highway 99. Perimeter transportation offers bus service from Vancouver International Airport ($20 U.S. one way); call 800/663-4265 24 hours in advance for reservations. B.C. Rail also provides service from the North Vancouver terminal (see B.C. Prospector, above).

Through **Whistler Resort Association** you can arrange for a variety of lodging and ski packages; call 800/944-7853 in the United States or Canada for their seasonal vacation planners, brochures, reservations, and information. Call the Whistler Activity and Information Centre, 604/932-2394, for recreation and sports information.

Scenic Route: Vancouver-Whistler-Lillooet-Fraser River

This route will give you a taste of the best of British Columbia in a few days. It takes you from sophisticated Vancouver northwest to recreation-rich Whistler along Highway 99, the Sea-to-Sky Highway, that overlooks Howe Sound. On a clear day, it's an absolutely knock-your-socks-off gorgeous drive. Spend time exploring the hiking, biking, golf, and fishing options around Whistler, then continue north to the village of Pemberton, a jumping-off spot into wilderness. Continue northeast on 99 and you'll reach the town of Lillooet, the beginning of the **Cariboo Gold Rush Trail**, across a road only paved in recent years. (Or with a four-wheel drive and a strong sense of adventure, you can take the Forest Service road northwest of Pemberton and make your way on primitive roads through the wilderness to Gold Bridge. A writer friend and I did this and spent time at **Tyax Mountain Lake Resort**, 250/238-2221, a destination in the Chilcotin Range wilderness that most folks reach by floatplane.) Continue on 99 to **Cache Creek** and visit nearby **Hat Creek Ranch**, a Provincial Heritage site that is a living history ranch. A former stagecoach stop,

WHISTLER-LILLOOET LOOP

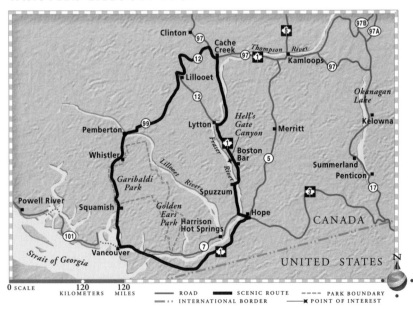

it gives you a feel for life in the late 1800s. Near Cache Creek you can pick up Highway 1 (Trans Canada Highway). Go north to dude ranch country around Clinton and into the Cariboo and Chilcotin regions. Or take it south along the Thompson and Fraser Rivers and stop at dramatic **Hells Gate** canyon on the Fraser. The drive is barren and dry until you reach the area around Hope, where the Fraser River Valley becomes a verdant farming region en route back to Vancouver. ◣

7

VANCOUVER

Vancouver may be the best example of a Northwest city combining sophisticated elements of urban life—the arts and architecture, culture, entertainment, fine dining—all in the lap of nature. And nature here is at her absolute tip-top, knock-your-socks-off best.

Stroll the perimeter of 1,000-acre Stanley Park, which lies in the heart of the city. Stop somewhere near the dramatic Lion's Gate bridge and look north across Burrard Inlet to the shore of North Vancouver. You can hike from that shoreline and in less than half an hour be in wilderness. You can drive north and in the same time reach a ski lift at Grouse Mountain. Continue around the park until you reach the skyline view, and you'll see a vibrant cosmopolitan city with a delicious international flavor. Fashion. Business. British heritage. The strong influence of native peoples. The incredibly rich migration—especially of talented chefs—from Hong Kong. There's a fabulous and large Chinatown with the Dr. Sun Yat Sen Chinese Garden (the only Chinese garden ever built outside of China and just one of the very special gardens in this city).

Artist Emily Carr, whose work you will see in the Vancouver Art Gallery, once made an observation about life that also applies to this city: "There is so much to see, so much to bite off and store and chew on . . ." ◼

VANCOUVER

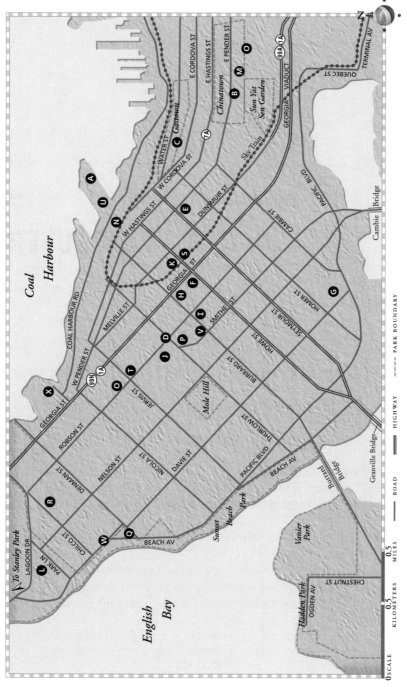

Coal Harbour

English Bay

To Stanley Park

Chinatown

Sun Yat Sen Garden

Sky Train

Mole Hill

Sunset Beach Park

Vanier Park

Hadden Park

E CORDOVA ST
E HASTINGS ST
E PENDER ST
TERMINAL AV
QUEBEC ST
GEORGIA VIADUCT
PACIFIC BLVD
CAMBIE ST
Cambie Bridge
Gastown
WATER ST
W CORDOVA ST
DUNSMUIR ST
W HASTINGS ST
GEORGIA ST
HOMER ST
SEYMOUR ST
HOWE ST
SMITHE ST
BURRARD ST
MELVILLE ST
COAL HARBOUR RD
W PENDER ST
JERVIS ST
THURLOW ST
NICOLA ST
DAVIE ST
NELSON ST
PACIFIC BLVD
BEACH AV
ROBSON ST
DENMAN ST
GEORGIA ST
CHILCO ST
PARK LN
LAGOON DR
BEACH AV
OGDEN AV
CHESTNUT ST
Burrard Bridge
Granville Bridge

99A / 1A
99A
7A
99N / 1

O
M
B
A
U
N
C
E
S
K
F
H
I
V
P
D
J
T
O
G
X
R
W
Q
L

SCALE
0.5 MILES
0.5 KILOMETERS
0

ROAD — HIGHWAY — — — PARK BOUNDARY

Sights

- **A** Canada Place
- **B** Chinatown/Dr. Sun Yat Sen Classical Chinese Garden
- **C** Gastown
- **D** Robson Street
- **E** The Umbrella Shop
- **F** Vancouver Art Gallery
- **G** Yaletown

Food

- **H** 900 West at the Hotel Vancouver
- **I** Bacchus
- **J** CinCin
- **K** Diva at the Met
- **L** Fish House at Stanley Park
- **M** Floata
- **N** Herons

Food (continued)

- **O** Hon's Wun Tun House
- **P** Piccolo Mondo
- **Q** Raincity Grill

Lodging

- **R** Buchan Hotel
- **S** Four Seasons Hotel
- **T** Hotel Vancouver
- **K** Metropolitan Hotel Vancouver
- **T** Pacific Palisades Hotel
- **U** Pan Pacific Hotel Vancouver
- **V** Sutton Place Hotel
- **W** Sylva Hotel
- **N** Waterfront Centre Hotel
- **G** Wedgewood Hotel
- **X** Westin Bayshore

Note: Items with the same letter are located in the same town or area.

A PERFECT DAY IN VANCOUVER

The perfect day in Vancouver is sunny and long. First thing in the morning, hop an Aquabus (one of the small foot ferries that skitter around the city's waterways) from the foot of Hornby Street across False Creek to Granville Island, where things come to life about 9 a.m.; grab some food—coffee or chai (latte-style tea served at JJ Roaster) or a Belgian waffle at the informal Market Grill—and then explore the island's market and art studios. Back downtown, make your way to Robson Street and have lunch at CinCin's (on the balcony, overlooking Robson's shoppers, is perfect). Don't miss the Dr. Sun Yat Sen Classical Chinese Garden, (especially in springtime) and the Museum of Anthropolgy. Make dinner reservations for a view table at the Teahouse at Stanley Park, and relax into your evening as the sun sets on English Bay.

SIGHTSEEING HIGHLIGHTS

✮✮✮✮ **Chinatown/Dr. Sun Yat Sen Classical Chinese Garden**—In the heart of Vancouver's Chinatown—the third largest in North America after San Francisco and New York—the garden is constructed almost entirely of materials from China: carved screens and woodwork, tiles, and stones. The first authentic classical Chinese garden ever built outside of China, it is particularly beautiful when spring cherry blossoms litter the garden.

    Details: 578 Carrall Street; 604/662-3207. Open daily throughout the year; there are tours, tea, and a gift shop. Admission is about $6. (1–2 hours)

✮✮✮✮ **Granville Island**—Bustling, chic, and colorful, this 20-acre island on False Creek in the heart of Vancouver draws most people to its public market. But the artisans and their work draw visitors again and again. Walk the island's web of small lanes and watch artists and craftsmen at work in their studios, often using old-world tools and techniques to create pottery or tapestries, jewelry, glass sculptures, and more. Some of the best artists in British Columbia can be found here, many since the late '70s and early '80s. To take a circular tour of the artists studios, a good place to start is the **Crafts Association of B.C.** "Crafthouse," 1386 Cartwright Street, 604/687-7270. Nearby **Gallery of B.C. Ceramics** shows the work of members of the **Potter's Guild of B.C.** Another place to start is the **Net Loft**, a complex of studios and shops near the public market. Outside, around its perimeter, you'll find artists' studios. Inside there are shops like **Nancy Lord**, which offers custom-designed coats, clothing, and purses in butter-soft leather. **Maiwa Handprints** has batiks, hand-printed clothing, gifts, artists supplies, and books. The **Emily Carr College of Art & Design** is on the island.

    *Details: The island is small, yet packed with so much it can be confusing. Pick up a map at the **Granville Island Information Centre** at the end of Anderson street near the public market. The island is busiest on weekends. In winter the public market is closed Mondays, as are many of the studios. Three-hour free parking spaces merely dot the island, and are especially hard to find on weekend mornings. You can take a ferry from downtown. The Aquabus, 604/689-5858, runs from the south end of Hornby Street to the Arts Centre on the island. (2–3 hours)*

✩✩✩✩ **Museum of Anthropology**—On a bluff overlooking the ocean, this Arthur Erickson (Canada's leading architect and a local resident) designed award-winning building contains open displays of totem poles; potlatch bowls, dishes, and boxes; Bill Reid's massive scultures *Raven* and *The First Men*; and traditional long houses. It is a don't-miss destination.

>   *Details: 6393 NW Marine Drive, on UBC campus, 604/822-3825. Call for information on special workshops and performances. (2 hours)*

✩✩✩✩ **Queen Elizabeth Park**—This 130-acre park claims a hill south of downtown Vancouver and offers one of the best views of the city, particularly from Seasons in the Park Restaurant (Clinton and Yeltsin dined here during the summit) or overlook nearby. The Plexiglas-encased Bloedel Conservatory is lit at night, filled with tropical plants.

>   *Details: Off Cambie Street and West 33rd Avenue; call 604/257-8570 for conservatory hours, 604/874-8008 for Seasons in the Park reservations. (1–2 hours)*

✩✩✩✩ **Robson Street**—Combines the chic and style of Beverly Hills' Rodeo Drive and the eccentric youthful energy of London's Carnaby Street. It's the fashion heartbeat of the city, where stylish folks of all ages come to explore. You'll find international designers—Ferragamo, Guess, Esprit, and more—British chain store Marks & Spencer (nicknamed Marks & Sparks), Roots, Murchie's Tea, Planet Hollywood, a Virgin Megastore, and plenty of hip coffee shops and restaurants. Counter-culture types and conservatives happily mingle, making this area a summer-time people-watching feast.

>   *Details: The main shopping segment is on Robson between Hornby and Cardero streets. (1–2 hours)*

✩✩✩✩ **Stanley Park**—At 1,000 acres this is Canada's largest city park, overlooking English Bay and Burrard Inlet. The Aquarium is here—be sure to see the fascinating beluga (white) whales—along with rose gardens, restaurants, hiking and horseback riding trails. The Nine O'Clock Gun is a sea cannon that's traditionally fired every evening to remind fishermen of fishing time limits.

>   *Details: Grounds are open 24 hours. Expect to pay a few dollars for parking at all locations including the restaurants; carry change for meters. (2–3 hours)*

★★★★ **University of British Columbia Botanical and Nitobe Memorial Gardens**—The beautiful Nitobe Memorial Gardens combine elements of a tea garden and a landscape garden and are part of the 70-acre Botanical Garden with its natural segments and its medicinal garden and gift shop.

Details: Botanical garden at 6804 SW Marine Drive, UBC campus, 604/822-9666. Admission about $4.50. (About 1 hour for each garden)

★★★ **Canada Place**—It's fun to explore this unusual building at the foot of Howe Street. You'll be able to see its design, like a white ship's sail, from all over the city. The Canadian Pavilion of Expo '86, Canada Place houses the Pan Pacific Hotel, restaurants, shops, an IMAX theater, and conference quarters. It's also the cruise ship terminal.

Details: At the foot of Howe Street. (1–2 hours)

★★★ **Capilano Suspension Bridge**—Soaring 25 stories and covering a 450-foot span over a rushing river, the Capilano Suspension Bridge, Vancouver's oldest commercial tourist attraction, still quickens the heartbeat and steals breath of visitors as it did over a hundred years ago. Millions have crossed it. A protected outdoors interpretive area on the grounds chronicles the park's growth; you'll also see about 30 totem poles, carved in the 1930s, clustered here in Totem Park. Native Tshimsian and Tlingit carvers work in the Carving Centre near the Trading Post (built in 1911 as a teahouse to honor the queen's birthday). West Coast tribal-style spirit masks, cedar carvings and other native crafts, and quality clothing, jewelry, and leather goods are for sale here. Cross the bridge and discover a nature exhibit and 15 acres of trails, ponds, and forest to explore.

Details: The park is about 10 minutes from downtown Vancouver. Go through Stanley Park, over the Lions Gate Bridge, and north 1 mile on Capilano Road., 604/985-7474. Guided tours. Admission is $8.25 for adults. The log Bridge House Restaurant on site is open for lunch and dinner. (2 hours)

★★★ **Gastown**—This historic district of Vancouver, with its cobblestone streets, lies between downtown and Chinatown, mainly around Water Street. Now home to antiques shops, galleries, and restaurants, it was in the late 1800s the thriving center of Vancouver's waterfront commerce. In September Gastown hosts a celebration honoring "Gassy Jack" Deighton, the district's namesake and first saloonkeeper.

Details: *For information on current events contact the Gastown Business Improvement Society, 604/683-5650. (2 hours)*

★★★ **Richmond**—A trip to this southern suburb of Vancouver, near Vancouver International Airport, is like going to Hong Kong without the airfare. Chinese families have settled in droves, and the result has been an explosion of new construction, hotels, and businesses. The Radisson President Hotel has a Buddhist shrine. Parker Place shopping center has a food court with an amazing selection of Chinese food. If you see 'pearl tea' on a menu, try it—you drink it with a wide straw, sucking up the gelatin-like 'pearls' at the bottom.
   Details: *Take Granville Street south from downtown Vancouver and follow the signs to Vancouver International Airport; near the airport you will see exit signs for Richmond. The Travel Information Centre is at 7888 Alderbridge Way, 604/271-8280. (2–3 hours)*

★★★ **The Umbrella Shop**—When it rains in Vancouver, as it often does—57 inches of annual rainfall to Seattle's 37—many of this store's brightly hued bumbershoots dot the streets. The owner is the third generation of his family to operate the store. If he has time, he'll give you a tour of the workroom and the ancient Singer sewing machines they still use.
   Details: *534 West Pender Street; 604/669-9444. (15 minutes)*

★★★ **Vancouver Art Gallery**—Designed in 1907 by Francis Rattenbury (Victoria's legendary architect), this is conveniently located on Robson Street and well worth a visit for the Emily Carr paintings that are part the gallery's permanent collection. Other Canadian artists are featured, as well. Changing special exhibits.
   Details: *750 Hornby Street, one block off Robson Street; 604/662-4719. Admission is $7.50. (1–2 hours)*

★★★ **VanDusen Botanical Garden**—Modern sculptures are a surprise in this 55-acre horticultural showplace made up of numerous specialized gardens. VanDusen features Canada's largest collection of rhododendrons; in spring, vibrant blooms fill Rhododendron Walk. Each June there is a large outdoor garden show. A restaurant and gift shop are on site.
   Details: *5251 Oak Street (at 37th Avenue), Vancouver; 604/878-9274. Admission is $5. (2 hours)*

★★★ **Yaletown**—Designers, architects, shop owners, and their customers quietly go about their business in this garment district. Delivery trucks at loading docks are noisy and the streets that are packed with cars, but it's a fun place to be, day or night. Formerly rundown and forgotten, Yaletown's renewal started with Expo '86. Now a mix of architect and design offices, shops, restaurants, and night spots, it's livlier than ever. Check out such shops as **Bernstein and Gold** in the 1100 block of Hamilton Street, 604/687-1535, which offers individually designed furniture, much of it down-filled, beautiful European cottons, and beeswax candles.

   Details: Located between Pacific Boulevard, Homer Street and Nelson Street. (1–2 hours)

SPECTATOR SPORTS

The Vancouver area offers a great selection of spectator sports. The Canucks hockey games are exciting to watch and the team is a perennial powerhouse. For a truly memorable experience, take in a **Canucks** hockey game played at GM Place. Arrive there early and have some food at the Orca Bay Bar and Grill, 604/899-7525; no reservations are accepted on game nights. While at the game, you'll see fireworks and all kinds of entertainment between periods. Maybe the Giant Orca will swoop down on you with a surprise offering!

   The **B.C. Lions** (Canadian Football League) offer up football Canada-style. If basketball is what you want, take in a **Grizzlies** game. Rounding things out are soccer as played by the **86ers** and baseball pitched to you by the **Canadians**. All individual tickets can be arranged through Ticketmaster; call 604/280-4400.

FITNESS AND RECREATION

Manfred Scholerman of **Rockwood Adventures,** 604/926-7705, a former Culinary Olympics chef, has created a series of unique city-to-wilds-type adventures and can lead you hiking in town, on the North Shore, to islands, and other spots. **Spectacular Adventures,** 604/925-8187, in North Vancouver, also offers interesting trips, like picnicking on a glacier.

   Shopping on Robson Street offers current European, Canadian, and American fashions and great people watching. Stroll **Granville Street** for antiques, **Granville Island** for art, **Main Street/Punjabi**

District for saris, **Commercial Street** for Italian food shops and the Italian community, and **Richmond** for Hong Kong–like Parker Place shopping center. Denman Street runs perpendicular to Robson's north end and is the main shopping street of the city's west end, which is adjacent to Stanley Park.

Vancouver has an outdoor summer theater series called **Bard on the Beach**; performances are in Vanier Park on English Bay.

FOOD

The food scene in Vancouver is dynamic and exciting. Choose from terrific Chinese food, seafood, and a wide variety of restaurants with many different personalities. Choices range from cheap and cheerful eateries, to expensive and elegant ones. And you might as well start where you started this chapter—at Stanley Park: The energetic feel of the **Fish House at Stanley Park,** 604/681-7275, extends to the lively saltwater fish prints that adorn the tomato-red walls of this gray clapboard. For an appetizer try the signature flaming prawns or a sampler of six West Coast oysters from the oyster bar. Palms, fig trees, and a conservatory give the **Teahouse at Ferguson Point**, 604/669-3281, on the edge of English Bay, a garden ambiance that's especially romantic at sunset. Weekend brunch entrees include wild rice pancakes and smoked salmon benedict. Tour buses often crowd the parking lot at **Prospect Point Cafe**, 604/669-2737, because the overlook here has terrific views of the boat traffic on Burrard Inlet and the soaring Lion's Gate Bridge; however, if you're in the park and looking for food on the go, there's a quick-stop kiosk offering grilled salmon sandwiches, hamburgers and hot dogs, espresso drinks, and ice cream; inside, a restaurant with a deck overlooks the inlet.

Stop by **900 West at the Hotel Vancouver,** 604/669-9378, and **Bacchus,** 604/608-5319, in the Wedgewood Hotel for after-shopping drinks or dinner. Both of these are a block away from Robson Street. For Chinese vegetarian (you wouldn't know if I hadn't told you) dim sum in a high-energy atmosphere, try the **Hon's Wun Tun House,** 604/688-0871, also on Robson—a fun way for shoppers to re-energize. **Piccolo Mondo**, 604/688-1633, is a quiet, romantic restaurant with an award-winning wine menu, a block off Robson. **CinCin**, 604/688-7338, feels like a rustic Italian villa and serves Mediterranean food on an outdoor terrace overlooking Robson.

For Chinese food, **Hon's,** 604/688-0871, has a location in

GREATER VANCOUVER

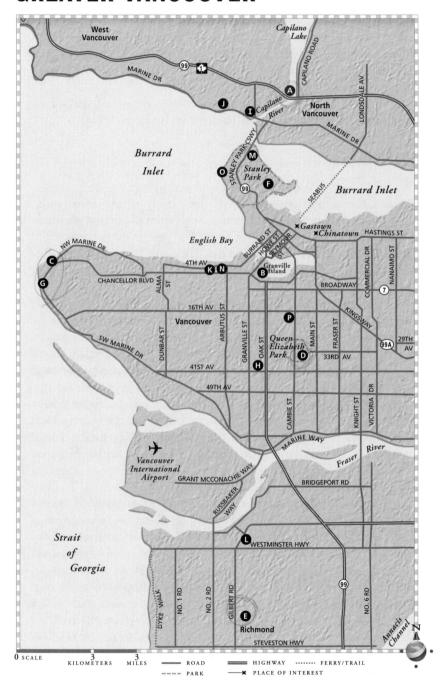

West
Vancouver

Capilano
Lake

MARINE DR

99

CAPILANO ROAD

A

LONSDALE AV

Capilano
River

North
Vancouver

MARINE DR

J

I

Burrard

Inlet

STANLEY PARK CSWY

M

Stanley
Park

O

99

F

SEABUS

Burrard Inlet

English Bay

BURRARD ST

HOWE ST

SEYMOUR ST

✕ Gastown
✕ Chinatown

HASTINGS ST

NW MARINE DR

C

4TH AV

K I N

Granville
Island

B

COMMERCIAL DR

NANAIMO ST

G

CHANCELLOR BLVD

ALMA ST

BROADWAY

7

16TH AV

ARBUTUS ST

Vancouver

GRANVILLE ST

OAK ST

P

MAIN ST

FRASER ST

KINGSWAY

99A

29TH
AV

DUNBAR ST

Queen
Elizabeth
Park

D

33RD AV

SW MARINE DR

H

41ST AV

CAMBIE ST

KNIGHT ST

VICTORIA DR

49TH AV

Vancouver
International
Airport

GRANT MCCONACHIE WAY

RUSSBAKER WAY

MARINE WAY

Fraser River

BRIDGEPORT RD

Strait
of
Georgia

L

WESTMINSTER HWY

DYKE WALK

NO. 1 RD

NO. 2 RD

GILBERT RD

99

NO. 6 RD

Annacis Channel

E

Richmond

STEVESTON HWY

N

0 SCALE   3   3
KILOMETERS   MILES

ROAD
PARK

HIGHWAY
PLACE OF INTEREST

FERRY/TRAIL

Sights

Ⓐ Capilano Suspension Bridge

Ⓑ Granville Island

Ⓒ Museum of Anthropology

Ⓓ Queen Elizabeth Park

Ⓔ Richmond

Ⓕ Stanley Park

Ⓖ University of British Columbia
     (UBC) Botanical and Nitobe
     Memorial Gardens

Ⓗ VanDusen Botanical Garden

Food

Ⓘ Beach Side Cafe

Ⓙ Beach House at Dundarave
     Pier

Ⓚ Bishop's

Ⓛ President Chinese Restaurant

Ⓜ Prospect Point Cafe

Ⓝ Sophie's Cosmic Cafe

Ⓞ Teahouse at Ferguson Point

Ⓟ Tomato Fresh Food Cafe

Chinatown. **Floata,** 604/602-0368 also in Chinatown, has a thousand seats, and is another great place to go for dim sum. Out in Richmond, near the airport, **President Chinese Restaurant,** 604/276-8181, in the Radisson President Hotel and Suites, offers great Cantonese food with some Szechuan offerings.

Herons, 604/691-1991, in the Waterfront Centre Hotel, is contemporary and elegant and has water views to go with dinner or cocktails. **Diva at the Met,** 604/602-7788, is a romantic and chic spot for dinner before the theater; weekend brunch is tops, too, and they have a great wine list that includes many outstanding British Columbia wines. **Raincity Grill,** 604/685-7337, on Denman Street with views of English Bay, is known for its long list of Pacific Northwest wines. **Bishop's,** 604/738-2025, just southwest of downtown in the community of Kitsilano, is a magnet for celebrities; yet host John Bishop has a reputation not only for excellent food (and to-die-for desserts), he also ranks high as a gracious host.

Funky, casual places for food any time are **Tomato Fresh Food Cafe,** 604/874-6020, at 3305 Cambie Street, where the room sizzles and there's clatter and noise and good food that's not expensive; and **Sophie's Cosmic Cafe,** 604/732-6810, at 2095 West Fourth Avenue, a great kitchy place for a pancake-and-egg breakfast. The North Shore of Vancouver offers water-view dining in the community of Ambleside with the **Beach Side Cafe**, 604/925-1945, and the lawn at **The Beach House at Dundarave Pier**, 604/922-1414, goes right to the beach, and is a great warm day place to relax before or after a delicious meal.

Or a unique way to dine is to take B.C. Rail's **Starlight Dinner Train** from North Vancouver to Porteau Cove, along the Sea to Sky Highway and Howe Sound, twice a week May to October, (800) 663-8238.

The **Vancouver Playhouse International Wine Festival** started more than 20 years ago with one founding winery—Robert Mondavi of California. Now each spring it draws over 100 top winemakers from more than 18 countries around the world for a week-long food and wine extravaganza each spring. It's one of the largest and most popular wine events in North America. You can choose from a variety of events— seminars, tastings, dinners, food pairings. Many take place in top restaurants or wineries in the area. For details, call 604/872-6622, or check the Web site: www.winefest.bc.sympatico.ca.

For the latest restaurant news, tune in to Vancouver's CFUN 1410 AM on Saturdays from 11 a.m. to 1 p.m. to hear food expert and author Kasey Wilson and one of Canada's leading wine authorities, newspaper columnist Anthony Gismondi, and their guests as they discuss up-to-the-minute food and wine news on *The Best of Food and Wine.*

LODGING

If you can, stay downtown or near Stanley Park. The Royals—Charles, William, and Harry—stayed at the Canadian Pacific's **Waterfront Centre Hotel** during their 1998 visit; the hotel offers tremendous water views at 900 Canada Place Way, 604/691-1991 or 800/441-1414, www.cphotels.com. The best water views are from the **Pan Pacific Hotel Vancouver**, #300–999 Canada Place, 604/662-8111 or 800/937-1515, www. panpac.com—worth a visit to the lobby whether you stay or not. Another waterfront hotel is the **Westin Bayshore**, 1601 Georgia Street, 604/682-3377 or 800/228-3000, www.westin.com; north toward Stanley Park, the Westin is set back from traffic and is a good spot for kids. The **Hotel Vancouver**, 900 West Georgia Street, 604/684-3131 or 800/441-1414, www. cphotels.com, is a Canadian Pacific hotel a block away from Robson Street, next to the Vancouver Art Museum; this is Vancouver's grand old hotel, and has recently been restored. The **Wedgewood Hotel**, 845 Hornby Street, 604/689-7777 or 800/663-0666, www.travel.bc.ca/w/wedgewood, is an excellent spot with European flair and good jazz in the lounge at Bacchus, its fine restaurant. The **Four Seasons Hotel**, 791 West Georgia Street, 604/689-9333 or 800/332-3442, www.fshr.com, is beautiful and modern with Oriental art and a Four Seasons reputation for service. **Metropolitan Hotel Vancouver**, 645 Howe Street, 604/687-1122 or 800/667-2300, www.metropolitan.com, is contemporary and spacious; Diva restaurant is off the lobby. **Pacific Palisades Hotel**, 1277 Robson Street, 604/688-0461 or 800/663-1815, has a great location in the midst of Robston Street activity. The **Sutton Place Hotel**, 845 Burrard Street, 604/682-5511 or 800/961-7555, www. travelweb .com/sutton.html, has had several names, but has always been a luxury property. The **Sylvia Hotel** overlooks English Bay, and is the favorite destination of the value-conscious seeking views and old English atmosphere. The **Buchan Hotel**, 1906 Haro Street, 604/685-5354 or 800/668-6654, www.budgethotels.com, is a inexpensive, comfy, no-frills spots in a good location.

NIGHTLIFE

Robson Street is always lively. There are restaurants, billiards, and coffee shops. There's good theater in town, too. The dramatic Ford Centre for the Performing Arts, 777 Homer Street, 604/602-0616, and Granville Island feature several theaters. There's a DJ in the pub and a party atmosphere prevails at the **Yaletown Brewing Co.**, 604/688-0039 1111 Mainland Street, in the Yaletown area. There are lots of billiard's clubs and restaurants here. One of the first to start this trend was **Soho Cafe and Billiards**, 1144 Homer Street, 604/688-1180. The **Automotive Club**, 1095 Homer, 604/682-0040, is in a frankly funky former auto dealership with refreshments like sandwiches, fruit juice, and rootbeer. Parking in Yaletown day or night is difficult; lots are scarce.

HELPFUL HINTS

Paper currency are in $5, $10, $20 and larger increments. There are $1 coins referred to as "loonies" (a loon is imprinted on it) and $2 coins called "toonies."

8

SAN JUAN ISLANDS

There are about 400 islands in the San Juan archipelago, but when people say "San Juans" they usually mean Washington's three most popular and populated: Lopez, Orcas, and San Juan Islands. Accessible by ferry, airplane, floatplane, or private and charter boats of all sizes, they form a verdant, watery crossroads between the waterfront cities of Seattle and Victoria, Anacortes and Sydney. Folks come here to see orca, explore small coves by boat and beaches by foot, bicycle long country lanes, or wander small villages. Thick with evergreens and interspersed with bucolic farms, meadows, ponds, and wetlands, the islands—particularly San Juan Island—are becoming more populated. Historic clapboard farmhouses and buildings do still mark the landscape, and you'll see old roses clambering over picket fences. Time slows down here, as if it's not measured digitally but in the graceful swings of an old pendulum clock.

In the best of all worlds you will have time to explore each island. If you must choose, here are some tips: **Lopez** is the first island reached by ferry from Anacortes and offers lots of flat roads for bicycling, a marina, and Lopez Village with eateries and shops to explore. Long known as the Friendly Island, residents give the "Lopez wave" to passing motorists. Lopez offers a winery to visit, berries, salmon, and other fresh and preserved foods. **Orcas** is the largest island with the highest peak, Mt. Constitution, and its irregular saddlebag shape creates East Sound and West Sound. The village of Eastsound is the largest community on the island. Historic

SAN JUAN ISLAND

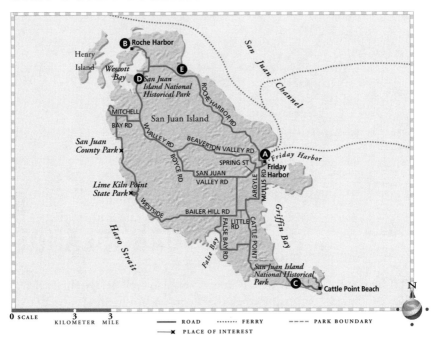

Sights

- **Ⓐ** Friday Harbor
- **Ⓑ** Roche Harbor and Hotel de Haro
- **Ⓒ** San Juan Island Historical Park (American Camp)
- **Ⓓ** San Juan Island Historical Park (English Camp)
- **Ⓐ** Whale Museum

Food

- **Ⓔ** Duck Soup Inn
- **Ⓐ** Friday Harbor House
- **Ⓑ** Lime Kiln Café
- **Ⓐ** Roberto's
- **Ⓑ** Roche Harbor Resort

Lodging

- **Ⓐ** Friday Harbor House
- **Ⓐ** Friday's
- **Ⓐ** Mariella Inn & Cottages
- **Ⓐ** Wharfside B&B

Note: Items with the same letter are located in the same town or area.

Rosario Resort and marina is located here. **San Juan Island** is the most populated island, and Friday Harbor, where the ferry lands, is the largest town in the San Juans. Its snug, east-facing village offers spectacular sunrise views for early risers and a daylong look at ferry and boat activity (with two customs houses here, this is an international crossroads for boaters). You'll see the historical military encampments at San Juan Island's American and English Camps; and there's history and wildlife to learn about at the Whale Museum and other island historical museums.

A PERFECT DAY IN THE SAN JUAN ISLANDS

A perfect day in the islands begins with a lazy breakfast and some pleasant conversation at an inn or B&B. Then bicycling is a perfect way to take in wildflowers, wildlife, and beautiful vistas. Wander the islands' small villages, and find an outdoor deck for lunch on a warm day (the Islander Lopez, Christina's on Orcas, or Roche Harbor Resort on San Juan are good bets). Sit outside to take in the crisp scent of salt air, the call of seagulls, and the pleasant hum of the good life.

SIGHTSEEING HIGHLIGHTS

★★★★ **Eastsound (Orcas)**—Located at the head of Orcas Island's largest bay, Eastsound is the largest town on the island. Look for historic buildings now housing bookstores, restaurants, and other local commercial enterprises. The Emmanuel Episcopal Church dates back to 1886. When you arrive on Orcas Island, don't forget to set your watch to "Orcas time"—the pace is relaxed.

Details: The ferry docks at the village of Orcas, at the south end of the island. Follow signs from here to Eastsound (about 7 miles). (1–2 hours)

★★★★ **Friday Harbor (San Juan)**—This is the largest town in the islands—population about 2,000—and the county seat. The ferry docks here. There are restaurants, a community theater and a movie theater, the whale museum, and a marina (the crab shack on the dock sells crab cocktails to go). In May the artists in the community and on the island host an open house; in July there's a jazz festival.

Details: About 1½ hours by ferry from Anacortes, there are a variety of ways to arrive here (see "Helpful Hints," below). (2 hours)

✮✮✮✮ **Lopez Village (Lopez)**—You'll see fine glass, jewelry, and artwork at Chimera Gallery, a cooperative of Lopez Island artists; wreaths and accessories at the Lopez Country Store; and fine scents, soaps, and gifts at the Willow Farm store. Visit the **Lopez Historical Museum,** 360/468-2049 or 360/468-2049 after hours; donations suggested. Here you will find maritime exhibits, pioneer displays, American Indian art, and what is thought to be the first automobile in San Juan County.

Details: Go 4 miles south of the ferry dock on Weeks Road. The museum is oen only in the summer; call for hours. (1 hour)

✮✮✮✮ **Whale Museum (San Juan)**—The museum is located in one of the island's oldest buildings and features exhibits depicting the biology, behavior, and sounds of whales. There are videotapes to watch, an interactive computer, and complete whale skeletons. Other whale-related exhibits include photographs, carvings, and paintings.

Details: Three blocks northwest of the ferry landing at 62 First Street North; 360/378-4710; www.whale-museum.org. Open daily from Memorial Day weekend to October 1 10 to 7, the remainder of the year 10 to 6. Admission is $5, $3.50 for seniors over 62; $2 for students with ID and kids 5 to 12. (1 hour)

✮✮✮ **Moran State Park and Mt. Constitution (Orcas)**—In 1926 Robert Moran, former mayor of Seattle and ship-building tycoon, donated the 5,000-plus-acre park to the state. Drive five miles up 2,409-foot Mt. Constitution for stunning views of the San Juans and the mainland.

Details: 5 miles southeast of Eastsound; 360/376-2326; www.orcasisle-.com. Open daily May through September 6:30 to dusk; 8 to dusk the remainder of the year. (1–2 hours)

✮✮✮ **Roche Harbor and Hotel de Haro (San Juan)**—Located on the northwest corner of the island, Roche Harbor is a resort town and a very popular boating destination. Once the site of the largest lime-producing company in the West, it has several historic attractions. The Hotel de Haro, the centerpiece of the Roche Harbor Resort, is on the National Register of Historic Sites and once hosted Teddy Roosevelt. A lovely rose garden lies in front of the inn. A newly expanded marina has doubled the number of boat slips.

Details: Northwest of Friday Harbor, 360/378-2155 or 800/451-8910. (1–2 hours)

★★★ **San Juan Island National Historical Park (American Camp and English Camp)**—This park was created to commemorate the 1872 settlement of the border dispute between the United States and England that began in 1859 with the Pig War. For these years two encampments were at different ends of the island. The **American Camp**, now a 1,200-acre site at the island's southeast tip, is about five miles from Friday Harbor. **English Camp,** 520 acres on Garrison Bay, on the northwest side of the island, is not far from Roche Harbor.

Details: Maps and brochures are available from the Park Superintendent's Office at 125 Spring Street in Friday Harbor; 360/378-2240. Rangers are at both sites Memorial Day weekend through Labor Day. Picnic sites, beaches, and trails are available; no overnight camping allowed. Visitors centers are on the grounds, hours 8:30–5 daily; grounds are open dawn to 11 p.m. (2 hours at each site)

FITNESS AND RECREATION

Orca-watching season runs May to September, yet July is peak month in the San Juans. This is a must-do if you visit during these months. Call **San Juan Excursions** in Friday Harbor, 800/80-WHALE; www.seawhales.com. **Island Institute's Marine Adventure Center**, 360/376-6720 or 800/956-6722, on Orcas Island, offers fully guided soft adventure programs that include classes in marine science and whale-watching and sea-kayaking outings for children and families. Base camp lodging with meals is at the center's **Beach House** onWest Sound.

The islands are also perfect for gallery hopping and summer cycling. Lopez is just a 45-minute ferry ride from Anacortes and its gently hilly terrain, long popular with cyclists, can easily be explored on a day trip. The other islands are good for cycling as well. Call in advance and you can reserve a bicycle from the **Bike Shop**, 360/468-3497, or **Lopez Bicycle Works**, 360/468-2847, on Lopez; on San Juan Island, contact **Island Bicycles**, 360/378-4941, **Susie's Mopeds**, 360/378-5244, www.rockisland.com/~sjmoped~/, or **Island Scooters and Bike Rentals**, 360/378-8811, www.rockisland.com/~sjmoped/.

Several day use parks make great locations for picnics. On Lopez, the rocky promontory at **Shark Reef Day Park** has a grassy knoll perfect for a simple sandwich picnic and offers a panoramic view of San Juan Channel (and Orcas if you're lucky). **Otis Perkins Day Park** on Fisherman's Bay has picnic tables and a long beach to stroll. Each May the artists of San Juan Island have an open house so you can explore the island by visiting the artists in their studios. Popular summer events are a jazz festival and Pig War BBQ. On those days the islands spill over with visitors.

FOOD

On Lopez, **Gail's Restaurant**,Village Center, 360/468-2150, www.pacificrim.net~gails/, is a great stop for oyster stew or a Greek salad; they grow most of their own produce and have an extensive wine list. Cinnamon rolls and sourdough bread are scrumptious picks from **Holly B's Bakery** (closed January to May), Lopez Plaza, 360/468-2133, but you can also get a scone, a slice of pizza, and many other baked goods here. At the **Lopez Island Pharmacy**'s real soda fountain, you can try a dish of chocolate raspberry swirl or coffee almond fudge, two favorite island ice creams produced by Lopez Island Creamery. The **Bay Cafe**, in the village, offers adventurous meals. Their menu changes frequently and includes creative items like Dungeness polenta appetizers and chicken satays with curried noodles. The restaurant in the **Islander Lopez**, 360/468-2233 is known for their Sunday brunch with special order omelets and plenty of seafood. At **Lopez Island Vineyards**, between the ferry landing and Lopez Village, Siegerrebe and Madeline Angevine grapes are grown on the property and made into wines. Open Wednesdays, Memorial Day to Labor Day, noon to 5. Call 360/468-3644 for a special appointment.

On Orcas, stop by **Christina's**, 360/376-4904, on Main Street in Eastsound, for a glass of Madeline Angevine (or another of the 50 Northwest wines on their list) and a mouthwatering platter of poached oysters, spot prawns, and cracked crab in season. Dinner only, but the bar opens at 4 p.m. for appetizers. Just east of Eastsound, **Ship Bay Oyster House**, 360/376-5886, offers baked, fried, and raw oysters and great chowder. On the west side of the island, try a seafood special, a salad, and the homemade bread at the **Deer Harbor Lodge and Inn,** 360/376-4110, www.sanjuanweb.com/DeerHarborInn/. **Rosario Resort's** dining room, 360/376-2222 or 800/562-8820, in the old Moran Mansion, overlooks the water and is a romantic destination for lunch or dinner.

On San Juan, the dining room at **Friday Harbor House,** 360/378-8455, is open to the public; dinners include fresh local products like island grown vegetables and Wescott Bay oysters. **Roberto's,** 360/378-6333, near the ferry in Friday Harbor, serves up generous

LOPEZ ISLAND

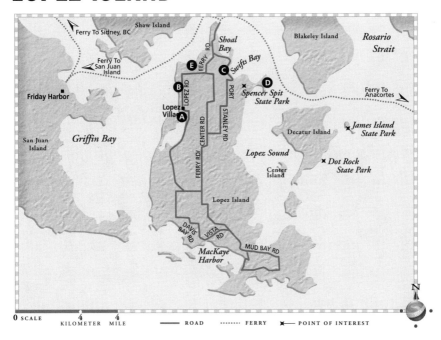

Sights

Ⓐ Lopez Village

Food

Ⓐ The Bay Cafe
Ⓐ Gail's Restaurant
Ⓐ Holly B's Bakery
Ⓐ Islander Lopez
Ⓐ Lopez Island Pharmacy
Ⓑ Lopez Island Vineyards

Lodging

Ⓐ Edenwild Inn
Ⓒ Inn at Swifts Bay
Ⓐ Islander Lopez

Camping

Ⓓ Spencer Spit
Ⓔ Odlin County Park

Note: Items with the same letter are located in the same town or area.

ORCAS ISLAND

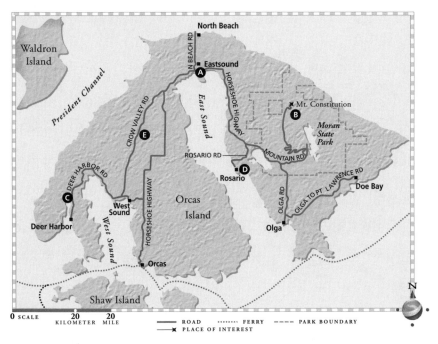

Sights

Ⓐ Eastsound

Ⓑ Moran State Park and Mt. Constitution

Food

Ⓐ Christina's

Ⓒ Deer Harbor Lodge and Inn

Ⓓ Rosario Resort

Ⓐ Ship Bay Oyster House

Lodging

Ⓓ Rosario Resort

Ⓔ Turtleback Farm Inn

Camping

Ⓑ Moran State Park

Note: Items with the same letter are located in the same town or area.

portions of satisfying Italian food. **Duck Soup Inn,** 360/378-4878, www.ducksoupinn.com, north of Friday Harbor about four miles, is a cozy spot with a stone fireplace and wooden booths that offers homemade breads and fine meals incorporating regional produce. **Roche Harbor Restaurant** at **Roche Harbor Resort,** 360/378-5757, views the marina, and the **Lime Kiln Café** on the dock offers informal meals, good for families.

LODGING

On Lopez, at the **Inn at Swifts Bay,** 360/468-3636, www.swiftsbay .com, a country hideaway near the ferry landing, guests are pampered with a wide variety of amenities, including slippers to wear to the hot tub and English walking sticks for hiking. Five rooms (available for adults only) include two upstairs suites with gas fireplaces. **Edenwild Inn,** 360/468-3238, www.edenwildinn.com, in Lopez village, looks like a vintage country farmhouse, yet it was built in 1990. Its sophisticated decor, antiques, and paintings provide a serene setting—though on warm nights you might hear the frogs in nearby ponds. The **Islander Lopez,** 360/468-2233, sports a totally rebuilt marina with a dock store offering provisions and supplies for boaters. Its great location on Fisherman's Bay (lodging is across the road from the bay) along with swimming pool, hot tub, and wide grassy play areas make it a great choice for families. This is a family-oriented resort with plenty of activities; 50 slips in the marina offer guest moorage. You can reserve fishing or sailing charters from the marina.

On Orcas, **Rosario Resort,** 800/562-8820, www.rosario-resort .com, centers around the historic 1909 Moran mansion, and in the lobby are some original Moran furnishings, like the Arts and Crafts–style conversation chairs. You'll have outstanding water views from 127 rooms (located not in the mansion but on the hillside nearby). There's a dock for visiting boats. A spa offers exercise and yoga classes, a weight room, swimming pool, and massage facilities. Tennis courts are nearby. **Turtleback Farm Inn,** 360/376-4914, is a restored turn-of-the century farmhouse located on 80 acres of farm and forest land and views of farm meadows where sheep graze and geese wander. One peek inside the inn's very own cookbook and you know you're in for a breakfast treat.

On San Juan, perched on the hillside above the marina, **Friday Harbor House,** 360/378-8455, www.karuna.com/fhhouse, a 20-room Mediterranean-style inn, new in 1994, claims the best of the views.

Rooms are elegant—all have fireplaces and Jacuzzis, most have views of the harbor. The dining room, where you can enjoy a continental breakfast of fruits and flaky scones, views the harbor too. If lodging aboard a boat appeals to you, the **Wharfside B&B,** 360/378-5661, www.rockisland.com/~pcshop/wharfside.html, an older 60-foot boat with two staterooms, right in the midst of the action at the marina in Friday Harbor, is a perfect choice. A stay at **Friday's** historic inn, 360/378-5848 or 800/352-2632, www.friday-harbor.com, in downtown, also puts you in the center of the action; deluxe rooms have water views. At the southern edge of town, **Mariella Inn & Cottages,** 360/378-6868 or 800/700-7668, www.mariella.com, is an impressive 1902 manse on a seven-acre peninsula of land. It has a garden and plenty of waterfront to explore. Three inn junior suites have jetted tubs, fireplaces, and a solarium that views the water; and there are other rooms as well. Cottages offer views and privacy and range from tiny log cabin rustic to modern two-level townhouse chic.

CAMPING

Where Salish Indians used to camp on Lopez Island's **Spencer Spit,** today you'll see the colorful tents of bicyclists, kayakers, and campers. A homesteader's abode for picnicking, eye-popping views of the islands, mountains, boat traffic, and shorefront and walk-in camping make this 129-acre state park a great destination for day-trippers as well as overnighters. **Odlin County Park** offers overnight camping on a first-come, first-served basis (check the sign at the Anacortes ferry for availability); for best luck in getting a spot, arrive before noon. **Moran State Park,** on Orcas (see above) has over a hundred developed sites for tents or motor homes, 360/376-2326; reservations are strongly suggested. Call the Washington State Parks reservation line, 800/452-5687, www.parks.wa.gov/rnw.htm. There are also numerous boat-in-only small island state parks.

NIGHTLIFE

Peace and quiet to enjoy the sounds of birds and lapping waves are the delights of the islands. However evenings are lively at pubs and restaurants in Friday Harbor on San Juan Island. There's a community theater on San Juan and on Orcas, and resorts like Rosario and Roche Harbor have entertainment.

HELPFUL HINTS

The islands are busy with visitors, and ferry lines are often long in summer. If you are traveling during high season and plan to catch a ferry to the islands from Anacortes, arrive an hour before the ferry departs. A good strategy is to overnight in Anacortes, and catch an early ferry. If you walk on or ride your bicycle you're almost assured of catching the ferry you aim for. **Washington State Ferries**, 800/843-3779, www.wsdot.wa.gov/ferries/default.cfm, offers five to seven daily sailings from Anacortes. The *Victoria Clipper*, 206/448-5000, www.victoriaclipper.com, offers high-speed passenger-only ferry service from Seattle, 800/888-2535, to Friday Harbor and to Rosario Resort on Orcas Island. **Island Shuttle Express**, 360/671-1137, provides passenger-only service from Bellingham to the San Juan Islands. During the summer months whalewatching cruises are offered. Also from Bellingham, a new catamaran service, **San Juan Island Commuter**, provides access to remote San Juan Islands areas; call 360/734-8180 or 888/734-8180. For daily air service through **West Isle Air** from Anacortes, Bellingham, and Seattle, call 800/874-4434. Floatplane service is available through **Kenmore Air** from Seattle, 800/543-9595, www.kenmoreair.com, and charter service from Seattle on **Sound Flight**, 800/825-0722.

Foot passengers have a variety of options on arriving at their island destination. For a cab on Lopez, call 360/468-2227; on San Juan, 360/378-3550 or 360/378-6777; on Orcas, 360/376-8294. Some inns and B&Bs have pick-up service; ask when reserving lodging. For island public transit information, call 360/376-8887 (or plan to rent a bicycle or moped; see "Fitness and Recreation" above.)

A couple of local tour operators offer personalized options. To see the island by bicycle on half-day or longer guided tours, call **Cycle San Juans**, 360/468-3251. **Easy Going Outings**, 360/757-0380, offers specialty food day trips and artists visits by van. And for a special, albeit more expensive, vacation, Captain John Colby Stone (of the Captain Whidbey Inn, 800/366-4097 or 360/678-4097) navigates his 52-foot classic ketch, the *Cutty Sark*, through the San Juan Islands on six-day cruises (starting in May and running once a month through September); these include stays in island country inns.

For additional information, contact **San Juan Visitor Information Service,** 360/468-3663 or toll free 888/468-3701, www.sanjuan.com; or contact the San Juan Island Chamber, 360/378-5240.

BELLINGHAM AND NORTHWEST WASHINGTON

A waterfront university town, Bellingham is the historic and cultural hub of Whatcom County, the fertile and forested northwest region of Washington. Although it is 90 miles north of Seattle and 50 miles south of Vancouver, the time it takes to cross the border into Canada makes Bellingham a logical halfway point between the two cities. Stop and sample the lifestyle that has earned Bellingham a spot as one of the nation's most liveable cities.

Its history includes a brief flurry with gold rush fever, a period of coal mining, and a constant relationship with logging. If the city (population over 60,000) feels spread out and disjointed, that's because it's a combination of four Bellingham Bay communities—Bellingham, Whatcom, Sehome, and Fairhaven—settled starting in the 1850s. Before that the Lummi, Nooksack, and Semiahmoo Indians occupied the coast along the bay.

Two spectacular old highway routes are connected to the city: Chuckanut Drive, an historic cliff-hugging road along the coast from the Skagit River delta in the south (which offers breathtaking views of the San Juan Islands en route to Fairhaven), and the Mt. Baker Highway, a winding, ever-climbing route that cuts through the Nooksack Valley to the east and winds through the foothills of Mt. Baker, ending at Artist Point, a spectacular viewpoint on the mountain.

Western Washington University, located in Bellingham, is a

NORTHWEST WASHINGTON

North Cascades National Park

North

Mt. Baker Wilderness

Mt. Shuksan ▲

North Fork

D

Noisy-Diobsud Wilderness Area

Baker Lake

Mt. Baker ▲

Mt. Baker National Recreation Area

Nooksack Falls

Lake Shannon

Concrete

20

G **J**
Glacier

MT. BAKER HWY

Silver Lake

R

SILVER LAKE RD

Maple Falls

Middle Fork

South Fork

542

C Van Zandt

H

Deming

River

Mt. Vernon

Sedro

9

Sumas

9

Nooksack

PARK RD

Lake Whatcom

Burlington

I

546

544

539

N SHORE RD

LAKEWAY DR

Larrabee State Park

E ✕

11

CHUCKANUT DR

L **K** **B**

M Bow

237

P

Bayview State Park

F
Lynden

MT. BAKER HWY

Samish Bay

Anacortes

20

CANADA

UNITED STATES

Peace Arch ✕

5

Lummi Indian Reservation

Bellingham

Bellingham Bay

HAXTON WAY

Lummi Island

O

N **A**
Blaine

548

Birch Bay

540

Q

Ferndale

Birch Bay State Park

0 SCALE 13
KILOMETERS
13 MILES

ROAD
HIGHWAY

PARK BOUNDARY
✕ PLACE OF INTEREST

INTERNATIONAL BOUNDARY

Sights

Ⓐ Blaine

Ⓑ Chuckanut Drive

Ⓒ Everybody's Store

Ⓓ Heather Meadows Interpretive Center

Ⓔ Larabee State Park

Ⓕ Lynden

Ⓖ Mt. Baker Highway and Scenic Byway

Ⓗ Nooksack Valley

Food

Ⓕ Dutch Mothers Restaurant

Ⓘ Edaleen Dairy

Ⓙ Milano's Market and Deli

Ⓚ Oyster Bar

Ⓛ Oyster Creek Inn

Ⓜ Rhododendron Cafe

Lodging

Ⓓ Glacier Creek Lodge & Cabins

Ⓝ Inn at Semiahmoo

Ⓞ The Willows

Ⓞ West Shore Farm Bed and Breakfast

Camping

Ⓟ Bayview State Park

Ⓠ Birch Bay State Park

Ⓔ Larabee State Park

Ⓡ Silver Lake Park

Note: Items with the same letter are located in the same town or area.

popular state university; its campus has a notable outdoor sculpture collection. Alaska Marine Highway System's southern terminus is at Fairhaven, and there is passenger ferry service to the San Juans and Victoria, British Columbia, from here, as well as an Amtrak station.

A PERFECT DAY IN NORTHWEST WASHINGTON

Spend the night in a B&B, and after breakfast explore Old Fairhaven (if you haven't had breakfast, stop at the Colophon Cafe). Plan to drive the Mt. Baker Highway, which takes you through the pastoral Nooksack Valley. Pick up a sandwich at Everybody's Store, a short detour from your route, and continue on to Picture Lake for a picnic lunch. Stop and marvel at the overlook at Heather Meadows and again at the end of the road at Artist Point. In the evening, I suggest a splurge on dinner at the Oyster Bar and a retreat to a mountain house or motel room.

SIGHTSEEING HIGHLIGHTS

★★★★ **Chuckanut Drive**—Take this route from I-5 if you're driving north from Seattle, as a slower way to Bellingham, particularly if it's lunch or dinnertime. Several restaurants on the drive feature oysters, some having started as oyster shacks decades ago. Taylor United, Inc.'s Samish Bay Oyster Farm has a retail outlet with shucked or in-the-shell oysters, clams, and other shellfish, as well as a video, recipes, and other information on the oyster.

Details: Going north, take Exit 231 off I-5. This is SR 11, which runs through the community of Bow and along the shores of Samish Bay winding north to Fairhaven. An access road to Taylor United is immediately next to the Oyster Creek Inn. Follow the signs. There is plenty of parking at Taylor United and great views of the bay. It's open daily 8 to 5. (45 minutes)

★★★★ **Heather Meadows Interpretive Center**—Nothing is quite as exhilarating or expansive to the senses as an alpine meadow on a hot, dry day with a crisp, blue sky overhead, wraparound views of mountain peaks and shimmering glacial lakes, and the sweet smell of mountain blueberries rising all around. Heather Meadows is such a setting and offers views of and trails to Bagley Lakes, mountain ridges dotted with bonsai-like silver fir, 500-year-old mountain hemlock, and glacial carved basalt formations bared to the sun. Challenging trails take off from here. (Note: If you do hike, keep in mind that you are in high-altitude terrain and the weather can change very quickly. Check with the ranger about conditions; take water, food, warm clothing, a map, and other hiking essentials.) The visitors center has interpretive displays about the natural and historical information of the area. Built as a warming hut by the Civil Conservation Corps in 1940, it was renovated in 1994. Just steps from the center you'll find a self-guided trail.

Details: Near the top of Mt. Baker at the end of SR 542. The center is open daily through mid-October 10 to 4:30; a ranger is on hand to answer questions. There are plenty of picnic tables nearby. (1 hour–full day)

★★★★ **Mt. Baker Highway and Scenic Byway**—Mt. Baker, in North Cascades National Park, dominates the horizon east of Bellingham and delights winter skiers (and snowboarders) and summer hikers. Along the 55-mile route to the mountain you'll meander through farmland and forest as you follow the north fork of the Nooksack River. The drive offers plenty to see and do. **Nooksack Falls**, about seven miles east of Glacier, drops 170 vertical feet; its proximity to the highway makes for an easy stop. From here the route is designated the Mt. Baker Scenic Byway. About 11 miles from Glacier, watch for a grove of towering Douglas fir, hundreds of years old. Several miles past here you will see a sign for Heather Meadows (see above). First you'll come upon the flower-filled meadows surrounding **Picture Lake,** which often reflects nearby **Mt. Shuksan** on its surface. Trails around the lake lead through wildflowers that include lupine and fireweed. Follow the road to its very end and you'll reach **Artist Point** viewpoint with stunning views of Mt. Baker and Shuksan. Trails take off from here and from Heather Meadows.

Details: Stop at the U.S. Forest Service/Glacier Public Service Center, 360/599-2714, about a mile east of the town of Glacier. Here you can get brochures, maps, and advice on the scores of hikes in the area available for all skill levels; many are wheelchair accessible. (3–5 hours)

★★★★ **Western Washington University**—Expansive views of the San Juan Islands and an extensive outdoor sculpture collection draw visitors to this campus on Sehome Hill, overlooking Bellingham Bay. The first large-scale sculpture, *Rain Forest*, a bronze fountain by artist James Fitzgerald, was installed in 1960. Now there are over 22 large-scale pieces on campus, including the work of Isamu Noguchi, Mark di Suvero, and Robert Morris.

Details: Take I-5, Exit 252 to Bill McDonald Parkway; audio phone tour and/or brochure available at the Western Gallery and Visitors Information Center while the university is in session. Call 360/650-3963. (2 hours)

★★★★ **Whatcom Museum of History and Art**—You will notice the unusual main building immediately, since it dominates the city's skyline. Built in 1892, the former city hall displays permanent exhibits of regional history, and hosts ever-changing shows of contemporary art. Additional buildings include Syre Education Center (201 Prospect) with exhibits on Northwest birds, Northwest Coast First Nations, and Inuit (Eskimo) peoples. The Arco Exhibit Gallery (206 Prospect) features contemporary art. The Whatcom Children's Museum (227 Prospect) has plenty of hands-on activities.

Details: The main building is at 121 Prospect Street, Bellingham, 360/676-6981. All buildings are open noon to 5 Tuesday through Sunday. Children's museum opens at 10 Thursday, Friday, and Saturday; admission is $2. Admission to other galleries by donation. (1–2 hours)

★★★ **Blaine**—This is the northwesternmost town in the continental United States, perhaps best known as home to the **Peace Arch**, a 67-foot classical Doric monument, reminding us with its inscription that the United States and Canada are "Children of a Common Mother." In 40-acre Peace Arch State Park, you can walk freely between the two borders. Semiahmoo Resort is at the tip of Blaine's Semiahmoo Spit, across the bay from downtown.

Details: Blaine Visitor Center is at 215 Marine Drive, Blaine; 360/332-4544 or 800/624-3555. (½–1 hour)

★★★ **Fairhaven**—Considered the historic old town of Bellingham, Fairhaven has its own colorful history as a boom town of the 1880s that never really quite exploded. Today its historic brick buildings house shops, eateries, and galleries. Don't miss Artwood, a fine woodworking gallery here. The Alaska Ferry terminal and Amtrak depot are here.

Details: From I-5, take Exit 250 south of downtown. (1 hour)

★★★ **Larabee State Park**—This was the first state park in Washington; it covers almost 2,000 acres of forest and park, with frontage on Samish Bay. Enjoy the tide pools, swim, hike, camp, and picnic. The park provides the southern access to six-mile Interurban Trail, a non-motorized path for hikers, bikers, and horses that parallels Chuckanut Drive through the forest.

Details: 245 Chuckanut Drive; 360/676-2093; State Parks reservations, 800/452-5687. There are 87 campsites, 26 full hookups. (2 hours)

★★★ **Lynden**—Founded by Dutch settlers, this farming community keeps its heritage alive with a working windmill, a pioneer museum, and a spring Holland Days festival. The **Dutch Village Mall** on the town's main street is accentuated by a 72-foot tall working windmill. The interior simulates a Dutch street scene with tulips, a flowing canal, and cobblestone streets. Inside is access to Dutch Village Inn, 360/354-4440, a motel in the windmill.

Details: *Exit 256 off I-5 and north on Highway 539; follow signs.* *Front Street is the town's main street. 655 Front Street for the mall. Open* *Monday through Saturday 10 to 9. Most of town is closed Sunday. (2 hours)*

★★★ **Mt. Baker Theater**—Opened in 1927, this 1,500-seat vaudeville movie palace features elaborate Moorish-Spanish–style architecture and is on the National Historic Register. A $1.6 million renovation project in 1995 returned it to its former glory. Live musical and theater performances, as well as movies, are held here.
    Details: 106 N. Commercial; 360/734-6080 for schedule information, 360/734-4950 for movie information.

★★★ **Nooksack Valley**—Small farming communitites dot the verdant Nooksack Valley east of Bellingham, including Everson, Deming, Nooksack, Nugents Corner, Van Zandt, and Lynden (see below). There are berry farms and an increasing number of orchards. The varieties grown here differ from those grown in the state's hotter eastern Washington apple region. You won't find Red Delicious or Granny Smiths, but tasty alternatives. The full-flavored Jonagold is the prominent apple. Two farms about 15 miles east of Bellingham, not far from Everson near Highway 9, open in the fall for harvest festivities. Also visit **Cloud Mountain Farm & Nursery**, 360/966-5859, and **Stoney Ridge Farm**, 360/966-3919—don't miss their caramel apple pie à la mode. **Mount Baker Winery** offers wine tasting, 360/592-2309.
    Details: To reach the Nooksack Valley, from I-5 in Bellingham, take Exit 255 (to the Mt. Baker Highway). Call for directions to the farms. Mt. Baker Winery's tasting room is open daily, except Monday, 11 to 5. You'll see their sign a mile before Deming on the Mt. Baker Highway. (4–6 hours)

★★ **Big Rock Garden**—Formerly a private nursery, Big Rock Garden has a fine collection of rhododendrons and Japanese maples and views overlooking Lake Whatcom. Special programs offered .
    Details: 2900 Sylvan Street 360/676-6985. Open April 1 through October. Admission is free. (45 minutes)

★ **Everybody's Store**—This is a small roadside store with everything from medicinal herbs to wine and wool socks. It's a fun detour en route to Mt. Baker from Bellingham—and a good place to get a made-to-order sandwich.
Details: Highway 9, Van Zandt; 360/592-2297. (15 minutes)

BELLINGHAM

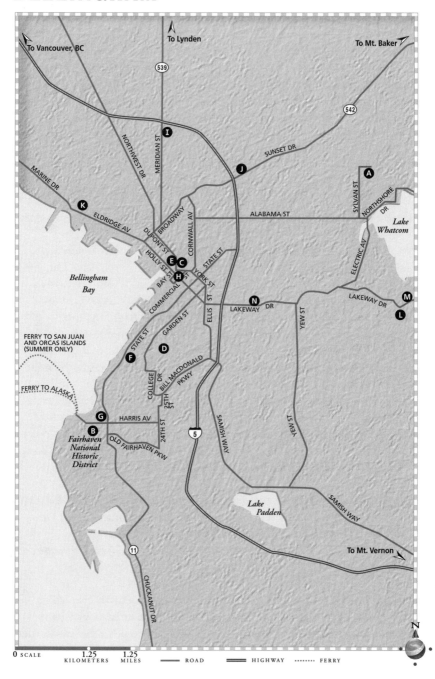

To Vancouver, BC

To Lynden

To Mt. Baker

539

542

NORTHWEST DR

MERIDIAN ST

SUNSET DR

MARINE DR

I

J

A

SYLVAN ST

NORTHSHORE DR

K

ELDRIDGE AV

ALABAMA ST

BROADWAY

DUPONT ST

CORNWALL AV

Lake
Whatcom

Bellingham
Bay

HOLLY ST

BAY ST

STATE ST

ELECTRIC AV

E C

H

YORK ST

LAKEWAY DR

M

COMMERCIAL ST

ELLIS ST

N

LAKEWAY DR

L

STATE ST

GARDEN ST

YEW ST

FERRY TO SAN JUAN
AND ORCAS ISLANDS
(SUMMER ONLY)

F

D

COLLEGE DR

BILL MACDONALD PKWY

FERRY TO ALASKA

25TH ST

G

HARRIS AV

24TH ST

B

5

SAMISH WAY

YEW ST

Fairhaven
National
Historic
District

OLD FAIRHAVEN PKW

Lake
Padden

SAMISH WAY

11

CHUCKANUT DR

To Mt. Vernon

N

0 SCALE   1.25   1.25
KILOMETERS   MILES   ━━ ROAD   ═══ HIGHWAY   ········ FERRY

Sights

Ⓐ **Big Rock Garden**

Ⓑ **Fairhaven**

Ⓒ **Mt. Baker Theater**

Ⓓ **Western Washington University**

Ⓔ **Whatcom Museum of History and Art**

Food

Ⓕ **Cliff House**

Ⓖ **Colophon Cafe**

Ⓗ **Il Fiasco**

Ⓘ **Orchard Street Brewery**

Ⓙ **Pastazza/Pastazza Presto**

Lodging

Ⓚ **DeCann House**

Ⓛ **Big Trees B&B**

Ⓜ **Schnauzer Crossing**

Ⓝ **A Secret Garden**

FITNESS AND RECREATION

Bellingham is known for the **Ski-to-Sea Race & Festival,** held each year on Memorial Day weekend. It's an 85-mile relay that includes seven events, parades, and a carnival. The six-mile **Interurban Trail,** a non-motorized path for hikers, bikers, and horses that parallels Chuckanut Drive through the forest, is south of Bellingham.

Whalewatching cruises can be taken through **Island Mariner** in Bellingham, 360/734-8866 or 888/373-8522, and through **San Juan Island Shuttle Express,** 360/671-1137. **Viking Cruises** out of La Conner, 360/466-2639, also offers whalewatching and sightseeing.

Whatcom Falls Park, 1401 Electric Avenue, located on 241 acres on Whatcom Creek has hiking trails, waterfalls, picnic shelters, barbecue pits, tennis courts, a juvenile fishing pond, and more. A highlight is the fish hatchery; for hours or information, call 360/676-2138. **Lake Padden Park**, 4882 Samish Way, on over 1,000 acres, has hiking and bridle trails around the lake and an 18-hole municipal golf course. For fishing and swimming, windsurfing, and seasonal kayak rentals, call 360/676-6985.

FOOD

The **Orchard Street Brewery**, 360/647-1614, is tucked away in an industrial strip north of downtown (call for directions), but well worth finding for yummy pizzas, salads, baked soups—and for their micro-brews. The **Colophon Cafe,** 1208 11th Street, 360/647-0092, a book-store café (located in Village Books) in Old Fairhaven, features homemade soups, sandwiches, quiches, and wonderful desserts. **Il Fiasco,** downtown at 1309 Commercial, 360/676-9136, is a favorite for Mediterranean and seafood with dinner daily. **Pastazza,** 360/714-1168, in Barkley Village (a new Bellingham residential community east of I-5 at Exit 255), offers homemade pastas and sauces. Their sweet potato ravioli with tomato fennel sauce is a favorite. Next door **Pastazza Presto** retail store sells pastas, sauces, and ice cream. The **Cliff House**, 331 N. State Street, 360/734-8660, offers a wide seafood selection (din-ner only served 5 to 10 daily). The whisky crab soup is reason enough to stop. Seating on their wraparound deck offers views of Bellingham Bay.

Along the Chuckanut Drive route (going south to north) the **Rhododendron Cafe**, 553 Chuckanut Drive, 360/766-6667, in Bow is small and casual, with fresh local ingredients. Perhaps the oldest oyster eatery, the **Oyster Bar**, 240 Chuckanut Drive, 360/766-6185, has a casual name and a rustic exterior, yet it's an elegant restaurant with fine linens, premium wines, waiters in black tie, and knock-out sunset views of Samish Bay. A classic entrée preparation features oysters crispy fried with an herbed parmesan crust and a lightly tart apple *aioli*. Dinner only. Bowls of oyster crackers and bottles of Tabasco sauce lend a casual touch to the **Oyster Creek Inn,** 360/766-6179, nearby. Menu choices include oysters raw on the half shell, a baked sampler, and a stew that is a delicate mix of extra small Samish Bay oysters, cream, milk, and herbs.

North of Lynden, stop at **Edaleen Dairy**, 9593 Guide Meridian Road (SR539), 360/354-3425, open 8 to 7:30 daily except Sundays, for fabulous ice cream cones. In Lynden, the **Dutch Mothers Restaurant**, 405 Front Street, 360/354-2174, is known for their Dutch cuisine. **Milano's Market and Deli**, 360/599-2863, in Glacier, offers hearty pastas and sandwiches and is a good stop for families.

LODGING

Many of Bellingham's B&Bs are in historic homes. **DeCann House**, 2610 Eldridge Avenue, 360/734-9172, is affordable, set in a Victorian home in an historic neighborhood. Set on a wooded lot on the east side of town, **Big Trees**, 4840 Fremont Street, 360/647-2850, is a post-Victorian, Craftsman-style home nestled amongst old-growth cedars and firs with views of Lake Whatcom. **A Secret Garden**, 1807 Lakeway Drive, 360/671-5327, is a turn-of-the-century Victorian-style home. A little more expensive, **Schnauzer Crossing**, 4421 Lakeway Drive, 360/733-0055 or 800/562-2808, is a stylish enclave with two guest rooms and a separate modern cottage with great views of Lake Whatcom. For a stay in the mountains, **Mt. Baker Lodging and Travel**, 360/599-2453, and **Mt. Baker Chalet**, 360/599-2405, are two reservation services that represent homes and cabins in the Mt. Baker area (specify if you're looking for a rustic cabin experience or a "house" experience). The **Glacier Creek Lodge & Cabins**, 360/599-2991, with rooms and small cabins with kitchenettes, is just off Mt. Baker Highway—perfect for skiers or hikers. On Lummi Island, **The Willows**, 2579 West Shore Drive, 360/758-2620, offers guest house lodging in a restful and refined cottage atmosphere. Rates include a full breakfast. Nearby on Lummi is the **West Shore Farm Bed and Breakfast**, 2781 West Shore Drive, 360/758-2600, an octagonal contemporary built in the 1970s by the owners, with a wood cookstove in the kitchen and a view deck. The **Inn at Semiahmoo**, 800/770-7992, is near Blaine and the Canadian border. Nature lovers explore the gently sloping beach along two sides of the mile-long spit or go whalewatching; golfers escape to the Arnold Palmer–designed course. The inn offers 198 rooms (16 are suites). Spa packages for two include accommodations.

CAMPING

Larabee State Park, on Chuckanut Drive, has 51 standard campsites, 25 full hookups, 8 walk-in campsites, and a great location. Near Anacortes are two other waterfront parks that offer camping: **Bayview State Park** (near Padilla Bay Interpretive Center) between Mt. Vernon and Anacortes, with about the same number of campsites; and **Birch Bay State Park**, southwest of Blaine. Reservations are needed May 15 through September 15; call 800/452-5687 to reserve at most state parks. Reservations can be made 11 months in advance of arrival date. West of Glacier, **Silver Lake Park** is a 411-acre Whatcom County Park that encompasses a former private resort and early homestead. There are 73 campsites; seven cabins are available for rental year-round. For cabin rentals, call 360/599-2776 well in advance. You can also rent a stall in the outdoor stable for your horse.

HELPFUL HINTS

Besides the Ski-to-Sea Race & Festival, Bellingham also hosts a music festival in August. Contact the Bellingham Whatcom County Convention and Visitors Bureau, 800/487-2032 (recorded message) or 360/671-3990. Their main office is at 904 Potter Street just off I-5 at Exit 253. **Alaska Marine Highway System's** port facility at Fairhaven is the southern terminus; call 800/642-0066 or 360/676-8445. **Island Shuttle Express**, 360/671-1137, provides passenger-only service to and from the San Juan Islands. During the summer months, whale-watching cruises are offered. A new catamaran service, **San Juan Island Commuter**, provides access to remote state parks such as Sucia, Matia, Jones, and Stuart Islands and is perfect transportation for hikers, campers, and kayakers; call 360/734-8180 or 888/734-8180. It departs from Bellingham Cruise Terminal in Fairhaven. Also from the terminal, mid-May through early October, **Victoria/San Juan Cruises**, offers passenger-only service to Victoria, leaving at 9 a.m. and returning at 8 p.m.; fare includes a salmon dinner, 800/443-4552.

SIDE TRIP: LUMMI ISLAND

Lummi Island is a quiet residential island that lies about 15 miles northwest of Bellingham. It's less than two miles wide and about nine miles long, has about 600 residents, no real town—just a store, library, and restaurant—and about 20 miles of country road for driving, cycling, or strolling. A private ferry provides island access from Gooseberry Point on the Lummi Indian reservation (the island is not part of the reservation). On the island, a pocket park and deck just north of the ferry terminal offers the only public beach access. Three times a year artists host open houses, and several studios can be visited year-round. To reach the island take Exit 260 from Interstate 5 and follow the signs west. The *Whatcom Chief* ferry holds about 20 cars and a handful of passengers and leaves the mainland at 10 minutes past the hour (round-trip $4). The **Beach Store Cafe**, 360/758-2233, lies near the ferry landing and serves local seafood and island-grown produce—including fruits and greens fresh from the orchard and garden. Open 8 a.m. to 9:30 p.m. daily in summer; closed some days in winter.

10

LEAVENWORTH

In little more than 30 years, Leavenworth has gone from ugly duckling to beautiful swan—from a dismal highway town to a Bavarian-style village that is one of the state's favorite visitor destinations and recreation areas. Located in the foothills of the Cascades, flanked by soaring snowcapped mountains, Leavenworth started the 1900s with prosperity and high hopes as a hub for the Great Northern Railroad. But in the 1920s, the railroad moved to Wenatchee, 30 miles further east. Leavenworth floundered for decades, depending on the timber and fruit industries for its survival. Finally, in the 1960s it reinvented itself as an alpine village, to fit its awe-inspiring geography. Since then visitors have come in ever growing numbers.

It can be a jam-packed tourist destination—there are more than 15 festivals every year, including favorites like Maifest, Autumn Leaf, and Christmas Lighting. It can also offer the serenity of a quiet small town, and a growing number of special lodgings are convenient to town but seem worlds away.

More and more, Leavenworth is becoming an arts town as well. The Icicle Creek Music Center offers chamber and other musical events year-round. The Leavenworth Summer Theater performs *The Sound of Music* outdoors. A summer festival features and accordian music competition and folk dancing. In the works for a spring event, are artists and artisan workshops and shows. ◼

LEAVENWORTH AREA

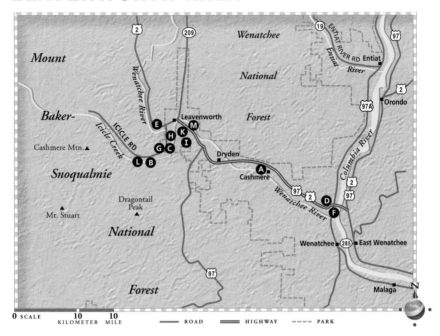

Sights

- **A** Chelan County Historical Museum and Pioneer Village
- **B** Icicle Creek Music Center
- **C** Leavenworth National Fish Hatchery
- **A** Liberty Orchards
- **D** Ohme Gardens
- **E** Tumwater Canyon
- **F** Washington Apple Commission Visitors Center

Food

- **A** Bob's Apple Barrel
- **G** Homefires Bakery

Lodging

- **H** All Seasons River Inn
- **I** Mountain Home Lodge
- **J** Sleeping Lady

Camping

- **K** Chalet Trailer Park
- **L** Icicle River RV Park
- **M** Pine Village Resort

Note: Items with the same letter are located in the same town or area.

A PERFECT DAY IN AND AROUND LEAVENWORTH

On a perfect summer day around Leavenworth you'll wake early in a cozy room, go for a hike in the woods and listen to the bird calls, and picnic by the river or on a promontory with views of the Cascades. Then you could play golf or go fishing. But be sure to save time for exploring Leavenworth and Cashmere. On a perfect winter day you may awaken to a new snowfall, then strap on cross-country skis to explore the very Bavarian landscape.

SIGHTSEEING HIGHLIGHTS

★★★★ **Icicle Creek Music Center**—Founded in 1995, the center features the music of the Kairos Quartet—the resident chamber musicians—and special performances by musicians from all over the country. Performances are in the Chapel Theater on the grounds of Sleeping Lady Conference center, west of Leavenworth. Lodging is also available at the conference center on Icicle Road west of Leavenworth. Don't miss the glass icicle sculpture by Dale Chihuly at the entrance to the conference center dining room.

Details: Tickets are $14 general admission, $12 senior, $7 for students and kids under 12. Call 800/574-2123 for Sleeping Lady and Icicle Creek Music Center or 509/548-6347 for information on individual performances as well as music retreat weekend packages (including lodging and fine food at the Sleeping Lady). Web site: www.cascade.net/~icicle. (3–4 hours for dinner and performance)

★★★★ **Ohme Gardens**—The view alone from here is worth the stop. The gardens, nine acres that overlook Wenatchee and the confluence of the Wenatchee and Columbia Rivers, are well known for their over 120 varieties of plants and flowers, the native stone path winding through the grounds, and many pools with waterfalls. Sit and contemplate the beauty from one of over 50 stone benches on the site.

Details: Immediately north of Wenatchee near the junction of Highways 2 and 97; look for the signs. Admission is $5 for adults and $3 for kids 7 to 17; 509/662-5785. Open daily April 15 through October 15 9 to 6. Web site: www.ohmegardens.com. (2 hours)

★★★★ **Tumwater Canyon**—In autumn this canyon west of Leavenworth is brilliant with fall color. Several turnouts provide unhurried views of the Wenatchee River ranging from tranquil pools to raging rapids. Look closely and you will see evidence of the devastating forest fires that raged out of control in the mid-1990s.

Details: A 9-mile stretch along Highway 2 just west of Leavenworth. (10 minutes)

✯✯✯ Chelan County Historical Museum and Pioneer Village—

A stop here offers an entertaining respite for travelers crossing Stevens Pass and a quick history lesson on the settlement of Central Washington. Besides a schoolhouse, blacksmith's shop, and railroad office, the village includes a hotel, saddle and print shops, a jail-house, a saloon, and an assay office—most built by pioneers before 1892.

Details: About 12 miles east of Leavenworth on busy U.S. Route 2; take the second Cashmere Exit. Located less than a block from Route 2, at 600 Cottage Avenue. The museum is open from April 1 to October 31 Monday through Saturday 9:30 to 5, Sunday noon to 5. Suggested donation $5 per family, $3 per person, $2 seniors and students, $1 kids 5 to 12. (1 hour)

✯✯✯ Liberty Orchards—

You can visit the home of Aplets & Cotlets, founded by two young Armenians who fled the unrest in Turkey in the early 1900s. In the gift store, you'll find generous samples of Aplets—inspired by a Turkish confection and first produced in 1918—and other of fruit gelatin candies.

Details: At 117 Mission Street, Cashmere; 509/782-4088 or www.libertyorchards.com. Open Monday through Friday 8 to 5:30, weekends 9 to 5. Visit weekdays and take a 20-minute guided tour of the kitchen. The store offers a wide variety of gifts. (30 minutes)

✯✯✯ Nutcracker Museum—

There are more than 3,000 different kinds of nutcrackers in this small museum upstairs on level with Leavenworth's main street. They range from thumbnail-size to larger than life. A 15-minute video offers a look at the history of nutcrackers.

Details: 735 Front Street; 509/548-4708 or 800/892-3989; www.nussnackerhaus.com. Open daily May through October from 2 to 5. Admission is charged. (45 minutes)

✯✯ Enzian Falls Championship Putting Course—

This 18-hole championship putting course in downtown Leavenworth provides a challenge for the pros and fun for the beginners; the pro-shop is an authentic alpine meadow cabin. Fun just to stop and look at.

Details: Located at 590 Highway 2 in Leavenworth (just across from the Enzian Inn); 509/548-5269. Open 4 p.m. to dusk weekdays, 9 to dusk on Saturday and noon to dusk on Sunday. There is a per person fee for 18 holes. (1½–2 hours)

☆☆ **Icicle Junction**—Great for families with kids of all ages. Bumper boat rides during summer months, an 18-hole miniature golf course, and an arcade filled with games. Try ice skating in winter.

Details: Located on the corner of Highway 2 and Icicle Road, 888/462-4242. (1–2 hours)

☆ **Leavenworth National Fish Hatchery**—Self-guided tours can be taken almost every day from 7:30 to 4. Kids love to watch the huge schools of fingerlings. During late spring and early summer, you may see spawning fish.

Details: Just west of town on Icicle Road; look for signs; 509/548-7641. Admission is free. (1 hour)

☆ **Washington Apple Commission Visitors Center**—Located near Ohme Gardens, they offer much information on the state's apple business. There are displays, free samples, and an informative video on the apple industry.

Details: 2900 Euclid Avenue, Wenatchee; 509/663-9600 weekdays; 509/662-3090 weekends. Open Monday through Saturday 9 to 5, Sunday 10 to 4. Admission is free. (1 hour)

FITNESS AND RECREATION

Hiking, white-water rafting, fishing, and boating are some favorite summer activities. There are numerous outfitters; call the chamber at 509/548-8807. Leavenworth may be best known for its winter activities. The family Ski Hill just east of town invites sledders and beginning skiers. For cross-country ski lessons and rentals, check out the **Leavenworth Nordic Center,** 509/548-7864. The hills around Leavenworth are alive with fun snow acitivities. Snowmobiling tours are offered by Mountain Springs Lodge, 509/763-2713. You'll find sleigh rides at **Red-Tail Canyon Farm,** 509/548-4512, or **Eagle Creek Ranch,** 509/548-4566, up Valley Road northeast of town.

There are plenty of shops—clock shops, galleries, a woodcarver, and more—to explore on and near Front Street, but don't miss **Cabin Fever Rustics**, a country home and accessories store a little off the beaten path on Commercial Street.

FOOD

For gourmet Austrian food that is lighter than traditional German food (you'll still find full-flavored entrées like savory lamb shanks), try **Restaurant Osterreich** on Front Street, below the Tyrolean Ritz Hotel, 509/548-4031. The menu changes frequently at **Lorraine's Edel House**, 320 Ninth Street, 509/548-4412, but you can expect piquant salads and fresh seafood dishes. In summer there's outdoor seating on the torch-lit patio of this comfortable 1920s house close to the heart of downtown. The pub, beer hall, and dining levels of the **Leavenworth Brewery,** 636 Front Street, 509/548-4545, overlook the brewing facility. Their Whistling Pig Wheat beer, known as "the Pig," is a favorite. A family atmosphere prevails in the dining area, where you can play cribbage and try the brewery's handcrafted honey-sweetened rootbeer. An extensive menu includes plump sausages and beer bread, soups, sandwiches, and vegetarian dishes. For dessert try a glass of porter and a chocolate brownie. The **Best of the Wurst** is an outdoor stand at 220 Eighth Street that offers grilled hamburgers and bockwurst sandwiches. Great on a cold day. **Homefires Bakery**, 509/548-7362, is on the west side of town; take the Icicle Road 2½ miles and watch for signs. Open Thursday through Monday.

East from Leavenworth to Wenatchee is a major apple growing area of the state. Fruit stands are open from May to October, where you'll find classics such as Red and Golden Delicious, Granny Smiths, Jonathans, and newer apples like Fuji and Gala, too. In Cashmere, **Bob's Apple Barrel** fruit stand marks the main entrance to town off Highway 2. You'll find large bins of apples, apple cider, butters, vinegars—even apple milkshakes.

LODGING

There are over 1,000 rooms within 20 miles of Leavenworth, and your choices range from a wide variety of in-town B&Bs to rustic cabins or elegant mountain retreats. Call the chamber at 509/548-5807. A very unusual lodging is **Cobblestone Cottage**, on the river in downtown

Leavenworth, 800/323-2920, where you can stay in an unusual fantasy room like the Medieval Castle Suite or rent the whole cottage. **All Seasons River Inn,** 8751 Icicle Road, about 1.5 miles (20-minute walk) out of Leavenworth, 509/548-1425 or 800/254-0555, is an adults-only, non-smoking bed-and-breakfast. E-mail them at allriver@rightathome.com. Affordable **Alpen Rose Inn,** about five blocks from downtown Leavenworth, 509/548-3000 or 800/582-2474, www.alpenroseinn.com, is an adults-only, non-smoking inn with full complimentary breakfast and desserts in the evening and a swimming pool. **Hotel ~ Pension Anna,** in downtown Leavenworth, 509/548-6273 or 800/509-ANNA, www.pensionanna.com, is an authentic Bavarian-style inn; a former church adjacent contains a large suite. **Abendblume Pension**, 509/548-4059 or 800/669-7634, e-mail: abendblm@rightathome.com, is an Austrian-style country home about a mile from downtown Leavenworth in the midst of a meadow with mountain views all around. It's an adult retreat with luxury amenities. Breakfast often includes tasty *Aebleskivers*, a unique Danish pancake. The amazingly reasonable **Haus Lorelei**, 347 Division Street, 509/548-5726 or 800/514-8868; www.hauslorelei.com, is just a short walk from downtown on a promontory over the Wenatchee River. All 10 guest rooms are individually decorated with antiques; two river-side rooms have four-poster canopy beds with lace hangings. **Haus Rohrbach Pension**, 509/548-7024 or 800/548-4477, is a comfortable chalet-style home (and separate suites) on the outskirts of Leavenworth. It has terrific valley views, Tumwater Mountain at its back door, a swimming pool in the front yard, and rates to meet every budget. **Mountain Home Lodge**, 509/548-7077 or 800/414-2378, in a comfortable contemporary building, lies three miles from the outskirts of Leavenworth up a primitive winding road to an alpine meadow with stunning views of the mountains. A massive stone fireplace is the focal point of the dining room. There are miles of hiking trails; in winter this is a cross-country ski destination. Call for rates, which vary with season. A good value, **Run of the River Inn,** 800/288-6491, is less than two miles from Leavenworth on the Icicle River. This comfortable country-style inn, with lots of attention to details—for example, hiking brochures and information await you—overlooks wetlands and is situated between two bird refuges, so it seems worlds away from everything. The **Enzian Motor Inn**, 509/548-5269 or 800/223-8511, www.enzianinn.com, is right on Highway 2. It has two pools, including a covered pool. A complimentary buffet breakfast is served.

LEAVENWORTH

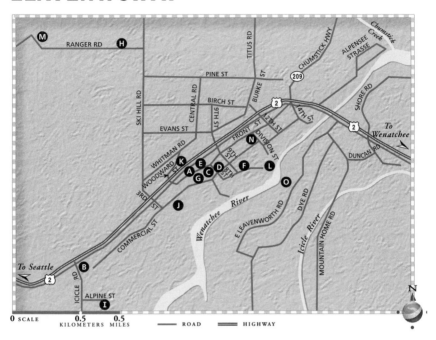

Sights

Ⓐ Enzian Falls Championship Putting Course

Ⓑ Icicle Junction

Ⓒ Nutcracker Museum

Food

Ⓓ Best of the Wurst

Ⓔ Leavenworth Brewery

Ⓕ Lorraine's Edel House

Ⓖ Restaurant Osterreich

Lodging

Ⓗ Abendblume Pension

Ⓘ Alpen Rose Inn

Ⓙ Cobblestone Cottage

Ⓚ Enzian Motor Inn

Ⓛ Haus Lorelei

Ⓜ Haus Rohrbach Pension

Ⓝ Hotel ~ Pension Anna

Ⓞ Run of the River Inn

CAMPING

There are three campgrounds around Leavenworth offering easy access to town and plenty of amenities: **Pine Village Resort,** 509/548-7709 or 800/562-5709, **Icicle River RV Park**, 509/548-5420, and **Chalet Trailer Park,** 800/477-2697. Cost for each is about $25 per night.

NIGHTLIFE

Leavenworth Brewery and the **Restaurant Osterreich**'s outdoor beer garden are lively evening spots in summer and on weekends. Also, check out performances at the **Icicle Creek Music Center** at Sleeping Lady retreat.

HELPFUL HINTS

Read *Miracle Town: Creating America's Bavarian Village in Leavenworth, Washington*, by Ted Price, published by Price & Rodgers (Vancouver, WA), 1997, tells the story of Leavenworth's rebirth. It's available through the Leavenworth Chamber of Commerce; 509/548-5807.

Alki Tours of Seattle offers train-trip packages for certain festivals; 800/895-2554.

Scenic Route: Cascade Loop

This is a Washington classic best planned for warmer months—from May to October—when the snows blocking the North Cascades Highway have melted. The loop offers a tour of the most beautiful mountain scenery and many of the best recreation options in the state and is a sure bet for sunshine. From Interstate 5, head east across Highway 2 to **Leavenworth.** Spend some time touring, hiking, or overnighting here.The apple town of **Cashmere** is about 10 miles east of Leavenworth and worth a detour for a look at the **Chelan County Historical Museum and Pioneer Village**, 509/782-3230, or a tour of Liberty Orchards, 509/782-2191, makers of Aplets and Cotlets. Traveling on you'll reach the city of **Wenatchee** at the confluence of the Wenatchee and Columbia Rivers, in the heart of one of the state's largest apple producing areas. You can visit the **Washington State Apple Commission Visitors Center**, 509/663-9600, for free apple samples and juice. Also take time to visit **Ohme Gardens** (you'll see signs from the freeway), overlooking the rivers and city.

Then, take Highway 97 or 97A north along either side of the Columbia River. Highway 97 on the east side passes several state parks with riverfront access and the popular **Desert Canyon** golf

CASCADE LOOP

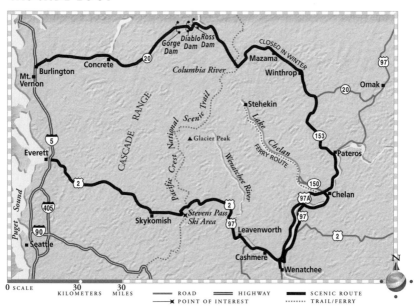

course, 509/784-1111. Highway 97A passes **Rocky Reach Dam**, 509/663-7522, with guided tours available. Both highways lead to **Lake Chelan** and the community of **Chelan**, 800/424-3526, www.lakechelan.com. This is a resort town destination for scores of sun and fun seekers. All summer long the lake is abuzz with boats, skiers, and jet skis. There are many beachfront resorts and condominiums, but the best known is **Campbell's Lodge**, 800/553-8225. Popular with families since 1901, it's right on the lake in the heart of Chelan, a Norman Rockwell–style small town. **Wapato Point**, 509/687-9511, about seven miles northwest of Chelan in the small town of Manson, is a popular condominium resort destination. From Chelan you can take an unusual detour to **Stehekin**, a remote village of about 70 year-round residents, 50 miles from Chelan at the northwest end of the lake in Chelan National Recreation Area. The **Lake Chelan Boat Company**, 509/682-2224 or www.ladyofthelake.com, runs boat and catamaran service here several times a day. You can also go by floatplane with **Chelan Airways**, 509/682-5555. Either way, you feel like you're journeying over a fjord. You can make it a day trip or an overnight. **Stehekin Lodge** is right at the landing. It offers motel-like rooms in the small main building and individual cabins nearby that have a more rustic flavor. A more luxury lodging is **Silver Bay Inn**, 509/682-2212 or 800/555-7781, with house and cabin rentals in a more private setting; a rolling lawn goes down to the water. **Stehekin Valley Ranch**, 509/682-4677 or 800/536-0745, offers cabins, fishing, horseback riding, and more. In summer there's plenty of hiking—trailheads leading into North Cascades National Park begin here—and a nearby waterfall to visit.

From Chelan, go north (first along Highway 97, then 153) to the Western-style town of **Winthrop** in the Methow Valley. In winter, this is a cross-country skiing mecca. In summer it's a great place to fish, mountain bike, and ride horses. Spend some time exploring main street here, or stop for lunch at the **Winthrop Brew Pub** 155 Riverside Ave., 509/996-313, in a quirky red schoolhouse-style structure along the river. There are numerous lodgings in the valley (call central reservations at 800/422-3048), however, **Sun Mountain Lodge**, a top-ranked destination resort 10 miles from town, 509/996-2211 or 800/572-0493, is a must visit if just for the view or a meal. From the dining room you'll have sweeping, eagle-perch views of the valley—enhancing the fine food. Continuing northwest of Winthrop on Highway 20 you'll come to Mazama, with

Mazama Country Inn, 509/996-2681 or 800/843-7951, a secluded lodge in the woods. Nearby is the newly built **Freestone Inn**, 800/639-3809, with inn rooms and cabin rentals. Then heading west you'll take the mountain route. Do this in early morning if possible or you'll face the sun while you're driving and lose some of the views. Stop at 5,447-foot **Washington Pass Overlook** for a spectacular view of the North Cascades. About 35 miles from the overlook you'll encounter Ross, Diablo, and Gorge Dams. All offer tours. The most unique is the four-hour guided tour of **Diablo Lake** by **Seattle City Light** that includes lunch, a boat cruise, powerhouse tour, and a vertical railway ride; this runs mid-June through September. Reservations are required, call 206/684-3030. Continue west through the lush and green Skagit Valley. You'll encounter I-5 access at Sedro Wooley.

For more information on the route, call the Cascade Loop Association, 509/662-3888 or www.cascadeloop.com. ◼

11
SPOKANE

Isolated by geography and situated far from other cities of its size, Spokane is the prosperous and historical hub of the Inland Empire, which skirts the thriving bread basket of Washington's great Columbia Basin. The city of 200,000 is known for hot summers, cold winters, and spring lilacs. The Lilac Festival in May kicks off with the annual Bloomsday Race, which attracts more than 50,000 participants.

The Spokane natives who fished for salmon were the primary residents until 1810, when the Northwest Fur Company built the first non-native trading post in the Northwest at Spokane House. In the 1870s grain and lumber replaced fur trading as a commercial focus. The town moved to Spokane Falls, 10 miles southeast of the post, where mills were built to harness the water power. This impressive falls is now the heart of Riverfront Park, the site of Expo '74. In the late 1800s Spokane experienced an "Age of Elegance" spurred by the wealth from silver mines in nearby Coeur d'Alene, Idaho. You'll see how the silver barons spent their money in the Victorian-style homes and mansions in Browne's Addition. A recent flurry of historic renovation in buildings and hotels around town may signal a new age of elegance for the city.

Spokane makes a great stopover if you're driving to the Northwest from eastern regions or traveling east to the prime resort areas of northern Idaho at Coeur d'Alene (a half hour away) or Priest Lake (two hours' drive northeast). It also works well to combine visits to Pullman, in the Palouse region to the south; to Lake Roosevelt and Grand Coulee Dam to the west; or into the interior of British Columbia.

SPOKANE

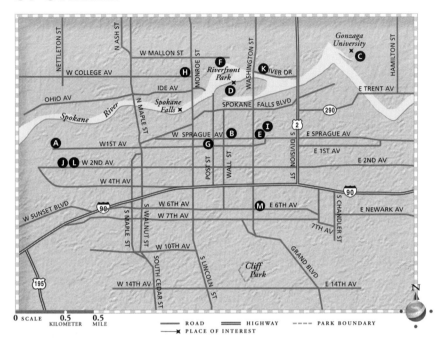

Sights

- **A** Cheney Cowles Memorial Museum
- **B** Douglas Gallery
- **C** Jundt Art Museum and Bing Crosby Collection at Gonzaga University
- **D** Riverfront Park

Food

- **E** Ankeny's
- **F** Clinkerdagger
- **G** Fugazzi Dining Room

Food (continued)

- **H** Milford's Fish House and Oyster Bar
- **I** The Onion
- **J** Patsy Clark's Mansion

Lodging

- **K** Cavanaugh's Inn at the Park
- **L** Fotheringham House
- **G** Lusso Hotel
- **M** Kempis Suites
- **E** The Ridpath Hotel

Note: Items with the same letter are located in the same town or area.

A PERFECT DAY IN SPOKANE

Exploring downtown's Riverfront Park is a must. Take the gondola ride above Spokane Falls. Picnic on the grounds or grab lunch at one of several restaurants nearby. Then head south of town to explore the Cheney Cowles Museum and tour Campbell House, which echoes the wealth of Spokane's early boom days. To end the day with some exercise, stroll through Manito Park or head to the Little Spokane River for a hike or a little canoeing.

SIGHTSEEING HIGHLIGHTS

✧✧✧✧ **Cheney Cowles Memorial Museum**—Spokane's best museum is ensconced amidst the elegant homes of Browne's Addition. It focuses on the pioneer history of the Inland Empire and includes an exhibit of Plateau Indian arts and an art gallery. Campbell House is a restored turn-of-the-century home located on the museum's grounds.

Details: 2316 West First Avenue; 509/456-3931. Open Tuesday through Saturday 10 to 5, Wednesday until 9, and Sunday 1 to 5. Admission $4, a tour of Campbell house included. (2 hours)

✧✧✧✧ **Jundt Art Museum and Bing Crosby Collection at Gonzaga University**—On the grounds of Spokane's well-known Jesuit University, you'll find a dramatic Dale Chihuly work, the Gonzaga Red Chandelier, and several other of his glass pieces and drawings at the Jundt Art Museum. Constantly rotating exhibits include local, regional, national, and international old master and contemporary artists; selections from their Rodin collection are always on exhibit. Crosby Center, a student enclave, has pictures and memorabilia from singer Bing Crosby, who attended Gonzaga, on display in the Crosbyana Room. His childhood home, with more displays, is on campus.

Details: The museum is on the west corner of Gonzaga's campus. Going north on Division Street take a right on DesSmet and a right on Pearl. Drive south on Pearl and you'll see the museum, a huge brick building with a copper roof; 509/323-6611. Summer hours Tuesday through Friday 10 to 4, Saturday noon to 4, closed Sunday, open Monday during the school year. The Crosby Center is at the foot of Standard Street off Boone Avenue; 509/323-4097. Summer hours 8:30 to 4:30; open later during the school year. Admission is free. (1–2 hours)

★★★★ **Riverfront Park**—The site of Expo '74 has been transformed into a lively 100-acre park that lies at the heart of the downtown, built around the Spokane River and Spokane Falls. The gondola ride leaves from the west edge of the park and carries riders over the Spokane River with a spectacular view of the falls and of Canada Island, the site of Canada's Expo exhibit. In addition to the outdoor art, including an intriguing series of joggers, visitors enjoy a tour train, an amusement park, ice skating in winter, and an IMAX theater on the grounds. The Spokane River Centennial Trail is a paved easy walk that parallels the river.

Details: In downtown along the Spokane River; 509/456-4386 for hours of operation, season pass rates, and special events; 509/625-6680 for IMAX show information. Admission to attractions varies. (2 hours or more)

★★★ **Cat Tales Endangered Species Conservation Park**—There are 30 species of rare and endangered big cats including lions, pumas, lynx, tigers, and leopards in this zoological park and training center that can be viewed up close (from about eight feet away).

Details: 17020 North Newport Highway, 509/238-4126. Open summers Tuesday through Sunday 10 to 6; otherwise Wednesday through Sunday 10 to 4. Admission $5 adults, $4 seniors (free on Sunday), $3 kids under 12. Guided tours are available. (2 hours)

★★★ **Manito Park**—There's a lilac garden here, of course, as well as rose, Japanese, perennial, and formal gardens, a conservatory with tropical foliage and seasonal flowers, and a duck pond. The park is best May through October; it offers a cool, green respite from high summer temperatures.

Details: South of downtown on Grand Avenue between 17th and 25th Avenues; 509/625-6622. The conservatory and Japanese garden are open 8 to dusk. Admission free. (1–2 hours)

★★★ **Silverwood Theme Park**—A Victorian-era theme park with food, shows, and games of skill. Thrilling rides like Skydiver, the Thunder Canyon river raft ride, and a 55-mile-per-hour wooden roller coaster called the Timber Terror—the names speak for themselves—attract teenagers and excitement seekers. Ferris wheels, carousels, and shows such as performances by international skaters round out the entertainment. Tinywood is a section for toddlers, complete with roller coaster, pump cars, and tree climbs. There's pizza and casual food at High Moon Saloon and all-you-can-eat–style family meals like chicken, mashed potatoes, and biscuits at Lindy's Country Restaurant.

Details: Fifty miles northeast of Spokane via Interstate 90; take highway 95 north from Coeur d'Alene and go 15 miles; 26225 North Highway 95, Athol, Idaho 83801; 208/683-3400. Open May through September; summer hours 11 to 8; check May and September hours. Admission $21 for ages 8 to 64. (full day)

★★★ **Spokane House Interpretive Center**—In 1810 Jaco Finlay was commissioned by the Pacific Fur company to set up a trading post where the Spokane and Little Spokane Rivers meet. It was the Northwest's first non-native trading post. Markers outline the site, and artifacts excavated in 1953 are on display in the interpretive center. An exhibit also traces the history of Northwest fur companies, including Pacific and Hudson Bay.

Details: Located in Riverside State Park, 9 miles northwest of downtown and less than a mile north of the community of Nine Mile Falls; 509/466-4747. Open mid-May to early September Wednesday through Sunday 9 to 6. Admission free. You can picnic on the grounds. (1 hour)

★★ **Douglas Gallery**—Bronze sculptures, hand-blown glass art, and fine paintings are a specialty of this 5,000-square-foot gallery. A lower level "vault" room showcases the works of many Northwest artists.

Details: 120 North Wall Street; 509/624-4179. Open Monday through Saturday 10 to 6. Admission free. (30 minutes)

★★ **John A. Finch Arboretum**—There are more than 2,000 labeled ornamental trees, shrubs, and flowers on this 65-acre park, somewhat hidden away in the north part of town, but worth a visit, especially in May when over 70 varieties of crabapples bloom.

Details: 3404 Woodland Boulevard; 509/624-4832. Open dawn to dusk daily. Admission free. (2 hours)

★★ **Red Shed Farm Museum**—This family-owned museum on a working wheat farm north of Spokane gives you a feel for farm life in the 1920s, '40s, and '50s, with re-created kitchens and a bedroom suite. There are over 500 farm implements and tools that have been passed down in the family. And the farm may have the largest collection of ironstone dishes in the Northwest.

Details: The farm lies 13 miles north of the city. Call 509/466-2744 for directions and to confirm they are open. At the farm, ring the bell to summon the owners. (1–2 hours)

KIDS' STUFF

On the grounds of **Riverfront Park** are several attractions that enthrall children: the **Childhood Express,** a huge two-story copy of a Radio Flyer wagon; a 1909 hand-carved **Charles Loof carousel**; and nearby, a garbage-eating goat sculpture (it's hard to tell who enjoys this more—kids or their parents). At **Cat Tales Endangered Species Conservation Park** kids can pet the young cubs. At the **Children's Museum of Spokane**, new in mid-1998, infants to 10-year-olds will enjoy interactive exhibits and games, including a splash through a hydroelectric power station exhibit. And kids and parents both enjoy a visit to the **Red Shed Farm Museum.**

SPECTATOR SPORTS

The **Spokane Indians** team plays minor league baseball. In winter the **Spokane Chiefs** hockey team plays in the Arena, often against Canadian teams.

FITNESS AND RECREATION

It's become less and less a well-kept secret that Spokane's municipal golf courses—**Downriver, Esmeralda, Indian Canyon,** and the **Creek at Qualchan**—offer attractively landscaped courses, great play, and great value. Call the City of Spokane, 509/625-6453, for details and tee times.

If the weather is inclement, you can explore 15 blocks of downtown where department stores such as **Bon Marché** and **Nordstrom** are connected by second-story skywalks.

Runners come here in May the annual **Bloomsday** run. Hiking and canoeing trails around the **Little Spokane River** west of town put you in a wetlands area reminiscent of a Lewis and Clark exploration. **Mt. Spokane** (at 6,000 feet), a 30-minute drive north of town, offers summertime hiking and mountain biking, and wintertime cross-country and downhill skiing—a great low-key ski destination for families. The **Spokane River Centennial Trail** is a 39-mile trail for walkers, runners, and bicyclists that runs from downtown east to the Idaho border.

Wine buffs can tour several wineries including Arbor Crest, Caterina, and Latah Creek. **Arbor Crest**, in the Cliff House, a national historic site on a bluff overlooking the Spokane River, is the one not to miss.

FOOD

Ankeny's, 515 West Sprague Avenue, 509/838-2711, on the top floor of the Ridpath Hotel downtown, offers expansive views of the city and river, beef and seafood meals, and late evening entertainment. Their entrées are moderately priced. The **Calgary Steak House**, 3040 East Sprague Avenue, 509/535-7502, is a good place for family dinners and has a children's menu, but expect to pay a hefty price for a New York steak. A lively place to go for a good hamburger and family dining is **The Onion**, 302 West riverside Avenue (downtown), 509/747-3852; and 7522 North Davidson (north), 509/482-6100. **Clinkerdagger**, 621 West Mallon Street, 509/328-5965, has some views of the river and tasty pasta dishes, but the draw here is the desserts. **Patsy Clark's Mansion**, 2208 Second Avenue, 509/838-8300, in Browne's Addition, is dark and romantic—a dressy spot to go for a special evening. Patsy Clark was a silver baron and his unusual mansion with Moorish overtones was designed by Spokane's most famous architect, Kirtland Cutter. The **Fugazzi Dining Room** at Hotel Lusso, 1 North Post Street, 509/624-1133, has an international menu with such offerings as wild mushroom ravioli and Moroccan chicken. **Luna**, 5620 South Perry, 509/448-2383, a European bistro–style restaurant tucked away in the pretty residential neighborhood of Southhill, is a little pricey, but the innovative food, using seasonal produce, is wonderful. **Milford's Fish House and Oyster Bar**, 719 North Monroe Street, 509/326-7251, is miles from the saltwater, but the fish is fresh from Puget Sound and simply and deliciously prepared. For budget-friendly options in fun settings, try **Knight's Diner**, 2909 North Market, 509/484-0015, located in an old Pullman train car (breakfast and lunch only); or the **Milk Bottle Restaurant**, 802 West Garland Avenue, 509/325-1772, located in a former dairy. Homemade ice cream is a great reason to go to the Milk Bottle.

LODGING

The most exciting news in recent years centers on historic renovation. Examples are two luxury boutique hotels new in the late 90s. West Coast Hotels' **Lusso Hotel**, 1 North Post Street, 509/747-9750 or

SPOKANE AREA

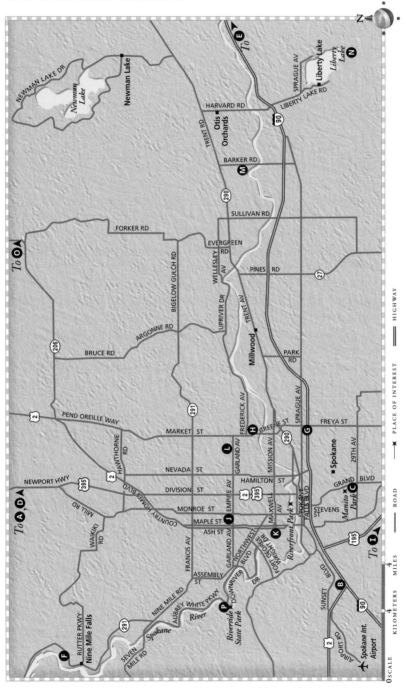

Sights

Ⓐ Cat Tales Endangered Species Conservation Park

Ⓑ John A. Finch Arboretum

Ⓒ Manito Park

Ⓓ Red Shed Farm Museum

Ⓔ Silverwood Theme Park

Ⓕ Spokane House Interpretive Center

Food

Ⓖ Calgary Steak House

Ⓗ Knights Diner

Ⓘ Luna

Ⓙ Milk Bottle Restaurant

Lodging

Ⓚ Twickenham Cottage

Ⓛ Waverly Place

Camping

Ⓜ KOA of Spokane

Ⓝ Liberty Lake Park

Ⓞ Mt. Spokane State Park

Ⓟ Riverside State Park

800/426-0670, combines two centennial buildings with an amazing renovation; the interior includes Italian marble archways and a five-story, hand-sanded cherry staircase. The **Kempis Suites,** 326 West Sixth Avenue, 509/747-4321, in the building that department store mogul Charles Kemp built in 1906, houses 15 apartment-size units with antique furnishings, kitchens, and dining rooms or offices. **Cavanaugh's Inn at the Park,** West 303 North River Drive across from Riverfront Park, 509/326-8000 or 800/843-4667, has over 400 rooms, seven floors, and a terrific location. Some rooms have fireplaces (the suites), whirlpool tubs, and river views. There are two pools (one indoors). Cavanaugh's also owns the **Ridpath Hotel,** 515 West Sprague Avenue, 509/838-2711 or 800/426-0670. For years the classic hotel in the city, it has an outdoor pool and over 300 rooms. **Fotheringham House,** 2128 West Second Avenue in Browne's Addition, 509/838-1891, was home to Spokane's first mayor, David B. Fotheringham. Now it's a historic B&B with four rooms; no phones or TVs, but plenty of Victorian character. Another B&B is **Waverly Place,** 709 West Waverly Place, 509/328-1856, a 1902 Victorian home located in

Corbin Park, an elegant older neighborhood north of the river. It offers central air conditioning and a pool. A comfortable, smaller B&B option especially attractive to joggers, bicyclists, and hikers is the **Twickenham Cottage**, 509/326-2397, located along the Centennial Trail at West 2809 Summit Boulevard. Two rooms rent for $80 each, and the whole cottage (with kitchen, laundry room, and attached garage) is available for weekly or longer stays. There are also a number of national chain hotel/motels convenient to downtown.

CAMPING

Mt. Spokane State Park, 509/238-4258, about 30 miles northeast of Spokane, offers a dozen or so sites for tents or self-contained RVs and a few primitive sites. **Riverside State Park,** 509/456-3964, is about six miles northwest of downtown. **KOA of Spokane**, 3025 North Barker Road, 509/924-4722, has over 150 sites for trailers and tents. It's located in Otis Orchards about 13 miles east of Spokane (take Exit 293 off Interstate 90). **Liberty Lake Park**, 3707 South Zephyr Road, Liberty Lake, 509/456-4730 for group reservations or 509/255-6861, offers swimming beaches with lifeguard, tent, and RV camping; there is a fee for park admittance.

NIGHTLIFE

There are a number of brewpubs around town, many with live entertainment on weekends. A popular newer spot is the **Bayou Brewery** with a New Orleans Mardi Gras theme, great Cajun food, bands, and comedy groups on weekends. Good for families weeknights. **The Ram** brewpub and restaurant is a lively watering hole with music and entertainment near the Arena. The **Cavallino Lounge** in the **Lusso Hotel**, with its blown-glass chandeliers from Italy and purple drapes, is a busy nighttime gathering spot; it's a non-smoking establishment, and folks come for the unique martinis.

HELPFUL HINTS

A walking map is available for self-guided tours of historic centennial buildings. The Spokane Area Convention and Visitors Bureau Visitor Information Center at 201 West Main Avenue, 800/248-3230, www

.spokane-areacvb.org, will provide maps and answer any questions you might have. The Spokane International Airport is seven miles southwest of town, off Sunset Boulevard.

SIDE TRIPS: PULLMAN, ROOSEVELT LAKE, GRAND COULEE DAM, COEUR D'ALENE

About 75 miles southeast of Spokane is **Pullman**, the site of Washington State University and home to the Cougars. This is a picturesque college town set against the rolling wheat fields for which the Palouse region of Washington is known. You can get an ice-cream cone or view cheesemakers at work at **The Creamery** on campus, known for producing Cougar Gold, a nutty white cheddar cheese that claims diehard fans. It comes packed in a can as it did during World War II.

About 50 miles south of Spokane, just off SR 195, is **Steptoe Butte State Park**. Take a winding road to the top of the 3,612-foot butte and on a clear day you can see into Montana.

Palouse Falls, about 100 miles southwest of Spokane (take SR 261 south off I-90 near Ritzville), is in an area called the Channeled Scablands, sculpted by the floods of the Ice Age. The falls drop almost 200 feet and offer an impressive contrast to the surrounding dry canyon.

Traveling west of Spokane along U.S. 2 leads you into bare, arid country, which is beautiful if you have the inclination to appreciate it. Take SR 25 north to see **Roosevelt Lake** stretching about 150 miles from Grand Coulee Dam to the Canadian border; houseboat rentals are available to explore this impressive lake. About 90 miles west along U.S. 2, then SR 174, is **Grand Coulee Dam**, perhaps the most famous of many Northwest dams and truly a spectacle to see, especially after dark when a laser light show showcases the spillway.

To the east is Idaho. Just over the border, **Coeur d'Alene Resort** is a prime destination for avid golfers anxious to try their hand—or club—on its renowned floating green. For area information, contact the visitors bureau at 800/286-5544.

12

WASHINGTON'S WINE COUNTRY

Directions to Washington's wine country? Sure. Go east from Seattle on I-90 to Ellensburg. In the middle of the state, hang a right on I-82 and follow it almost to the Oregon border. You've just followed the Yakima River, the wine country's main artery and a rich agricultural path through former desert. Home to more than 40 wineries, Washington's wine region is the second largest in the country. At the Tri-Cities—Richland, Kennewick, and Pasco—the Yakima meets the Columbia and Snake Rivers and the wine appellations fan out along these waterways.

In all, the route is about 250 miles—a bit of a drive on an ordinary day, but special winery events, warm weather, summer and fall produce, and some pretty interesting Western towns, museums, the Yakama reservation (the tribe uses the original spelling of the word), and a special excursion up the Columbia River to Hanford Reach are reasons enough to go. Yakima and the Tri-Cities are the large population centers.

Not far from Yakima, the Western town of Toppenish is the valley's "mural town." It's home to over 50 historical murals done by well-known Western artists. Prosser, 50 miles southeast of Yakima, is the birthplace of the state's modern wine industry; wine grape varieties were developed and tested at Washington State University's Extension Center north of town by Dr. Walter Clore, who's considered the father of Washington's wine industry.

Come to the valley in summer when the more than 400 crops raised here, such as apricots, Rainier cherries, Bing cherries, peaches,

WASHINGTON'S WINE COUNTRY

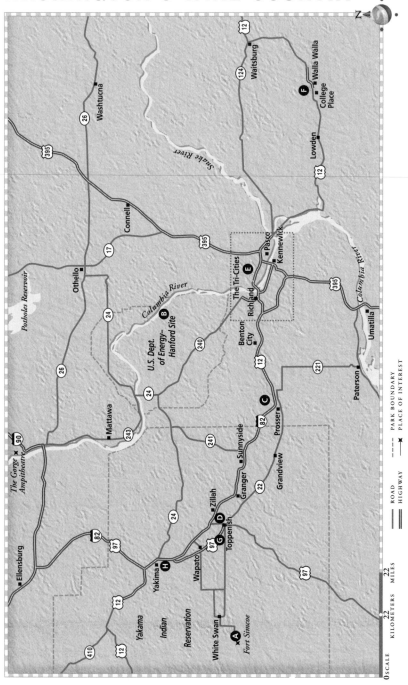

Sights

- **Ⓐ** Fort Simcoe
- **Ⓑ** Hanford and Hanford Reach
- **Ⓒ** Prosser
- **Ⓓ** Toppenish
- **Ⓔ** Tri-Cities
- **Ⓕ** Walla Walla
- **Ⓖ** Yakama Nation Reservation
- **Ⓗ** Yakima
- **Ⓗ** Yakima Valley Museum

Note: Items with the same letter are located in the same town or area.

and corn are plentiful. Apples are harvested August through October—this valley vies with the Wenatchee area as the state's apple capital—and wine grapes shortly thereafter in time for Octoberfest celebrations.

A PERFECT DAY IN THE WINE COUNTRY

Take an early stroll, bike ride, or drive through the countryside. Visit some country wineries and plan to picnic on the grounds. Explore the produce stands. If it's July, a perfect day includes a peach sundae from the Donald Mercantile south of Yakima. In the heat of summer, book lodging with a swimming pool nearby.

SIGHTSEEING HIGHLIGHTS

✯✯✯✯ **Hanford and Hanford Reach**—In the mid-1940s Hanford, near the Tri-Cities town of Richland, was designated as a site for development of the atomic bomb. A segment of the Columbia River where the first reactors were built was closed to the public. Only reopened in the 1970s, this free-flowing segment of the Columbia, particularly an area called the Hanford Reach, can be visited by jet-boat excursion with **Columbia River Journeys.** This is a special trip that sends shivers down your spine, revealing a beautiful and historic wildlife-rich area, with the defunct reactors rising eerily in the background.

Details: Call Columbia River Journeys; 509/943-0231. Cost is $36 for adults, $19 for ages 4 to 11, under 4 free. (4 hours)

★★★☆ **Prosser**—Washington's modern-day wine industry started at Washington State University's Extension Center outside this classic small town. A new wine museum and interpretive center planned for Prosser. Watch for it after the year 2000. The museum in the city park is a worthy and shady stop. Each August the town draws thousands of folks to the outdoor wine and food festival. In September a hot air balloon rally fills the skies with color.

Details: About 50 miles southeast of Yakima on I-82. (2–3 hours)

★★★☆ **Toppenish**—The murals on Toppenish's Old Timers Plaza show the Yakama natives picking hops and getting them to market. Other murals portray the life of the tribes and the settlement of the region. One depicts the signing of the treaty of 1855, still in effect today. In all the town has over 50 murals that show the area's history and enliven the buildings (most by noted Western artists). One depicts the treaty signing with Territorial Governor Issac Stevens. The project restored the town and gives a visually stimulating look at the history of the valley. Toppenish is also home to the **Yakima Valley Rail and Steam Museum**, 509/865-1911, with summer train excursions, and the **American Hop Museum, 509/865-4677. Kraff's** clothing store has a wide selection of Western-style Pendleton pillows and blankets.

Details: 20 miles southeast of Yakima between I-82 and Highway 97. (1–2 hours)

★★★☆ **Walla Walla**—This is a gracious old college town—home to Whitman College—that owns a goodly share of Northwest history. Lewis and Clark stopped here in 1805, and after that, fur trappers traveled here, finally setting up a fort. West of town, Marcus Whitman built a mission in the 1830s. The Whitman Massacre in 1847 occurred when the Cayeuse tribe attacked the missionaries, blaming them for a deadly attack of measles. You can visit the **Whitman Mission National Historic Site** interpretive center. The exhibits at **Fort Walla Walla Museum** look at pioneer life. Walla Walla has a festival to celebrate its famous sweet onion. And several of the state's highly regarded wineries are here.

Details: *The Whitman Mission is 7 miles west of town. For general information contact the Walla Walla Area Chamber of Commerce; 509/525-0850. (4–6 hours)*

★★★★ **Yakima**—This city of 60,000 is the major commercial gateway to the Yakima Valley's rich agricultural region. Irrigation in the early part of the century turned the desert of mixed volcanic sediment into richly fertile land. Stop at **Washington's Fruit Place** for a closer look at this agricultural story. **Historic Front Street** downtown offers a look at the city's past, as does the **Yakima Electric Railway Museum,** which offers rides on its antique trolleys.

Details: *Request a brochure from the Yakima Valley Visitors & Convention Bureau; 509/575-3030 or 800/221-0751, email: yvvcb @televar.com. Washington's Fruit Place, 105 South 18th Street, 509/576-3090, is less than a mile from I-82 at Exit 33. (4 hours to explore the town, 45 minutes at the fruit interpretive center)*

★★★ **Tri-Cities**—These are the towns of Richland, Kennewick, and Pasco, spread out broadly around the Columbia River. Hanford Atomic

Wine Grapes in the Yakima Valley

Yakima Valley C & V Bureau

Works is near Richland. There are shopping centers, business districts, colleges, wineries, and more here. The Atomic Cup hydroplane races are held here each summer. In early September Pasco hosts a unique salsa festival.

Details: *Contact the Tri-Cities Visitor and Convention Bureau in Kennewick; 509/735-8486 or 800/254-5824. (A day or longer)*

★★★ **Yakama Nation Reservation**—Blanketing nearly 1.5 million acres in southeastern Washington, a cultural center, state park, teepee camping, powwows, and mural town convey the history and way of life of the 14 tribes that make up the Yakamas and the role they play in the Yakima Valley. (Note that the tribe and town spellings are different.) The Indian Nation Cultural Center includes a museum, theater, library, gift shop, restaurant, and camping facilities. Browse the 12,000-square-foot museum's dioramas, artifacts, rock art, tule shelters, and clothing. At the museum store you can find small dream-catchers, some wrapped in white buckskin; check out the moccasins and baskets, too. Many items are made locally by members of the Yakama Nation. Sample frybread and other native foods in the museum restaurant.

Details: *Located just off Highway 97 and Buster Road in Toppenish; 509/865-2800. For visitor information, call 509/865-5121, ext. #436, or write Odessa Johnson, Yakama Nation, P.O. Box 151, Toppenish, WA 98948. Call 509/865-2000 for information on camping, teepees, and RV hookups. Open Monday through Saturday 9 to 5, Sunday 10 to 5. Admission is charged. (2 hours)*

★★★ **Yakima Valley Museum**—This is a really fine museum (and getting better all the time) with a large carriage display, changing exhibits, and a display on apple industry label art. One of the best exhibits here is the working soda fountain on the lower level that re-creates one of Yakima's popular 1950s-style drugstore fountains. Go to have a Green River Soda or a big, fat hot fudge sundae.

Details: *2105 Tieton Drive, Yakima (in Franklin Park). (1–2 hours)*

★★ **Fort Simcoe**—This was home to the infantry who watched over the area in the mid-1800s. Restored officers quarters are open to the public. Plan to picnic on the old parade ground. The annual Treaty Day Pow Wow in White Swan the first week of June includes arts displays and dancing demonstrations, as does Toppenish's Fourth of July Pow Wow and Rodeo.

Details: Near the town of White Swan 30 miles west of Toppenish. (2 hours)

FITNESS AND RECREATION

Floating the Yakima River, especially along the Ellensburg Canyon route, is a favorite summertime activity. You can bicycle or jog the **Yakima River Greenway**. The **Apple Tree Golf Course and Restaurant** in Yakima is worth a stop, just to see their 17th signature hole, Apple Island. Farm stand shopping and winery touring are good ways to meet the local vintners and producers. The jetboat trip up to **Hanford Reach** offers not only a look at the original nuclear reactors and the site of White Bluffs—the town that was removed when Hanford was built—but a rich look at the wildlife of the river, including beaver and white pelicans.

FOOD

In Yakima **Deli di Pasta**, 509/453-0571, in the historic district on Front Street, is a great choice for fine Italian meals. Nearby in the restored train station is the state's first brewpub, **Grant's Brewery Pub**, 509/575-2922, where you'll find tasty local microbrews. **Birchfield Manor**, 509/452-1960, a short drive east of town, offers weekend gourmet dinners worth planning around. This B&B is also a good place to overnight. This region has a large Hispanic population; at the east end of Zillah you'll find **El Ranchito Restaurant and Bakery**, 509/829-5880, offering an informal self-serve restaurant where dishes are served with fresh tortillas made in the factory behind the store; call ahead to arrange a tour. There's also a large assortment of authentic Mexican wares including metal *camales* (tortilla presses) and all kinds of terra cotta. **Snipes Mountain Brewery**, 509/837-2739, is a new brewpub in Sunnyside, in an unexpectedly grand new building, that makes a good lunch stop. You can watch cheesemaking at the **Darigold Dairy Fair** in Sunnyside, 509/837-4321, a fun stop for the whole family with sandwiches, ice cream, and cheeses, including soft curds, to sample and buy.

The **Donald Mercantile**, at Donald off I-82 near Wapato, is a fun stop for old-time atmosphere and fresh produce; but if you love fresh peaches, you *must* stop in July for their fresh peach sundaes. (I do this in lieu of lunch!) The **Rocky Mountain Chocolate Factory**,

WASHINGTON'S WINE COUNTRY

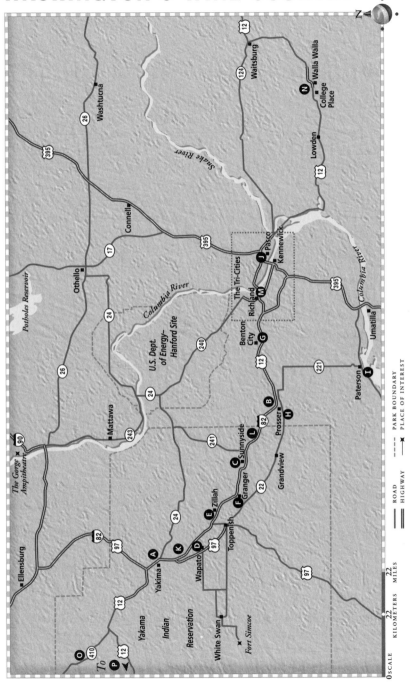

Food

- (A) Birchfield Manor
- (B) Chukar Cherries
- (C) Darigold Dairy Fair
- (A) Deli di Pasta
- (D) Donald Mercantile
- (E) El Ranchito Restaurant and Bakery
- (F) Granger Berry Patch
- (A) Grant's Brewery Pub
- (G) Rocky Mountain Chocolate Factory
- (H) Snipes Mountain Brewery

Wineries

- (B) Chinook Winery
- (I) Columbia Crest Winery
- (J) Gordon Brothers Cellars
- (G) Hedges

Wineries (continued)

- (H) Hinzerling Winery
- (B) Hogue Cellars
- (J) Preston Winery
- (K) Staton Hills Winery
- (L) Tucker Cellars

Lodging

- (A) Birchfield Manor
- (M) DoubleTree/Hanford House
- (N) Green Gables Inn
- (M) Shilo Inn
- (C) Sunnyside Inn

Camping

- (O) American River
- (P) Packwood
- (P) Rimrock Lake

Note: Items with the same letter are located in the same town or area.

509/829-3330, carries chocolate raspberry fudge among a dozen delicious varieties for about $8 per pound, and offers samples of its daily specials. Frozen red and golden raspberries, boysenberries, loganberries, and huckleberries are sold in gallon containers (about $35 per gallon). Outside Granger at the **Granger Berry Patch,** 509/854-1413, you can pick up raspberry, blackberry, or other preserves. Just outside Prosser, don't miss the free tastings of dried Bing, Rainier, and tart cherries; blueberries; and cranberries at **Chukar Cherries,** 320 Wine Country Road, 509/786-2055. The Truffle Chocolate Cherries (dried sweet cherries coated in milk chocolate) make great gifts, if you can bear to give them away.

WINERIES

There are more than 40 wineries in this region, many with tasting rooms located at the vineyards or in the small towns of the valley. Many have picnic spots. You'll need at least three days to seriously explore the area that breaks roughly into four areas: the Yakima Valley, Benton City, Tri-Cities area, and Walla Walla wineries. Below are just a few of the wineries you can visit. Call ahead for tasting hours and tour information.

Traveling southeast from Yakima, the first winery sign you'll likely see is for **Staton Hills Winery**, 509/877-2112, east of Yakima, in an attractive building with a great valley view. **Tucker Cellars**, 509/837-8701, between Sunnyside and Grandview, offers free tastes of their fresh popcorn daily and sells bags of popped corn and small jars and gallon jugs of unpopped corn, as well as Tucker's honey-pickled asparagus and other food products. **Hinzerling Winery,** 509/786-2163, in Prosser, is the Yakima Valley's oldest family-owned and -operated winery, and winemaker Mike Wallace is a highly visible member of the valley winemaking community. At the **Hogue Cellars,** 509/786-4557, east of Prosser, you'll find jars of pickled asparagus, snap peas, carrots, and spicy beans, as well as other gift items in their newly redone tasting room. Nearby, in a charming clapboard farmhouse, is **Chinook Winery**, 509/786-2725, known especially for their excellent Merlot wine. The biggest, most impressive wine facility in the region is **Columbia Crest Winery**, 509/875-2061, at Paterson, about 30 miles east of Prosser near the Columbia River.

Near Benton City is the Red Mountain area (with its own unique microclimate), along Sunset Road, and a number of wineries worth a detour, including the elegant new **Hedges** chateau. **Gordon Brothers Cellars** tasting room is in Pasco, off I-182 at Exit 9. The **Preston Winery,** 509/545-1990, is one of the pioneer grape growers in the state and a delightful country winery with expansive vineyard vistas.

And there are special events like **Spring Barrel Tasting** on the last weekend of April, coinciding with asparagus season. The **Tri-Cities Northwest Wine Festival** is held in mid-November in Pasco. And each year Yakima Valley wine producers host an open house right after Thanksgiving offering samplings of varietal wines along with foods prepared to match; recipe cards of the dishes are also available. For a brochure and map to all the wineries, call the **Yakima Valley Wine Growers Association** at 800/258-7270 or pick up *The Grape Vine,* a free seasonal guide to valley activities, available in many restaurants, stores, and area lodgings. Or for touring information contact the **Washington Wine Center** in Seattle, 206/667-9463; www.washingtonwine.org.

LODGING

Birchfield Manor, 509/452-1960 or 800/375-3420, a Victorian-style B&B in the country just outside Yakima, offers gourmet meals and a pool. Down the valley try the pleasant, surprisingly affordable **Sunnyside Inn,** 509/839-5557 or 800/221-4195, a 12-room (eight with Jacuzzis, two with fireplaces) inn. There are a number of convenient **Best Western** motor inns along the route, 800/528-1234. The **DoubleTree/Hanford House** in Richland is right on the Columbia, as is a nearby **Shilo Inn,** 509/946-4661 or 800/222-2244. In Walla Walla the **Green Gables Inn** B&B, 509/525-5501 or 888/525-5501, www.greengablesinn.com, is a grand home on a quiet street close to Whitman College.

CAMPING

Although there are some campgrounds scattered around Yakima and the Tri-Cities, it can get so hot here in the summer that the best option for campers is to tour the valley, then head west of Yakima along U.S. 12, the White Pass Highway, to **Rimrock Lake** or **Packwood** (this puts you close to Paradise on Mt. Rainier). Or take SR 410 over Chinook Pass (closed in winter) from U.S. 12 to the campgrounds along the **American River.** These are in the William O. Douglas and Goat Rocks wilderness areas, where the Wenatchee National Forest, 509/653-2205, and the Gifford Pinchot National Forest meet.

HELPFUL HINTS

To do justice to the area, plan a four-day, three-night visit. For more lodging options, call the **Yakima Valley Visitors & Convention Bureau,** 800/221-0751, or the **Tri-Cities Visitor and Convention Bureau** in Kennewick, 800/254-5824 or 509/735-8486.

You can reach the Columbia Gorge and Portland from Toppenish. Highway 97 leads south through the small town of Goldendale (there's an observatory here) into the gorge; the road passes Maryhill Museum (see the Portland chapter).

Farmers spruce up tractors, combines, and grape harvesters with lights for the **Sunnyside Farm Implement Parade** early in December. It's a unique valley celebration that has drawn national media attention and a growing number of fans. Winter is not the best time to visit the valley (it can be cold and dismal), but if you're here, check out the parade. For information, call 509/837-5939. Also, the town of Toppenish has added a lighted Western parade with two dozen horse- and mule-drawn wagons, Conestogas, buggies, and stagecoaches in early December.

13
CENTRAL OREGON

When Sunriver Resort south of Bend, Oregon, was built in the late 1960s, it changed the whole destiny of central Oregon. It was a new concept then—a planned community of residences, bicycle trails, a small airport, restaurants, and a village, set around lakes, rivers, and two beautiful golf courses. And that was just the beginning of this high-desert region's modern-day resort wonders. Now this area is a haven for summer recreation and for private residential communities.

There are golf courses galore—more than 24 just around Bend—and a whole slew of resorts. Mix that with hot, dry summers, a wildlife-rich landscape, rivers to float, caves to explore, dramatic geologic formations, some wonderful museums, plenty of art, music festivals—and you've got a destination that's a delight for the whole family.

Bend is the epicenter of this resort wonderland. The Western-style town of Sisters, northwest of Bend, and nearby Black Butte Ranch combine small-town charms with major recreational opportunities. When the snow falls, this is one of the Northwest's most popular winter resort areas, famous for the skiing opportunities on Mt. Bachelor.

There are spectacular geologic features in the area, such as Newberry National Volcanic Monument south of Bend, which includes Lava Butte and Lava Lands, and the John Day Fossil Beds National Monument northeast of Bend. The High Desert Museum between Sunriver and Bend and the Museum at Warm Springs are attractions that offer plenty of exploring on less glorious days. ◪

CENTRAL OREGON

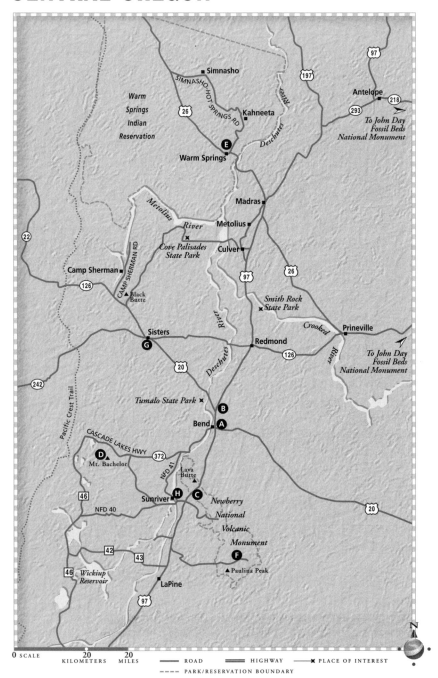

Simnasho

SIMNASHO-HOT SPRINGS RD

Warm
Springs
Indian
Reservation

26

Kahneeta

197

97

Antelope

218

293

To John Day
Fossil Beds
National Monument

Deschutes River

E

Warm Springs

Metolius River

Madras

22

Metolius

Cove Palisades
State Park

Culver

Camp Sherman

CAMP SHERMAN RD

126

▲ Black
Butte

97

26

Smith Rock
State Park

Crooked River

Prineville

To John Day
Fossil Beds
National Monument

Sisters

G

20

Deschutes River

Redmond

126

242

Pacific Crest Trail

Tumalo State Park ✕

B

Bend ▲ A

CASCADE LAKES HWY

372

D
Mt. Bachelor

NFD 41

Lava
Butte

20

46

NFD 40

Sunriver

H

C

Newberry

National

Volcanic

Monument

42

43

F

46

Wickiup
Reservoir

▲ Paulina Peak

LaPine

97

N

0 SCALE   20   20
         KILOMETERS   MILES   ━━━ ROAD   ═══ HIGHWAY   ✕ PLACE OF INTEREST
                                  ---- PARK/RESERVATION BOUNDARY

Sights

Ⓐ   **Bend**

Ⓑ   **High Desert Museum**

Ⓒ   **Lava Butte and Lava Lands Visitor Center**

Ⓓ   **Mt. Bachelor**

Ⓔ   **Museum at Warm Springs**

Ⓕ   **Newberry National Volcanic Monument**

Ⓖ   **Sisters**

Ⓗ   **Sunriver Resort**

A PERFECT DAY IN CENTRAL OREGON

For a perfect warm-weather day, rise early with the sun so you can capture the fresh, dewy sensation left by a cool night before temperatures rise. You can bicycle, play golf (set up a tee time well in advance), or fish, depending on your preference. As the day heats up, float the Deschutes River (use *lots* of sunscreen) or hang out by a pool. To get out of the sun, spend time inside the High Desert Museum, the Museum at Warm Springs, or shopping in the galleries in Bend or Sisters.

SIGHTSEEING HIGHLIGHTS

✦✦✦✦ **High Desert Museum**—This museum combines historical artifacts, living history presentations, and wildlife with indoor and outdoor exhibits. It also features Western and Native American artifacts; new in 1999 is a Native American wing with more than 7000 items on display. You can also stroll through time in the Earle A. Chiles Center, which re-creates the sounds and sights of historical events in Central Oregon. There are wildlife demonstrations and interpretive talks throughout the day. Outside, view live demonstrations in the sawmill and a settlers cabin.

   Details: Located 6 miles south of Bend at 59800 S. Highway 97; 541/382-4754. Open 9 to 5 daily, except major holidays. Admission is $6.25, $5.75 for seniors and youths between 13 and 18, $3 for ages 5 to 12, 4 and under free. (3 hours)

★★★★ **Mt. Bachelor**—This 9,065-foot mountain draws skiers and snowboarders from mid-November through the Fourth of July for its 300-plus inches of dry powder, 70 runs, and seven express chairs. In summer, rides to the summit showcase views of the high desert and the Cascades. The route to the mountain from Bend is the Cascades Lake Highway, a National Scenic Byway.

Details: About 22 miles and less than 30 minutes west of Bend.

★★★★ **Museum at Warm Springs**—Over 7,500 square feet of exhibits include more than 600 items—photographs, rare documents, artifacts, and displays—detailing the history of the Warm Springs, Wasco, and Paiute tribes. Outside, an amphitheater features living history, storytelling, crafts, and dance demonstrations.

Details: On the Warm Springs Indian reservation, off Highway 26, an hour north of Bend; 541/553-3331. Open daily 10 to 5. Admission $6. For more information write: Confederated Tribes of Warm Springs, P.O. Box C, Warm Springs, OR 97761. (3 hours)

★★★★ **Newberry National Volcanic Monument**—Just east of LaPine is a five-mile-wide caldera containing Paulina and East Lakes—two of Oregon's best fishing areas—lava formations, a large obsidian field, and waterfalls. The view from Paulina Peak is breathtaking.

Details: Naturalist walks are offered in spring and summer through the Deschutes National Forest. Information center on County Road 21 has information, maps, and displays. (4–6 hours)

★★★★ **Sunriver Resort**—This is one of the Northwest's best year-round resort destinations. The 35,000-square-foot main lodge re-opened in 1998 after $5.5 million was spent renovating the Cascadian style structure. This is worth a visit, as it overlooks beautiful meadows and mountain scenery typical of central Oregon. The resort includes three 18-hole championship courses, 35 miles of paved bike paths, 28 tennis courts, an indoor racquet club a marina for canoeing and white-water rafting, a shopping village, and more.

Details: 15 miles south of Bend, call 541/593-1000 or 800/547-3922 for information and reservations. (2–4 hours)

★★★ **Bend**—This city bustles but retains a small town feel with Mirror Pond, flanked by Drake Park, at the heart of downtown. There are shops, restaurants, and galleries. The best view of the city is from Pilot

Butte State Park, a 500-foot cinder cone. You'll spot nine Cascade mountain peaks as well.

Details: There's a visitors center on U.S. 20 a mile northwest of Bend, or contact Bend Chamber Visitor and Convention Bureau at 800/905-2363. (2 hours)

★★★ **Lava Butte and Lava Lands Visitor Center**—Lava Butte, part of Newberry National Volcanic Monument, is one of about 300 cinder cones that errupted on the flanks of 500-square-mile Newberry Volcano (Newberry caldera is the site of the eruption). One trail goes over molten land created from lava flow; another leads to native plants. Displays include touch tables, videos talk about geology, and attractions of the area.

Details: 12 miles south of Bend off Highway 97, 541/593-2421 (April through October; otherwise call the Bend Ft. Rock Ranger Station, 541/388-5664). Guided tours include panoramic views from the butte. Operated by the U.S. Forest Service. The visitor center is open daily 9:30 to 5 from Memorial Day to Labor Day. Admission charge per car and small charge for shuttle bus to top of butte. (1–2 hours)

★★★ **Sisters**—This Old West-style town west of Bend was established in 1885 as an outpost for Company A of the First Oregon Volunteers. The town hosts a stunning quilt show each summer, when quilts are displayed on the main street of town. They've held a rodeo each June for almost 60 years. Near Sisters is the largest llama breeding ranch in the world.

Details: Sisters lies on Highway 20 about 22 miles northwest of Bend. (2 hours)

FITNESS AND RECREATION

For much of the year this is the golf resort capital of the Northwest. Acclaimed resorts like **Sunriver**, **Black Butte**, **Eagle Crest**, and **Kah-Nee-Ta** focus on the sport. However, a wide variety of other activities and facilities make these great destinations for families. There are 24 courses—public and private—around Bend for all levels of expertise; most offer stunning scenic views that please whether or not your game does.

The **Metolius River** northwest of Bend is a National Wild and Scenic River and the area around it offers fly fishing, horseback and llama riding, mountain lodges, moutain biking, and more. Lakes here offer water sports such as water skiing and windsurfing. The **Metolius Recreation Area** encompasses Black Butte Ranch; call 541/595-6117 for more information or access their website: www .ohwy.com/or/m/metolrec.htm. The **Deschutes River** has Class I to Class V river-rafting options.

Mt. Bachelor, southwest of Bend, has six-day lodges, runs of up to two miles in length, and a vertical drop of 3,100 feet. Mountain bikers will find hundreds of miles of single track trails and plenty of high country areas to explore. With stunning rock spires that tower above Crooked River Canyon, **Smith Rock State Park** is one of the state's most popular destinations for rock climbers. There are also more do-able hiking trails and picnic spots. The park is located nine miles northeast of Redmond.

The summertime Cascade Festival of Music in Bend showcases jazz, pop, rock, blues, and the classics and draws plenty of music fans to riverside **Drake Park** for picnics and good sound. There's also the Sunriver Music Festival each August.

Sisters is a great destination for shopping; quilts are a specialty— each summer the town hosts a popular outdoor quilt show. In Bend there's shopping along Wall and Bond streets. The Blue Spruce Gallery, south of town, specializes in the pottery of Oregon artists, including richly textured Raku items.

FOOD

Bend offers more restaurants than any other town in the area. Choices include the historic **Pine Tavern Restaurant**, 967 Northwest Brooks Street, 541/382-5581, with its outdoor terrace and river view, featuring a salad bar and other healthy choices for lunch and dinner. **Jake's Diner & Truck Stop**, 6120 South Highway 97, 541/382-1041, is popular with locals for its huge portions at regular prices; breakfast is served 24 hours. The **Broken Top Club** restaurant, 61999 Broken Top Drive, 541/383-8210, in the sparkling clubhouse outside Bend, offers mountain views and fine dining options like grilled salmon with a sauce of red peppers. And for a great ice cream cone, get in line at **Goody's Soda Fountain**, 957 NW Wall Street, 541/389-5185. **Scanlon's**, 61615 Mt. Bachelor Drive (just off Century Drive), also offers fine dining and yummy savories like focaccia bread with olive oil for dipping. The place for special meals at Sunriver Lodge is **Meadows** restaurant 541/593-1000, with its fabulous views—a good Sunday brunch destination. Takeout or sit-down Chinese and pizza meals can be had in **Sunriver Village**. In Sisters, the **Hotel Sisters and Bronco Billy's Saloon** at 105 Cascade Street, 541/549-7427, re-creates the atmosphere of a Western town in the early 1900s; seafood and lighter choices are available, but Western-style food like the lip-smackin' ribs are the specialty here.

LODGING

The most famous lodging destination in the area is **Sunriver Resort** (see above), 541/593-1000 or 800/547-3922. **Sunriver Vacations**, 800/874-7644, can arrange private condominium, cabin, or home rentals. **Black Butte Ranch**, located on the high meadows of the mid-Cascades on 1800 forested acres near the Deschutes National Forest, is a residential community, like Sunriver, with two golf courses, tennis courts, swimming pools, and bicycle and jogging trails. It offers views of seven mountain peaks and is quieter and more low-key than Sunriver; a restaurant and accommodations can be found at The **Lodge at Black Butte Ranch** 800/452-7455. The **River House**, 3075 N. Highway 97 in Bend, 800/547-3928, is near the River's Edge Golf Course, has indoor and outdoor pools and a convenient main thoroughfare location, and offers good value. **Eagle Crest Resort**, 800/682-4786, is set on 700 acres of high desert just west of Redmond on Highway 126 and offers hotel-style rooms, or two- to three-bedroom townhome rentals. The **Inn of the Seventh Mountain**, 18575 SW Century Drive, Bend, 97702, puts you up close to Mt. Bachelor, and offers all-inclusive vacation packages, 800/452-6810. There are more economical motels, some bed-and-breakfast inns, and a hostel. Contact the Central Oregon Visitors Association, for more information, 800/800-8334.

CAMPING

One of the special camping features of the area is the collection of teepees at **Kah-Nee-Ta Resort** on the Warm Springs Reservation in dry, rugged country 11 miles north of Warm Springs, off Highway 26. Accommodations range from the village RV park, camping sites, and teepees to lodge rooms. Try their Bird-in-Clay dinner (a specialty) and their special salmon bake. For reservations, call 800/554-4786.

CENTRAL OREGON

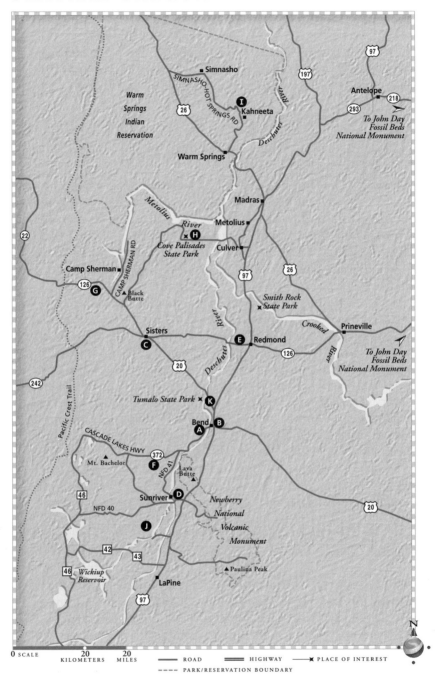

Simnasho

Warm
Springs
Indian
Reservation

SIMNASHO HOT SPRINGS RD

26

I
Kahneeta

Deschutes

197

97

Antelope
218

293

To John Day
Fossil Beds
National Monument

Warm Springs

Metolius

River

Madras

Metolius

22

CAMP SHERMAN RD

H ×
Cove Palisades
State Park

Culver

97

26

Camp Sherman

126 **G**

▲ Black
Butte

Smith Rock
× State Park

Crooked

Prineville

Sisters

C

20

E
Redmond

126

River

To John Day
Fossil Beds
National Monument

242

Pacific Crest Trail

Deschutes

River

Tumalo State Park ×

K

Bend **B**
A

CASCADE LAKES HWY

372

F

NFD 41

Mt. Bachelor ▲

Lava
Butte ▲

Newberry

46

NFD 40

Sunriver **D**

National

Volcanic

20

J

Monument

42

43

▲ Paulina Peak

46

Wickiup
Reservoir

LaPine

97

N

0 SCALE
KILOMETERS 20   MILES 20

ROAD   HIGHWAY   ×PLACE OF INTEREST

- - - - PARK/RESERVATION BOUNDARY

Food

- **Ⓐ** Broken Top Club
- **Ⓑ** Goody's Soda Fountain
- **Ⓒ** Hotel Sisters and Bronco Billy's Saloon
- **Ⓑ** Jake's Diner and Truck Stop
- **Ⓓ** Meadows
- **Ⓑ** Pine Tavern Restaurant
- **Ⓑ** Scanlon's
- **Ⓓ** Sunriver Village

Lodging

- **Ⓔ** Eagle Crest Resort
- **Ⓕ** Inn of the Seventh Mountain
- **Ⓖ** The Lodge at Black Butte Ranch
- **Ⓑ** River House
- **Ⓓ** Sunriver Resort

Camping

- **Ⓗ** Cove Palisades State Park
- **Ⓘ** Kah-Nee-Ta Resort
- **Ⓙ** LaPine State Park
- **Ⓚ** Tumalo State Park

Note: Items with the same letter are located in the same town or area.

Southwest of Madras, the Deschutes, Metolius, and Crooked Rivers merge at Lake Billy Chinook, which is the recreational hub of **Cove Palisades State Park**, named after the basalt formations (palisades) that tower over the lake. For reservations, call 800/452-5687. Just five miles northwest of Bend is **Tumalo State Park**, 541/388-6055, reservations 800/452-5687. It offers more than 80 sites, good fishing, and lies along the Deschutes River. The river also runs along the outskirts of the campsites at **LaPine State Park**, 30 miles southwest of Bend. It's open year-round and has more than 140 sites, three yurts, and five cabins; call 800/452-5687 for reservations. A day use cabin on picnic grounds accommodates group gatherings and is centrally located to Cascade Lakes Highway, half an hour from Newberry Crater. For more information, call the ranger at 541/536-2428.

NIGHTLIFE

Folks gather at the **Deschutes Brewery & Public House**, 1044 N.W. Bond Street, 541/382-9242, Bend's first brewpub, for light midday meals, but the place comes alive at night. Or try the **Bend Brewing Co.**, 1019 Brooks Street, 541/383-1599.

HELPFUL HINTS

Golfers can request a copy of the *Oregon Golf Guide* from the state tourism department. For a packet of information on lodging and recreation, contact the Central Oregon Visitors Association, 630 North Highway 97, Suite 104, Bend, Oregon 97701, 800/800-8334, or the Bend Chamber Visitor and Convention Bureau, 800/905-2363. The Redmond Municipal Airport offers flight connections to the area, and there is a small-plane airport at Sunriver.

SIDE TRIP: JOHN DAY FOSSIL BEDS NATIONAL MONUMENT

Fifty million years ago, the 14,00-acre site of John Day Fossil Beds National Monument, northeast of Bend, was almost a tropical forest. Today it contains one of the world's most complete records of natural history. Bones, leaves, wood, nuts, and seeds have been preserved in deposits of volcanic ash. They tell a more fascinating story than *Jurassic Park*—of camels, rhinoceroses, three-toed horses, and huge animals that have no modern-day counterparts. Three separate units make up the national monument. Each has unique landscapes, attractions, and scientific importance. It's best to start your exploration at the main visitor center at the Sheep Rock unit. It's open daily from March through October. Here you'll get dramatic views of Picture Gorge and can explore the Cant Ranch House visitors center with its displays of prehistoric animal fossils, including the skull of a sabre-tooth cat. The ranch house was built in the early 1900s and is on the National Historic Register. The stunning red and yellow accents to the cone-shaped Painted Hills were created by volcanic ash. This unit is located 10 miles north of the town of Mitchell. The dramatic pinnacles of the Clarno Unit were created from mudflows. All three units are located north of U.S. 26; Clarno lies east of U.S. 97. For more information, contact John Day Fossil Beds National Monument, HCR 82, Box 126, Kimberly, OR 97848; 541/987-2333.

The **Kam Wah Chung Museum**, on Ing Hay Way in the community of John Day (call City Hall for information, 541/575-0028) celebrates the herbal medicine practices of Chinese mine and railroad workers in the area.

Scenic Route: Oregon Trail Towns

This is perhaps the oldest scenic trail in the Northwest. It was the final approach to the Willamette Valley—"the land of milk and honey"—for thousands of settlers who made their way west in the huge 2,000-mile migration that began in 1847. More than 300,000 settlers crossed this wagon route in what is called the biggest overland migration ever. In 1998, Tamustalik, the last of five major cultural centers marking significant aspects of this journey, was completed. Some of the centers are building restorations; most are impressive new facilities. This drive primarily follows Interstate 84 from the Idaho border to Portland. The route leads through rolling dry hills, along the dramatic Columbia Gorge to the forests and valleys of western Oregon. As you drive, remember all those weary pioneers who crept along the trail in wagons into a mysterious wilderness and a new life. Thank your automobile and the highway gods. And keep your gas tank full.

Our route begins 50 miles northwest of Boise, Idaho at Ontario, Oregon, where the Malheur, Payette, Owyhee, and Snake Rivers converge. Here you'll find **Four Rivers Cultural Center**, 676 S.W. 4th Avenue, Ontario, 888/211-1222 or 541/889-8191,

OREGON TRAIL TOWNS

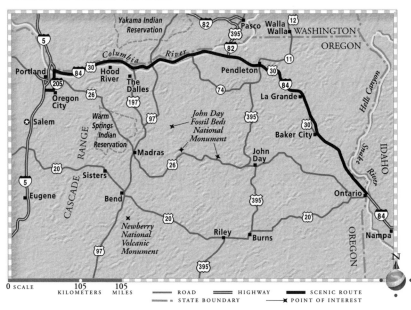

email: frcc@micron.net, nestled in Treasure Valley beneath the Elkhorn Mountains. Exhibits in the 10,000-square-foot museum reflect the mix of cultures residing in this area—the Paiute Indians, the Basque descendants of early settlers (many raised sheep), and Japanese Americans released from WWII internment camps to work in the growing farming industry along with the Hispanics who migrated north from Mexico. Outside the center is a Japanese garden designed by internationally renowned landscape artist Hoichi Kurisu.

The next stop is at the **National Historic Oregon Trail Center at Flagstaff Hill**, six miles east of I-84, just north of Baker City, 541/523-1843 or 800/523-1235. This is where the pioneers caught their first real glimpse of the promised land, a sweeping vista that is much the same as it was 150 years ago. The museum tells the pioneers' story through exhibits and living history presentations. Nearby are nearly five miles of interpretive trails where you can see actual ruts left by the wagon wheels.

New in 1998, the **Tamustalik Cultural Institute**, east of Pendleton at the base of the Blue Mountains, 541/276-3873, chronicles the history and culture of the Confederated Umatilla Tribes and looks at the impact the thousands of settlers had on their cultures up through the mid-1900s. The museum store features native arts and crafts.

Continuing northwest on I-84, the next stop is at the **Columbia Gorge Discovery Center/Wasco County Historical Museum**, one mile west of the Dalles off I-84, 541/296-8600, watch for signs. This facility opened in 1997 and features special exhibits and programs chronicling the geologic story that began more than 40 million years ago when the Columbia Gorge was born of volcanoes, earthquakes, and raging floods. It looks, too, at the 10,000 years or so of known history of the Native Americans along the river.

And finally, just as the pioneers did, you'll come to the **End of the Oregon Trail Interpretive Center in Oregon City**, 10 miles south of I-84 just west of Portland (off Interstate 205 at Exit 10). Here, three 50-foot-high covered wagon–shaped buildings dominate Abernethy Green, the main arrival area for the emigrants. The center is a living history exhibit with eight performances daily in the summer (call in advance for times, 503/657-9336). Each year, mid-July through early August, the Oregon Trail Pageant (a separate group) presents an outdoor historical drama. For ticket reservations, call 503/657-0988, or check out their Web site at www.teleport.com/~norrisa/otp_home.shtml. ∎

14

MEDFORD, ASHLAND, AND SOUTHWESTERN OREGON

The mesmerizing deep blue depths of Crater Lake, the magic of Shakespeare, and the seductive thrill of riding the Rogue River are what draw many to this southwest corner of Oregon. Gold, discovered in the Rogue Valley in 1852, is what orginally drew the white settlers. Until then the residents were the Rogue Indians.

Once the bustling center of gold fever, Jacksonville, a National Historic Landmark town, lost out in a business disagreement with the Oregon & California Railroad when it reached southern Oregon in 1883, and the railroad built their station five miles east of Jacksonville in what's now known as Medford. Jacksonville is home to the Peter Britt Music Festival, during which outdoor performances turn summer nights into melody. Medford, a city of about 50,000, is the commercial hub of the region's fruit growing industry, the home of mail order fruit marketer Harry & David, and rose purveyor Jackson & Perkins. Nearby in Ashland, the Oregon Shakespeare Festival delights theater and non-theater buffs alike, who enjoy classic and contemporary performances in this picturesque village setting.

The sleeping giant is the amazing Siskiyou mountain range that stretches west to the ocean. Millions of years ago it was an island in the Pacific that eventually folded up and reconnected to the continent. There are misty crumpled valleys, foreboding rivers (the Illinois River has even more challenging rapids than the Rogue), torrentially wet

SOUTHWESTERN OREGON

N

Klamath National Wildlife Refuge

Winema National Forest

Collier Memorial State Park

Chiloquin

Klamath Falls

Lower Klamath National Wildlife Refuge

97

97

97

62

Fort Klamath

Agency Lake

Upper Klamath Lake

66

B

K

Kimball State Park

Crater Lake

Crater Lake National Park

H

Pacific Crest Trail

Crater Lake

Rogue River National Forest

230

Prospect

CASCADE RANGE

140

Umpqua National Forest

62

Eagle Point

J

A

Mt. Ashland

E

I

Ashland

Talent

Medford

Rogue River

C

D

238

Jacksonville

MT ASHLAND SKI RD

Myrtle Creek

Valley of the Rogue State Park

Applegate River

Murphy

5

Grants Pass

99

Oregon Caves National Monument

F

Rogue River National Forest

46

G

199

Cave Junction

Siskiyou National Forest

42

OREGON
CALIFORNIA

0 SCALE 20
KILOMETERS

0 20
MILES

——— ROAD
——— HIGHWAY
– – – PARK/AREA BOUNDARY
✕ PLACE OF INTEREST
═══ STATE BORDER
········ TRAIL

Sights

A   Ashland

B   Crater Lake National Park

C   Harry & David's Country Village

C   Jackson & Perkins

D   Jacksonville

E   Mt. Ashland Ski Area

F   Oregon Caves National Monument

C   Southern Oregon History Center

Food

G   Caves Fountain

H   Crater Lake Lodge

Food *(continued)*

I   New Sammy's Cowboy Bistro

F   Oregon Caves Lodge

Lodging

H   Crater Lake Lodge

C   DoubleTree Hotel

F   Oregon Caves Lodge

C   Under the Greenwood Tree

Camping

J   KOA Glenyan

K   Mazama Village

Note: Items with the same letter are located in the same town or area.

winters, blistering summers, and unusual flora like the insect-eating pitcher plant. The Rogue River, protected by the Wild and Scenic Rivers Act, winds its way through here. It's no wonder that a 30-mile stretch of it is one of the remotest in the country.

A PERFECT DAY IN THE ROGUE VALLEY

A perfect day would dawn clear and warm and almost the whole of it would be spent out of doors. After a night in a cozy B&B in or near Ashland, head to Lithia Park for an early morning walk along Ashland Creek to breathe in the warm summer scent of the forest and stop to see the swans on its lake. Then drive to Crater Lake, stopping at Beth's for lunch or a piece of pie, but eating light. Back in Ashland splurge on an early dinner at Primavera. End your day with a performance at the Oregon Shakespeare Festival's outdoor Elizabethan Theater (remembering to take a cushion along, or plan to rent one, for the hard outdoor seats).

SIGHTSEEING HIGHLIGHTS

★★★★ **Ashland**—Nestled in the forest-rich foothills of the Siskiyou Mountains, Ashland is a charming village-like town filled with historic homes and many top-notch restaurants. The **Oregon Shakespeare Festival** draws visitors from all over the world (and has done so for more than 50 years). Most theater buffs make their reservations a year in advance (see Southern Oregon Reservation Center below). **Lithia Park,** a beautiful 100-acre area, provides a perfect accent for the festival's theater complex that rises above it. A small historic plaza downtown is a gathering spot. Ashland's intimate atmosphere makes you want to park the car and explore. Southern Oregon State University is here. Small galleries, shops, and interesting book stores beckon for browsing. Nearby jet boats and river rafts ply the wild and scenic Rogue and Klamath rivers.

Details: 12 miles south of Medford following I-5. Contact the Oregon Shakespeare Festival, 541/482-4331 or www.mind.net/osf/. (2–4 hours, or overnight for a theater visit)

★★★★ **Crater Lake National Park**—Oregon's only national park is a humdinger. The deepest lake in the United States, it is a caldera formed thousands of years ago when Mt. Mazama collapsed in explosive volcanic eruptions. It lies on the crest of the Cascade Range 80 miles northeast of Medford. Built in 1915, the impressive Crater Lake Lodge was completely renovated and reopened in 1995. Activities here include hiking and bus tours of Rim Drive, narrated boat trips to Wizard Island (in the middle of the lake), launch trips to the lodge and exhibit building at Rim Village, nature trails, and naturalist programs. **The Pinnacles** are surrealistic spires of eroded volcanic rock near the lake.

Details: 72 miles east of Medford off I-5 to SR 62. Pets are not allowed in public buildings or on trails. For information: Chief of Interpretation, Crater Lake National Park, P. O. Box 7, Crater Lake, OR, 97604; call 541/594-2211 for current road and weather information. Admission is $5 per private vehicle per day; $2 per bicycle. (half day minimum)

★★★★ **Oregon Caves National Monument**—These 480 acres of marble caves with columns and curtains of calcite form a series of beautiful underground galleries and rooms; just be prepared to climb a lot of steps. Above ground, the historic **Oregon Caves Lodge** is a classic, offering rustic rooms.

Details: *80 miles southwest of Medford. Guided tours conducted daily. Admission charged; children under 6 not admitted. Open year-round. Call the lodge at 541/592-3400. (2 hours)*

★★★ **Harry & David's Country Village**—Probably you or someone you know has received a fruit basket filled with juicy pears and more from this leading mail order fruit and gift company. You can tour their plant and visit their Country Store, packed with fruits, gourmet foods, and samples. Jackson & Perkins flowers (owned by the same company) are available here.
    Details: *1314 Center Drive, South Gateway Center (off I-5 at Exit 27), Medford; 541/864-0221. Call for reservations for free tours of plant and bakery (1 hour)*

★★★ **Jackson & Perkins**—Gardeners will recognize this mail order company as the world's largest private rose grower. Their test and display gardens near Medford are worth a visit.
    Details: *The gardens can be seen any time of day at 2518 South Pacific Highway, Medford (just down the road from the Country Village); May through September are prime bloom months. You may picnic on the grounds. (15 minutes–1 hour)*

★★★ **Jacksonville**—There are more than 80 historic homes and buildings in this National Historic Landmark Town, five miles west of Medford, that boomed in the mid-1800s as a gold town.
    Details: *Just minutes from Medford, take State Route 238 west off of I-5, 541/899-8118. For information on self-guided tours, go to the Rogue River Valley Railway Depot located at Oregon and C Streets. Open from June to August daily 10 to 4; Saturday to Monday 10 to 4 the rest of the year. (1 hour)*

★★ **Mt. Ashland Ski Area**—This 7,500-plus-foot mountain showcased within the Siskiyou's is a smaller, low-key family skiing and snowboarder's destination, with beginner to advanced slopes; four chair lifts provide access to more than 23 runs.
    Details: *18 miles south of Ashland, 541/482-2897. (All day)*

★★ **Southern Oregon History Center**—Historical and cultural exhibits of the Southern Oregon Historical Society are on display at this center in downtown Medford.
    Details: *Follow I-5 to approximately 30 miles from the California*

border. Medford Convention and Visitors Bureau, 101 East 8th Street;
541/779-4847. (1 hour)

FITNESS AND RECREATION

Theater is big recreation in this region, and outdoor evening theater
performances at the **Oregon Shakespeare Festival** run from mid-
February through October. There are 11 plays presented each season.
For tickets or information, call the box office, 541/482-4331. The
Peter Britt Music Festival runs June to September, for schedule and
information, call 800/882-7488.

Movies have immortalized the Rogue—think Meryl Streep in *The*
River Wild and John Wayne in *Rooster Cogburn*. Outfitters offering river
trips are plentiful. **Raft Trips Adventure Center** in Ashland,
541/488-2819 or 800/444-2819, schedules adventure tours for white-
water rafting and biking; they also rent bikes.

The **Southern Oregon Reservation Center,** 800/547-8052,
offers one-call information on theater reservations, lodging, river trip
reservations, and more.

FOOD

In Ashland, **Primavera**, 241 Hargadine, 541/488-1994, has great appetizers, pasta, seafood and vegetarian dishes, and a consistent and well-
deserved reputation as a must-go—as does the **Chateaulin**, 50 East
Main Street, 541/482-2264, fun for hors d'oeuvres and wine before the
theater. For yummy Italian food, try **Il Giardino**, 5 Granite Street,
541/488-0816. Many restaurants have café or bistro menus, lighter
choices for before-theater meals. For a quick lunch downtown, try
Pangea, 272 East Main, 541/552-1630, which offers delightful grilled
or wrap sandwiches. **The Standing Stone Brewing Company**, 101
Oak Street, 541/482-2448, is a light, airy brewpub and a reasonable
stop for lunch or dinner.

North, halfway between Ashland and Talent on Highway 99, **New**
Sammy's Cowboy Bistro, 541/535-2779, serves dinners only Thursday
through Sunday (fewer days in winter), seats only a handful of people,
and has no sign (call for directions and reservations), but plenty of
gourmets know about it; it's funky, tiny, and booked months ahead.

Crater Lake Lodge offers great views with dinner; whether

ASHLAND

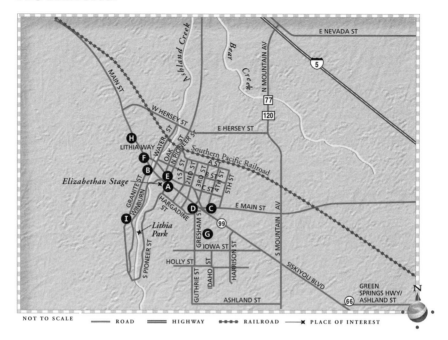

Food

Ⓐ Chateaulin

Ⓑ Il Giardino

Ⓒ Pangea

Ⓓ Primavera

Ⓔ The Standing Stone Brewing Company

Lodging

Ⓕ The Bard's Inn

Ⓖ Chanticleer Inn

Ⓗ Iris Inn Bed and Breakfast

Ⓘ Lithia Rose Lodging-on-the-Park

you're staying there or not. Sample regional fare in the dining room at **Oregon Caves Lodge** or try an ice cream cone from the **Caves Fountain**, a 1930s-style soda fountain, at 20000 Caves Highway, Cave Junction 97523, 541/592-3400.

LODGING

Ashland is known for its many bed-and-breakfast lodgings. Most homes are older, and sometimes the rooms are small. However, it's fun to be walking distance from the theater. The **Lithia Rose Lodging-on-the-park**, 163 Granite Street, 541/482-1882 or 800/354-9914, across from Lithia Park, boasts a well-deserved reputation for great breakfasts and a charming back garden. The bungalow-style **Chanticleer Inn**, 120 Gresham Street, 541/482-1919 or 800/898-1950, a long-time lodging that's comfortable and quiet, and the Victorian-style **Iris Inn Bed and Breakfast**, 800/460-7650, are a bit further away but also popular. Most B&Bs have a two-night minimum. **The Bard's Inn**, 132 Main Street, 800/528-1234, is a Best Western lodging that has a swimming pool— very inviting in the heat of summer.

Out of town toward Jacksonville, **Under the Greenwood Tree**, 3045 Bellinger Lane, Medford, 541/776-0000, is a 125-year-old historic country B&B with huge trees, a beautiful garden, and the feel of a plantation; breakfasts are the creation of owner Renate Ellam, a Cordon Bleu–trained chef.

These are a few suggestions, however there are hundreds of rooms in Ashland and Jacksonville inns, and two services can provide more information: the **Ashland Area Association of Oregon Bed & Breakfast Guild** offers reservations, information, and brochures, 800/983-4667; the **Ashland B&B Clearinghouse**, 541/488-0338, lists not only B&Bs but old hotels, motels, and new inns. The **Southern Oregon Reservation Center**, 800/547-8052, offers ticket and lodging package combinations—great for visitors who haven't planned ahead for theater tickets that are hard to come by.

The **Oregon Caves Lodge**, 20000 Caves Highway, Cave Junction, 97523, 541/592-3400, is a classic, offering rustic rooms; it's fun to stay here even if the guest rooms have paper-thin walls. The patio of **Crater Lake Lodge**, 541/830-8700, offers one of the best views in the whole state; a stay at this refurbished national park lodge is a real treat.

Located centrally in Medford, the **DoubleTree Hotel** at 200

North Riverside Avenue, 800/222-8733 or 541/779-5811, has 180-plus rooms and two outdoor swimming pools.

CAMPING

To camp near Ashland, contact **Glenyan Campground**, which offers more than 60 sites near Emigrant Lake about six and a half miles southeast of Ashland on Highway 66; call 541/488-1785 for reservations. **Mazama Village**, 541/594-2255, x3705, at Crater Lake's south entrance, offers almost 200 campsites on a first come/first served basis.

HELPFUL HINTS

The **Medford Visitor and Convention Bureau's** visitors center is located just off Interstate 5 at Exit 27, and is open during the summer; its office downtown at 304 S. Central Avenue, Medford, 97501, is open year-round. For information, call 541/779-4847 or 800/448-4856. **Ashland Visitor and Convention Bureau** is at 541/482-3486.

If you're on a long road trip, stop by Blackstone Audiobooks, south of Ashland. You can rent books for 10 to 45 days and return them in mailers provided by Blackstone. Call for directions, 541/482-9239.

Scenic Route: Southwest Oregon

This route takes you from high mountain views at Crater Lake to where the Rogue River meets the Pacific. On Interstate 5, halfway between Medford and Grants Pass, take Exit 40 at Gold Hill and head north on Highway 234, then east on Highway 62 to **Crater Lake**, where you can drive the rim loop in summer. Tour boats visit **Wizard Island**, in the center of the caldera (a crater with a diameter many times that of the original volcanic vent). Historic **Crater Lake Lodge**, restored and reopened in 1995, sits on the rim.

From here go north to **Diamond Lake Resort** on Highway 138. Continue west to **Roseburg**, along the Umpqua River. Visit wineries, fish or raft here. From Roseburg go north on I-5 and take Exit 136, Highway 138 to Elkton. West of Elkton you reach the ocean and the wildlife-rich area around **Reedsport**. Explore the **Dean Creek Elk Viewing Area** east of Reedsport, or whalewatch in **Winchester Bay**.

Highway 101 takes you through coastal forests and along beaches and dunes through **Coos Bay, Bandon, Port Orford**, and **Brookings**. The route dips into California, then follows the Smith River northeast along Highway 199 to Cave Junction; visit **Oregon Caves National Monument.** ◪

SOUTHWEST OREGON

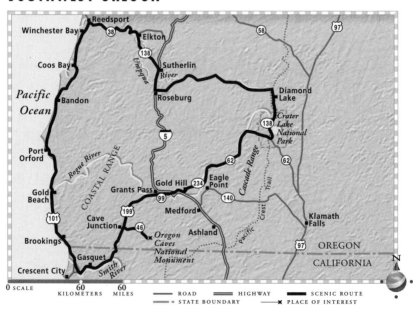

15
WILLAMETTE VALLEY

After crossing the endless Midwestern flatlands and battling the uncompromising Rockies, the pioneers of the 1840s surely must have thought they had reached the Promised Land when their dusty Conestoga wagons rolled into the Willamette Valley—the fabled Oregon Territory. Before them was a vision that could have been brushed by an eighteenth-century landscape artist. Grasslands stretched 100 miles north and south in fertile elegance, mixed generously with majestic fir trees, and here and there commanding Oregon oaks lent dignity to the pastoral scene.

A century and a half later this elegant, bucolic valley, cradle of much of Oregon's history, nurtures a different influx of pioneers: winemakers. Along with the wineries, a good crop of bed-and-breakfast and a growing number of restaurants have developed.

Summer is the most rewarding time to visit. Wildflowers are out, fruits and produce are at their peak, and the wineries have new releases and longer tasting-room hours. Produce stands, historic small towns, charming inns, picturesque covered bridges, and college towns (there are three universities here) offer plenty to explore.

Many travelers take I-5 for speed and miss the real beauty of the Willamette Valley. A loop drive, beginning at Portland, Eugene, or Springfield, exploring 99E and 99W (which parallels Interstate 5), gives you the feel of the region at a slower pace. It's definitely worth the side trip, and it's even more rewarding if you stay overnight. ◾

WILLAMETTE VALLEY

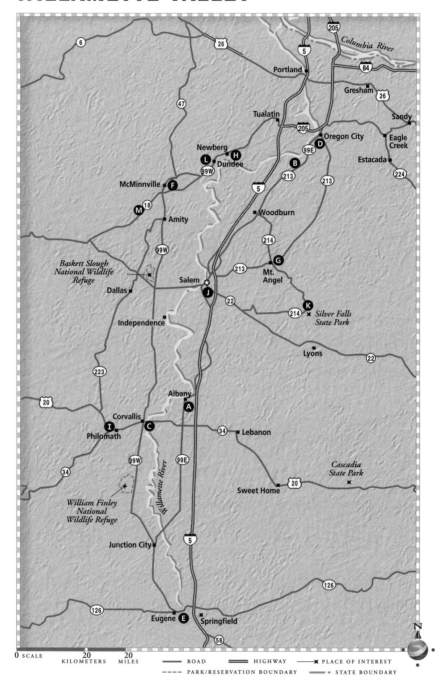

Columbia River

6
26
205
5
84
Portland
Gresham
26
Sandy
47
Tualatin
205
Newberg
99E
Oregon City
D
Eagle
Creek
L
Dundee
H
B
Estacada
McMinnville
F
99W
213
213
224
M
18
5
Amity
Woodburn
99W
214
Baskett Slough
National Wildlife
Refuge
213
G
Dallas
Salem
Mt.
Angel
J
22
K
Independence
214
Silver Falls
State Park
223
Lyons
22
20
Albany
A
22
Corvallis
C
34
Lebanon
I
Philomath
Cascadia
State Park
34
99W
99E
Sweet Home
20
William Finley
National
Wildlife
Refuge
Junction City
5
126
126
Eugene
E
Springfield
58
N

0 SCALE 20 20
KILOMETERS MILES ——— ROAD ═══ HIGHWAY —✕ PLACE OF INTEREST
‐ ‐ ‐ ‐ ‐ PARK/RESERVATION BOUNDARY ═ ▪ STATE BOUNDARY

Sights

- Ⓐ Albany
- Ⓑ Champoeg State Park
- Ⓒ Corvallis
- Ⓓ End of the Oregon Trail Interpretive Center-Oregon City
- Ⓔ Eugene
- Ⓕ McMinnville
- Ⓖ Mt. Angel
- Ⓗ Newberg
- Ⓘ Philomath
- Ⓙ Salem
- Ⓚ Silver Falls State Park

Food

- Ⓘ Firestone Farms
- Ⓕ Golden Valley Brewery & Pub
- Ⓒ Nearly Normal's
- Ⓕ Nick's Italian Cafe
- Ⓛ Red Hills Provincial Dining
- Ⓔ Sweetwaters Restaurant and Lounge
- Ⓘ Tina's
- Ⓘ Your Northwest

Wineries

- Ⓗ Duck Pond Cellars
- Ⓜ Oregon Wine Tasting Room
- Ⓗ Rex Hill Vineyards and Winery

Lodging

- Ⓒ Hanson Country Inn
- Ⓕ Orchard View Inn
- Ⓗ Partridge Farm
- Ⓗ Spring Creek Llama Ranch
- Ⓗ Springbrook Hazelnut Farm
- Ⓕ Steiger Haus
- Ⓔ Valley River Inn
- Ⓕ Youngberg Hill Ranch

Camping

- Ⓑ Champoeg State Park
- Ⓚ Silver Falls State Park

Note: Items with the same letter are located in the same town or area.

Corvallis Convention & Visitors Bureau

The Coastal Range as seen from the Willamette Valley floor

A PERFECT DAY IN THE WILLAMETTE VALLEY

Stay in the country in a B&B. And whether it has a great view or you drive to a high viewpoint or take a hot-air balloon ride, make sure you get a panorama of the valley with Mt. Hood looming to the east. A perfect summer day will include exploring produce stands and wineries, many of which offer great views of the valley and picnic spots. Explore the small towns and try an out-of-the-way excursion to the Briggatine Monastery to buy fudge or to Mt. Angel for a look at the beautiful church. Find a country restaurant for dinner and retire to your cozy B&B, and that's the end of a perfect day.

SIGHTSEEING HIGHLIGHTS

★★★★ **Albany**—This town boasts about 700 Historic Register buildings; self-guided walking tour brochures help you locate them. Several areas feature construction from the 1840s onward. A half-dozen covered bridges lie near town.

> ***Details:*** *Albany Convention and Visitors Center, 300 2nd Avenue SW, 541/928-0911 or 800/526-2256. (2–4 hours)*

☆☆☆☆ **Champoeg State Park**—On the banks of the Willamette River, Champoeg State Park offers hiking and biking trails, a garden with native plants, a visitors center and museum with historic exhibits, and a mueum store. Picnic sites and overnight camping are available.

Details: *Halfway between Portland and Newberg, off Interstate 5 at Exit 278. For general information call 503/678-1251; for camping reservations call 800/452-5687. Day use admission fee about $3. (2–4 hours)*

☆☆☆☆ **Corvallis**—Life in this quintessential college town centers on Oregon State University; guided campus tours are offered Monday through Friday, 541/737-2626 or 800/291-4192. Downtown is a thriving area of shops and restaurants. The **Benton County History Center**, 110 NW Third Street, 541/758-3550, offers a look at this farming region's history. *Da Vinci Days*, a stimulating festival of art, science, and technology, is held here each July.

Details: *Corvallis Convention & Visitors Bureau, 420 NW Second Street, 541/757-1544 or 800/334-8118; www.visitcorvallis.com. (2–3 hours)*

☆☆☆☆ **Covered Bridges**—About 50 covered bridges of the more than 400 built in Oregon still exist, and most are in the Willamette Valley. Several lie around Albany and Eugene. The Covered Bridge Society of Oregon, 541/265-2934, offers more information.

Details: *Touring maps are available from the Albany Convention and Visitors Center (see above). (Time varies)*

☆☆☆☆ **End of the Oregon Trail Interpretive Center-Oregon City**—Three 50-foot-high covered wagon–shaped buildings dominate Abernethy Green, the main arrival area for the emigrants reaching the Willamette Valley. The center is a living history exhibit with eight performances daily in summer (call in advance for times).

Details: *Oregon City is 20 minutes southeast of Portland, off Interstate 205 at Exit 10. For center details call 503/657-9336. (1–2 hours)*

☆☆☆☆ **Eugene**—This city, at the southern end of the valley, is the seat of scenic Lane County and the cultural hub of Willamette Valley. This is home to the **University of Oregon**, 541/346-3027, www.uoma.uoregon.edu., where you can visit the university's famed Asian art collection in the Museum of Art Wednesday through Sunday. Downtown, the **Hult Center for the Performing Arts**, 541/682-5000, is a striking modern building with a permanent collection of local fine art; it also features guest performers, musical theater, and dance. **Fifth Street Public Market**, 541/484-0383, is lively and filled with galleries and restaurants. **Sawmill Ballroom Lavendar Farm**, 29251 Hamm Road, 541/686-9999 or 888/686-8169, specializes in Tuscan Lavendar.

Details: Information is available through the Convention & Visitors Association of Lane County, 115 W. Eighth, Suite 190, 541/484-5307 or 800/547-5445; www.cvalco.org/travel.html. (4–6 hours)

✸✸✸ **McMinnville**—Home to Linfield College, site of the annual International Pinot Noir Festival. In the historic downtown, a six-block section between Third and Fourth Streets, there are shops and galleries and a handful of restaurants and wineries.

Details: Chamber of Commerce, at the corner of Adams (southbound 99W) and Fourth Streets, 503/472-6196, has a free walking guide of the district and map detailing Yamhill County's major towns.

✸✸✸ **Mt. Angel**—This east Willamette town is a German community founded in the late 1800s. It is unusual and special and worth a detour if you're in the area. Each fall they host a boisterous Oktoberfest, but the reason to come is to visit Mt. Angel Abbey, built by Benedictine monks on a stack-like hilltop overlooking the town. The three-day Bach Festival is held here in late July (inquire early if interested). The library designed by Alvar Aalto is worth a visit for its unique architecture and for its view.

Details: On SR 14, east of Salem. Mount Angel Chamber, 503/845-6882. (2 hours)

✸✸✸ **Newberg**—At the north end of the valley, this area has a couple dozen wineries and is the gateway to Willamette Valley wine touring. Rex Hill, Duck Pond Cellars, Amity, Ponzi, Sokol Blosser, Champoeg, Oak Knoll, and Adelsheim wineries are here.

Details: From I-5 in Portland, go west 20 miles on State Route 99W. Contact the Newberg Area Chamber of Commerce, 115 N. Washington Street; 503/538-2014.

✸✸✸ **Philomath**—This small town west of Corvallis is in tree-farming country. Home to the Benton County Historical Museum, Philomath is a good stop en route from Corvallis to ocean beaches. The town hosts the Shrewsbury Renaissance Fair the second weekend in September.

Details: *About 6 miles west of Corvallis on SR34. The museum can be reached at 541/929-6230 or www.peak.org/~lewisb/museum.html.*

★★★ **Salem**—The state capitol and second largest city in Oregon, Salem is also home to Willamette University. The art-deco style **State Capitol Building**, built in 1938, is on the National Register of Historic Places and has free tours available (hours vary) and grounds to explore. The **Mission Mill Village**, 1313 Mill Street SE, 503/585-7012 or 800/874-7012, is a five-acre park, home to a historic woolen mill, a museum, and several historic houses; it's open daily, admission is charged. **Made in Salem** gallery, an artist's cooperative, 189 Liberty Street NE, 503/399-8197, in the Reed Opera House shopping mall, is well worth a stop. **Deepwood Estate** is a historic home on several acres with gardens to tour. **Schreiner's Iris Gardens**, 3671 Quinaby Road North, is only open bloom season, May through June; however, a catalog is available by calling 800/419-4747, x71. The **Wheatland Ferry** north of town gives you an old-fashioned way to cross the Willamette River.

Details: Salem Visitors Center, 1313 Mill Street SE (at the Mission Mill Museum), 503/581-4325 or 800/874-7012. (4–6 hours)

★★★ **Silver Falls State Park**—Oregon's largest state park near Salem has 10 waterfalls and hiking in Silver Creek Canyon. Swimming, guided horseback riding, and camping facilities are also available (see below).

Details: Five miles east of Salem on Highway 22. Contact the park at 503/873-8681. For reservations, 800/452-5687.

FITNESS AND RECREATION

This is bicycling country, and good maps of routes are available. Bicyclists will appreciate the path that parallels 99W. The free Willamette Valley bicycle loop guide covers a 195-mile cycling and driving route; call 800/526-2256 for information. There are two large wildlife refuges here. **Baskett Slough National Wildlife Preserve** is a 2500-acre wintering ground for the dusky Canada goose that lies just west of 99W on Highway 22; it's a great place to stretch your legs, but there are no tables or restrooms. **William L. Finley National Wildlife Refuge** is a 5,000-acre-plus habitat for geese, elk, and other animals; the entrance is about eight miles south of Corvallis. There are plenty of trails to hike.

Great antique shopping can be had at the **Lafayette Schoolhouse Antique Mall**, 748 Highway 99W, 503/864-2720. The small historic town of **Aurora** has many antique shops to explore, as well.

FOOD

Summer is berry time in the valley, and there are all kinds: strawberries, loganberries, gooseberries, blueberries, red and black raspberries, Marion and boysenberries. You'll see roadside stands, but be sure to watch for **Firestone Farms,** just south of Dundee, 503/864-2672. www.firestonefarms.com. They sell a wide selection of berries and other produce, plus a vast array of Northwest gourmet foods (sample some at the tasting bar). Their peach or berry milkshakes alone are worth the stop. Newly opened in Dundee, **Your Northwest**, 110 SW Seventh Street, 503/554-8101, a retail store featuring the Northwest's finest foods & artisan products. Two restaurants in the north end of the valley are worth remembering: **Tina's,** in Dundee at 760 Highway 99W, 503/538-8880; and **Red Hills Provincial Dining,** 276 SW Highway 99W, 503/538-8224, where the setting is elegant. Reservations are suggested at restaurants; many do not take credit cards. **Nick's Italian Cafe**, 521 East Third Street, in McMinnville, 503/434-4471, is a perennial favorite and has an extensive wine list with many Oregon vintages. À la carte and five-course price-fixed menus include favorites like homemade pastas and grilled salmon. **Golden Valley Brewery & Pub,** 980 East Fourth Street, also in McMinville, 503/472-2739, offers British-style brews (you can view production), homemade sausages, and jazz and blues on weekend evenings. **Nearly Normal's,** in Corvallis, 541/753-0791, serves up vegan and vegetarian fare in a fun, rustic setting. Fresh seasonal produce and a creative chef make **Sweetwaters Restaurant and Lounge** at the Valley River Inn, 1000 Valley River Way, in Eugene a good destination, 541/687-0123; locally caught salmon is a specialty.

WINERIES

Tasting facilities at the wineries range from elegant or rustic. Many offer free samples; a few charge a small fee, often good toward a purchase. Most are friendly and family-owned, making a few thousand cases per year that are primarily consumed in-state—a great reason to visit. While many wineries are clustered in towns right on 99W, some of the best are tucked away in the hills, down long, winding and often rutted roads. Watch for the blue signs along 99W, which point the way to most wineries. A map is a necessity. Pick up a copy of the Oregon Wine Advisory Board's free brochure, "Discover Oregon Wineries," 800/242-2363, with details on nearly all locations, plus comprehensive maps.

The **Oregon Wine Tasting Room,** southwest of McMinnville on SR 18, 503/843-3787, has a changing sampling from many Oregon wineries (including ones without tasting rooms). The adjoining Lawrence Gallery, featuring Northwestern art and a restaurant make this a great stop.

If you can only make a short visit to the wine country, you'll find many fine wineries to visit in Yamhill County. From Portland, one of the first you'll encounter is **Rex Hill Vineyards and Winery**, a great facility with picnic grounds at 30835 Highway 99W, 503/538-0666. Call for a schedule of the hot air balloon rides that embark from here. South of here **Duck Pond Cellars** is just off the highway (their T-shirts make great souvenirs). Memorial Day weekend, wineries kick off peak season with open houses, live music, food, and new wine releases. Admission prices and hours vary, but most, including some not generally open to the public, welcome visitors Friday to Sunday from at least 11 to 4. Wineries are also open for tours Thanksgiving weekend. *Oregon Wine* newspaper, available free at wineries, publishes complete details.

LODGING

Accommodations here are plentiful and diverse. The Willamette Valley offers more than two dozen bed-and-breakfast options. You can stay in the midst of an orchard at **Orchard View Inn**, 16540 NW Orchard View Road, outside McMinnville, 503/472-0165 or ride llamas at **Spring Creek Llama Ranch**, 503/538-5717, in rural Newberg. Alpine-style **Steiger Haus**, 503/472-0821 or 800/445-7744, is a contemporary home with five rooms in McMinnville near Linfield College. **Youngberg Hill Ranch,** 503/472-2727, has a panoramic valley view. It's a contemporary home with period styling.

Near Newberg and McMinnville, you can pet the llamas at the **Partridge Farm**, 503/538-2050. Learn about hazelnuts at **Springbrook Hazelnut Farm,** 503/538-2050 or 800/793-8528, an historic home with a lap pool.

Near Corvallis, **Hanson Country Inn,** 503/752-2919, is an historic estate home with a real country feel. Most inns have restrictions regarding children, smoking, and pets. Some require two-night stays over weekends. For a complete list of B&Bs and other lodging call the Willamette Valley Visitors Association, 800/526-2256.

The **Valley River Inn,** West Coast Hotel in Eugene, 1000 Valley River Way, 541/687-0123 or 800/543-8266, overlooks the Willamette River. You can check out bicycles at the front desk, or arrange to go fishing for salmon or winter steelhead (catch a fish and the hotel chef will cook or smoke it for you).

CAMPING

Champoeg State Park, between Portland and Newberg (Exit 278 off Interstate 5), offers year-round camping in a variety of facilities: tent, walk-in, group, and RV campsites. Yurts are also available. Scenic **Silver Falls State Park**, near Salem, is Oregon's largest state park, covering about 8,000 acres. There are 51 tent sites and 53 electrical and water sites. For fees and reservations for both parks call Reservations Northwest, 800/452-5687.

HELPFUL HINTS

The Willamette Valley Visitors Association (associated with the Albany Convention and Visitors Association) provides general touring maps and valley information; call 541/928-0911 or 800/526-2256, or check the Web site: www.albanyvisitors.com.

16
OREGON COAST

Dunes resembling sugar. Dramatic Haystack Rock. Depot Bay's signature bridge. Salishan Lodge. Great seafood and public beaches that are some of the finest in the country. These are just a few of the attractions of the Oregon coast. No wonder the nearly 400 miles of Highway 101, from Brookings in the south to Astoria in the north, is a world-renowned vacation destination. Most of the coast highway, officially designated as a Scenic Byway in 1998, misses very little shoreline (cutting inland primarily south of Tillamook and at Coos Bay). You have views much of the way.

The drawbacks? Well, Highway 101 can slow to a crawl in the height of summer, when the crowds descend. Set aside at least five days if you plan to explore the whole coastline. Still, you'll spend a lot of time on the road. Most folks pick a spot and stay for a while, a good idea if relaxing is your goal. Accommodations vary widely from posh and luxurious resorts to simple and spartan vacation rentals.

One suggestion that's purely a taste issue: Consider the "personality" of your beach town destination and accommodation. What's your preference? A quintessential gray-shingled beach and arts community like Cannon Beach? A classic saltwater taffy, walk-the-promenade-and-ride-the-carousel community like Seaside? A lively and busy spot like Newport that hosts the largest seafood festival on the coast?

The best advice of all: Reserve accommodations well in advance. ◪

OREGON COAST

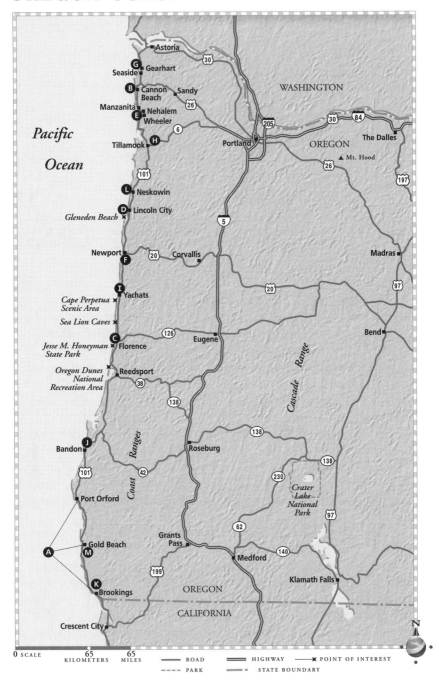

Pacific

Ocean

WASHINGTON

OREGON

The Dalles

▲ Mt. Hood

Astoria

G Gearhart
Seaside

B Cannon
Beach   Sandy

Manzanita   Nehalem
E Wheeler

Tillamook   **H**

Portland

L Neskowin

D Lincoln City
Gleneden Beach ✕

Newport
F   Corvallis

Madras

I Yachats
Cape Perpetua ✕
Scenic Area

Sea Lion Caves ✕

Jesse M. Honeyman ✕   **C** Florence
State Park

Oregon Dunes ✕   Reedsport
National
Recreation Area

Eugene

Bend

Cascade Range

Bandon   **J**   Roseburg

Coast Ranges

Port Orford

Crater
Lake
National
Park

Grants
Pass

A   Gold Beach
M

Medford

K
Brookings

Klamath Falls

OREGON

CALIFORNIA

Crescent City

N

0 SCALE   65   65
KILOMETERS   MILES   ——— ROAD   ════ HIGHWAY   ——✕ POINT OF INTEREST
--- --- PARK   ════ STATE BOUNDARY

Sights

Ⓐ Brookings/Gold Beach/Port Orford

Ⓑ Cannon Beach

Ⓒ Florence

Ⓓ Lincoln City

Ⓔ Manzanita/Nehalem/Wheeler

Ⓕ Newport

Ⓖ Seaside

Ⓗ Tillamook

Ⓘ Yachats

Food

Ⓙ Bandon's Cheddar Cheese

Ⓒ Blue Heron Bistro

Ⓗ Blue Heron French Cheese Co.

Ⓔ Blue Sky Cafe

Ⓓ Chez Jeanette

Food (continued)

Ⓚ Chives

Ⓔ Newhalem Bay Winery

Ⓖ Pacific Way Cafe & Bakery

Ⓓ Salishan Lodge

Ⓕ Tables of Content

Ⓗ Tillamook Cheese Factory

Lodging

Ⓛ The Chelan

Ⓓ Salishan Lodge

Ⓑ Stephanie Inn

Ⓕ Sylvia Beach Hotel

Ⓜ Tu Tu Tun Lodge

Camping

Ⓒ Jessie Honeyman State Park

Note: Items with the same letter are located in the same town or area.

A PERFECT DAY ON THE OREGON COAST

A perfect day is lazy and beautiful. Have breakfast in your room overlooking the beach, then find a long stretch of sand and go barefoot. Play in the surf. Or sunbathe. Pick a seaside town—Cannon Beach is a good one—and explore. Watch for glass art, crafts, pottery, and other artisan-created specialty items. For lunch, crab anything or clam chowder are good options. And, if regulations permit, build a beach fire at night and gather around it with your loved ones.

SIGHTSEEING HIGHLIGHTS

★★★★ **Cannon Beach**—Known for its impressive sand-carving contest and Haystack Rock, one of the world's largest monoliths, Cannon Beach is a quirky, with-it arts village. It's a popular destination, so expect to find crowds. There are over 20 galleries here, most along Hemlock Street, interesting shops to browse, and eateries. Stephanie Inn is here. **Haystack Rock** is about a mile's hike down the beach south from town. Nearby, **Ecola State Park** is a day use park whose scenic cliff trail is well worth the stop.
     Details: Ecola State Park is 2 miles north of town off the coast highway. Admission $3 per vehicle; pedestrians free. (2 hours)

★★★★ **Florence**—About 5,000 people live in this gateway to the **Oregon Dunes National Recreation Area**. Nearly half of this 30,000-acre area is open sand dunes, some reaching up to 400 feet high and about a mile in length. It's stunning. A few miles south of Florence is **Jessie Honeyman State Park** (see below). Nearby **Heceta Head Lighthouse** is perhaps the most photographed on the Oregon coast. About 11 miles north of town are the **Sea Lion Caves,** 541/547-3111; take an elevator to a huge, impressive cave to see huge and impressive sea lions.
     Details: Florence Chamber, 541/997-3128 or 800/524-4864; www.florencechamber.com. (2–4 hours)

★★★★ **Newport**—This historic community is the largest port on the central coast and known for its annual seafood festival. It's home to the **Oregon Coast Aquarium,** 541/867-3474, which in turn is home to seals, sea lions, otters, and other large sea animals like a giant Pacific octopus. You can see the dozens of smaller critters that hang out in tide pools. The **Mark O. Hatfield Marine Science Center**, 541/867-0100, is a major center for marine studies. The new public wing here is part of a recent $5 million renovation. There are displays and tide pool animals to touch. **Rogue Ales**, 2320 OSU Drive, 541/867-3660, with tours and tastings, is located on the historic bayfront.
     Details: Greater Newport Chamber, 541/265-8801 or 800/262-7844; www.newportnet.com. (4–6 hours)

★★★ **Brookings/Gold Beach/Port Orford**—This southern part of the Oregon coast, sometimes referred to as Curry County, backs up to the Siskiyou Forest. Beaches are smaller, and there's more of a Big Sur feel. You can hike here any time of year and have wide chunks of beach all to yourself. Jetboat trips from Gold Beach up the Rogue River are a famous way to explore this area (Rogue River Mail Boat Trips have been operating since 1895). Increased ecotourism offerings also make it a prime destination for beach adventures. Take a self-guided forest and beach hike or for insider's expertise, hire a guide. Port Orford is the site of a battle between Native Americans and the first whites attempting to settle the area. Brookings is referred to as Oregon's "banana belt" as temperatures are warmer here than anywhere else on the coast.

Details: *Rogue River Mail Boat Trips, 800/458-3511, www.mailboat.com. Gold Beach Chamber of Commerce, 800/525-2334, www.goldbeach.org. Brookings-Harbor Chamber of Commerce, 800/535-9469 or www.brookings-harbor.com. (2–4 hours)*

★★★**Lincoln City**—This is the closest city to Portland. Conditions are great for kite flying, and you'll see these colorful wisps all over town. It boasts 2,500 ocean-view rooms and is a prime location to watch storms or sunsets. It's also busy and commercial, with a large factory store outlet and Chinook Winds Casino. **Salishan Lodge**, 888/725-4742, www.dolce.com, the coast's most famous resort, is a few miles south at Gleneden Beach.

Details: *Lincoln City Visitor and Convention Bureau, 541/994-8378 or 800/452-2151. (2–4 hours)*

★★★ **Manzanita/Nehalem/Wheeler**—This three-town area, spread around Newhalem Bay, is only a dozen or so miles south of Cannon Beach. It offers ocean beaches, a warm water lake to swim in, river recreation, and lots of rustic vacation rentals, *and* it's relatively undiscovered. Manzanita is a secluded beachside area with an 18-hole golf course. There's an antique mall to explore in Newhalem right on 101. **Newhalem Bay Winery** has wine tasting in an historic cheese factory. Resident elk can be seen around the Nehalem River estuary. **Nehalem Bay State Park** extends to the tip of the spit enclosing the bay and offers over 200 campsites and yurt camping. Wheeler is south of the bay and offers fishing and boating.

Details: *Contact the Nehalem Bay Chamber of Commerce, 503/368-5100; e-mail: nehalembay@pdx.oneworld.com. For state parks reservations, call 800/452-5687; www.prd.state.or.us. (3–4 hours)*

★★★ **Seaside**—Lewis and Clark's party came here in 1806 to take salt from the sea by erecting a salt cairn, and you can see a replica of it at the south end of the **Promenade** that fronts the wide beach. Feed the seals at **Seaside Aquarium** on "the Prom." There's a museum in town as well. **Gearhart**, a quiet community of residential homes and a couple golf courses north of Seaside, is a favorite of well-to-do Portlanders.

Details: Seaside Visitor's Bureau, 888/306-2326; www.seasideor.com. (1–2 hours)

★★★ **Tillamook**—You'll see pastureland and dairies and cattle all around Tillamook. Most of the county's milk goes into the production of cheese, particularly at **Tillamook Cheese** factory. Kids love the ice cream sold on site, and it's fun for the whole family to watch the cheese-makers at work. You can also visit **Blue Heron French Cheese Co.** for cheese and wine tasting. The **Naval Air Station Museum**, housed in a rare WWII blimp hangar that is the largest wooden structure in the world, displays a collection of war planes and a jet simulator you can climb into.

Details: Tillamook Cheese is at 4175 Highway 101 N.; 800/542-7290. Summer hours are daily 8 to 8; winter daily 8 to 6. Blue Heron is 1 mile south of the Tillamook Cheese factory; 800/275-0639. Open summer 8 to 8; winter 9 to 5. The Naval Air Station Museum, 503/842-1130, is open during the summer 9 to 6. Admission is $5. (1 hour for each)

City of Newport

Autumnal storms pound Oregon's coast.

★★★ **Yachats**—This is a small, low-key village at the mouth of the Yachats River. Between June and September smelt come ashore to spawn. A July Smelt Fry Festival celebrates the event. Several thousand acres of rain forest make up **Cape Perpetua Scenic Area,** and the visitors center south of town displays exhibits on the natural forces that shaped the Oregon coast. It also offers Saturday environmental programs, such as tide pool explorations great for families. **Cape Perpetua Overlook** is the highest point on the Oregon coast and has great views.

Details: Yachats Chamber of Commerce, 541/547-3530 or www .pioneer.net. Cape Perpetua visitors center is 3 miles south of Yachats and 2 miles off U.S. 101; 541/547-3289. Summer hours daily 9 to 5. Admission is $3 per vehicle. (1–2 hours)

FITNESS AND RECREATION

The beaches are rich with recreational opportunities such as hiking, horseback riding, golfing, dune buggying, and lighthouse exploring. Kite flying is popular—particularly in Lincoln City. Wildlife watching is good all along the coast. Anywhere the forests meet the rocky headlands, you may see deer or sometimes elk. In Newport, a visit to the Oregon Coast Aquarium lets you touch sea stars and other tide pool animals. Also in Newport, you can learn more about the many lighthouses on the coast at the new interpretive center at **Yaquina Head Lighthouse**, 750 Lighthouse Drive, 541/574-3100. On the south coast, in **Reedsport**, there's a Marine Discovery area on the bayfront.

Fishing and boating excursions abound. Charters are available for halibut fishing in May and June, Chinook salmon through the summer, and ling cod, sea bass, and other rockfish all year. Major ports are at Garibaldi, Depoe Bay, Newport, Winchester, Charleston, Gold Beach, and Brookings. Prices range from $40 to over $150 for half to full day trips. And you don't have to join a charter to fish. You can throw in a line or crab year-round anywhere there's a bay. Marinas and bait shops sell bait and rent crabbing rings (about $4) and boats (price varies).

Depoe Bay, known as having the world's smallest harbor, is a whalewatching destination, as a number of whales make the central coast their year-round home. Guided Zodiak boat ecotours give visitors a look at nearby secluded coves and beaches.

A note for inveterate shoppers: The **Factory Stores**, 888/746-7333, in Lincoln City (there are 65 outlets) include an L.L. Bean store among many others.

Select your destination and check with the chamber for a list of additional local recreation options.

FOOD

There are 20 food festivals on the Oregon coast, and seafood is plentiful. Depoe Bay is famous for its salmon bakes, Yachats hosts an annual smelt festival, and the Newport Seafood Festival is the biggest on the coast. So, not surprisingly, casual meals are a breeze. Every town has cafés or little hole-in-the-wall eateries where you can buy fish and chips made with fish caught fresh that morning. So, with the exception of the **Pacific Way Cafe & Bakery**, (closed Tuesday and Wednesday) in Gearhart north of Seaside, 503/738-0245, which makes great basic fare such as sandwiches, soups, and seafood pizzas, the following are some special places to watch for along the coast. The **Blue Sky Cafe**, in Manzanita, 503/368-5712, offers a creatively diverse menu—both a Thai chicken entrée and bread pudding can be found on their menu—that draws plenty of fans. The dining room at **Salishan Lodge**, in Gleneden Beach, 541/764-2371, offers a soothing decor and a view of Siletz Bay. Menu selections emphasize locally harvested seafood and produce. **Chez Jeanette**, also in Gleneden Beach, 541/764-3434, serves French food in an intimate atmosphere. Try dinner (set menu by reservation) at the **Tables of Content** restaurant at the Sylvia Beach Hotel, 541/265-5428, if you're in Newport. The **Blue Heron Bistro**, 100 Commercial Street, 541/267-3993, in Coos Bay is a good dinner choice as well. In Brookings, **Chives**, 541/469-4121, is a surprisingly sophisticated eatery—linen tablecloths, art on the walls—with excellent service and a big city menu that might include items like roast pheasant and polenta.

If you catch a fish or crab during the day, yet want to dine out that night, check in advance with your restaurant of choice. Many restaurants along the coast will prepare your own fish or crab and serve it to you.

In Tillamook (see above), visit the **Tillamook Cheese Factory** for tasting and **Blue Heron French Cheese Co.** for cheese and wine tasting. In Newhalem, the **Newhalem Bay Winery**—the only winery on the coast—has wine tasting in an historic cheese factory. On the southern coast, you can also visit **Bandon's Cheddar Cheese** outlet, 800/548-8961, for samples and to see cheese being made.

LODGING

The beachfront **Stephanie Inn** in Cannon Beach, 800/633-3466, www.stephanieinn.com, a modern 46-room inn with fireplaces in all the rooms and great views, is a favorite coast getaway destination for romantic couples. There's a restaurant with two dinner seatings by reservation only. The best suites are pricier so check on package offerings. The funky and comfortable **Sylvia Beach Hotel,** 541/265-5428, is a renovated clapboard inn in Newport, named after the owner of a famous Paris bookstore in the 1920s. Each of the 20 rooms is named after a well-known writer. It sits on a small bluff overlooking the beach. The Colette, Mark Twain, and Agatha Christie rooms have fireplaces and are wheelchair accessible. **Salishan Inn,** at Gleneden Beach, 541/764-3600 or 888/725-4742, is across the street and up the road from the waterfront, but that doesn't deter the legions who love this golf and tennis resort with a well-deserved reputation for comfort and fine dining. **The Chelan,** 503/392-3270, a small condominium unit at Neskowin and a family favorite, is tucked away in this low-key beach community. Rooms have fireplaces and views of the beach. **Tu Tu Tun Lodge,** on the Rogue River near Gold Beach, 541/247-6664, www.tututun.com, offers fishing and rafting, yet is a romantic destination.

CAMPING

There are 19 state park campgrounds, with options like yurt and cabin rentals, and 72 day use properties that provide a special way to experience the natural beauty of the coast. **Jessie Honeyman State Park**, 541/997-3641 or 800/452-5687, www.prd.state.or.us, three miles south of Florence in the Oregon Dunes National Recreation Area, is the largest beachside state park. It also has a lake that provides warm swimming waters and paddleboat recreation. Camping spots are plentiful all along the coast and include yurts and rentals. The only caveat here, worth repeating: reserve well in advance.

BEACH SAFETY AND TIDE POOL ETIQUETTE

Winter storm watching is a favorite activity of Northwest beachgoers. The waves can grow to 30 feet or more as they crash to shore, and it's best to watch them from a safe distance. Keep safety in mind at all times at the beach. But be especially careful in the spring, and make sure that children stay safely away from logs or other debris in the surf.

When exploring tide pools it's fine to touch starfish and anemones, but consider the health of these critters and leave them in their habitat.

Oregon's beaches belong to the public, so you can explore any of them. And, unless otherwise advised, beach fires are permitted.

HELPFUL HINTS

The Oregon Coast Visitors Association, 541/574-2679 or 888/628-2101 (toll free), www.netbridge.net/ocva, is a good place to start getting information. You'll see distinctive "Oregon Welcomes You" signs with a yellow sun, green trees, and blue water that indicate visitors centers located in almost every community. These are open daily and maps and brochures are available, whether or not a host is on duty.

17
ASTORIA

Fans of Lewis and Clark, history buffs, sailors, hikers, kayakers—explorers of all breeds—will have a field day roaming the history-rich seaport town of Astoria and the Columbia River estuary. As you drive into town, the unremarkable 1920s-era buildings lining Commercial Street give no clue that this is the oldest white settlement west of the Mississippi. John Jacob Astor sent fur traders here to set up shop in 1811. The town thrived as a coastal port from the mid-1800s to the early 1900s. But in 1922 a fire leveled the downtown, at the time built on wooden pilings over the Columbia River. Fortunately, the Victorian homes that popped up in the boom days of the 1800s and at the turn of the century were spared. You'll easily spot the most imposing one—the red-roofed mansion built in 1885 by Captain George Flavel, pioneer Columbia River bar pilot and colorful entrepreneur. From the three-story octagonal turret, Captain Flavel watched his ships ply the waters of the Columbia. Nearby at Fort Clatsop, Lewis and Clark reached the end of their voyage years earlier.

It rains a lot in Astoria, and it doesn't have the "beach town" feel of other spots on the coast. Yet a walking tour along Franklin Avenue takes you back in time, and exploring the huge Columbia River Maritime Museum will fill your mind with high seas fantasies, as well as keep you dry in a drizzle or downpour. And when the sun shines, ahh, it's glorious. Meanwhile, think of Astoria as a mystical seaport—a dream-catcher snagging men's visions at the mouth of the West's mightiest river. ◣

ASTORIA AREA

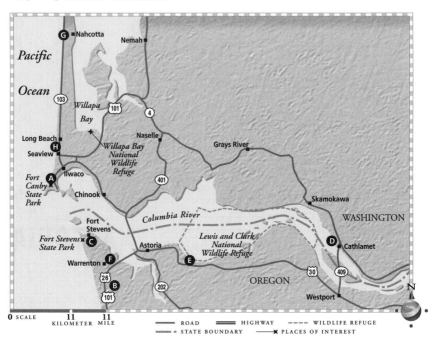

Sights

- **A** Fort Canby State Park
- **B** Fort Clatsop National Memorial
- **C** Fort Stevens and Fort Stevens State Park
- **D** Julia Butler Hansen Columbia White-tailed Deer Refuge
- **E** Twilight Eagle Sanctuary and Burnside Area
- **F** Warrenton

Food

- **G** The Ark
- **H** The Shoalwater

Lodging

- **F** The Shilo Inn

Camping

- **A** Fort Canby State Park
- **C** Fort Stevens State Park

Note: Items with the same letter are located in the same town or area.

A PERFECT DAY AROUND ASTORIA

Spend the night in an historic B&B. After breakfast, drive to the **Astoria Column** to climb 166 steps to the top of the 125-foot-tall monolith for a bird's-eye view of the town and the Columbia estuary. Visit the **Captain George Flavel House**, then head to the **Columbia River Maritime Museum**. Drive to **Fort Clatsop** to watch historical reenactments of Lewis and Clark's winter there. A map will lead you to this and other historic forts (such as **Fort Stevens State Park**), viewpoints, and beachfront communities. Back in Astoria, choose a waterfront spot to dine and watch boats ply the river as the sun sets.

SIGHTSEEING HIGHLIGHTS

★★★★ **Captain George Flavel House**—Considered by many to be the finest example of the Queen Anne style of architecture in Oregon, the house was a gift to the town in 1934 by Flavel's great-granddaughter and is now a museum. The Clatsop Historical Society has refurbished it as it was during Captain Flavel's time. Inside, the woodwork and much of the furniture is in the Eastlake style. There are six different fireplaces with handcarved mantels in varying woods and tile from different countries. There are also paintings by maritime artist Cleveland Rockwell and Astoria native John H. Trullinger.

Details: The home is at Eighth and Duane Streets; 503/325-2203. Open daily 10 to 5. Admission $5, includes admission to the Heritage Museum. (1 hour)

★★★★ **Columbia River Maritime Museum**—24,000 square feet of maritime exhibits take you from the time of dugout canoes to submarine technology. Displays focus on Chinook Indian artifacts, navigation, marine safety, and whaling. Another exhibit looks at the period when Astoria was considered the "Salmon Capital of the World." Waterfront location with great views. Tour a lightship, the *Columbia*, that once guided ships to safety at the mouth of the river.

Details: 1792 Marine Drive; 503/325-2323. Open daily 9:30 to 5. Admission $5. (1½ hours)

★★★★ **Fort Clatsop National Memorial**—This is the westernmost point reached by the Lewis and Clark expedition to expand knowledge of the Louisiana Purchase and open the West. The fort, basically two log cabins with seven small rooms, is a re-creation of the site where Meriwether Lewis and William Clark made camp during the miserable, rainy winter of 1805–06. It was built in 1955 from a drawing on the cover of Clark's field book. Historical re-enactments, a visitors center, and plenty of hiking trails make this a great stop for the whole family.

> *Details: Six miles southwest of Astoria, off Highway 101; 503/861-2471; www.nps.gov/focl. Open mid-June through Labor Day 8 to 6, the rest of the year 8 to 5. Re-enactments are held during the summer. Admission $2 for adults 17 and up, $4 per carload. (2 hours or more)*

★★★★ **Fort Stevens and Fort Stevens State Park**— Commissioned as a Civil War fortification in 1863, military here guarded the entrance to the Columbia until shortly after World War II. Gun emplacements still exist. A museum, gift shop, and Chinook long house are on the grounds. The *Peter Iredale*, shipwrecked in 1906, can always be seen but accessed only at low tide. The park's attractions include the fort, South Jetty Overlook, located where the ocean and river meet, a wildlife viewing platform, and 8.5 miles of paved bike and hiking trails (bicycle rentals from Memorial Day through Labor Day).

> *Details: Off Highway 101, 5 miles northwest of Astoria; call 503/861-3170 or 503/861-2000 for the museum; www.ohwy.com/or/f/ftsteven.htm. Park admission $3. (2–3 hours)*

★★★ **Fort Canby State Park**—On the Washington side this park overlooks the mouth of the Columbia River. The **Lewis and Clark Interpretive Center** tells the story of the 1804–1806 expedition. The **Cape Disappointment Lighthouse** here, built in 1856, is the oldest in Washington and open for tours. The park has many trails that pass through forest on the way to isolated coves and sandy beaches.

> *Details: 3 miles southwest of U.S. 101 at Ilwaco, Washington; 360/642-3078. Admission is free. (2 hours)*

★★★ **Julia Butler Hansen Columbia White-tailed Deer Refuge**— This reserve on the Washington side of the river is home to the endangered Columbia white-tailed deer and also provides habitat for bald eagle, raptors, river otter, and water fowl.

> *Details: Northwest of Cathlamet on SR 4 in Washington. (1 hour)*

✩✩✩ **Twilight Eagle Sanctuary and Burnside Area**—An observation platform overlooks protected eagle habitat and Cathlamet Bay. And there's kayaking on the John Day and Columbia Rivers.
    Details: Just east of Astoria, off Highway 30. (1–2 hours)

✩✩✩ **Warrenton**—A waterfront community with two mooring basins, charters, pleasure-boat facilities, and a waterfront trail.
    Details: West of Astoria on Highway 30, across Youngs Bay. (1 hour)

✩✩ **Heritage Museum**—This museum looks at maritime culture and the salmon canning industry, as well as exhibits on the Chinese who lived here early in this century and worked in the fishing industry.
    Details: 1618 Exchange Street; 503/325-2203. Open daily 11 to 4. Admission $5, includes admission to Flavel House. (1 hour)

FITNESS AND RECREATION

Twilight Eagle Sanctuary and Burnside Area, just east of Astoria, offers water trails for canoeing or kayaking and spots for eagle viewing. You can also see wildlife at the **Julia Butler Hansen Columbia White-tailed Deer Refuge** across the river in Washington. Forts on both sides of the river offer plenty to explore

A block south of the Flavel House you'll find Franklin Avenue, the town's primary residential street in earlier times. Over 20 historical homes lie in the eight blocks that stretch east to Exchange Street. You can pick up a walking tour booklet and audio tape at Flavel House, the Heritage Museum, or the Chamber of Commerce Information Center.

Shoppers can putter through shops such as **Let It Rain**, 1269 Commercial Street, 503/325-7728, for umbrellas and rain-gear, or **Finn Ware**, 1116 Commercial Street, 503/325-5720, for Scandinavian gifts.

FOOD

The reputation of the **Columbian Cafe**, 1114 Marine Drive, 503/325-2233, for great vegetarian dishes, seafood stews, and creative surprises is so great folks come to Astoria just to eat here. It's quirky and often packed. The café at the **Pacific Rim Gallery**, 108 10th Street, 503/325-5450, serves coffee, ice cream, and light fare to enjoy while you take in the work of regional artists. The **Cannery Cafe**, Sixth Street at the river, 503/325-8642, in an historic salmon cannery, and is the best place to go for Sunday brunch. The **Ship Inn Restaurant & Pub**, 1 Second Street, 503/325-0033, is known for fish and chips and river views. Two renowned restaurants on the Long Beach Peninsula (on the southwest Washington coast) offer fancier fare—**The Ark,** in Nahcotta, 360/665-4133, and **The Shoalwater**, at the Shelburne Inn in Seaview, 360/642-2142.

NIGHTLIFE

The **Wet Dog Cafe,** 144 11th Street, 503/325-6975, is a riverfront brewpub featuring music and dancing Thursday, Friday, and Saturday nights until 1:30 a.m. The menu—steaks, pastas, and an awesome soft taco grande—also includes burgers such as the Blues Burger and the Hip Hop Burger (bacon or ham with choice of cheese). Four different beers are brewed on site. The other popular spot for music and dancing is the the **Red Lion**, 400 Industry Street, 503/325-7373 or 800/547-8010, featuring nightly entertainment in the Seafare Lounge.

LODGING

Astoria's historic-home B&Bs offer good value and are close to town. Many are on Franklin Avenue. Some rooms offer great views of the river. The very affordable **Rosebriar Hotel,** 636 14th Street, 503/325-7427 or 800/487-0224, once a convent, was Astoria's first B&B. In the next block is slightly more expensive **Franklin Street Station,** 1140 Franklin Street, 503/325-4314 or 800/448-1098, a popular and homey inn. Also a good value, **Clementine's,** 847 Exchange Street, 503/325-2005 or 800/521-6801, is a two-house complex near Flauel House. Try other historic and easy-on-the-wallet B&Bs like **Captain's Inn,** 1546 Franklin Street, 503/325-1387 or 800/876-1387; **Columbia River Inn,** 1681 Franklin Street, 503/325-5044 or 800/953-5044; and **Martin & Lilli Foard House,** 690 17th Street, 503/325-1892.

Motel lodging includes the **Red Lion Inn,** 400 Industry Street, 503/325-7373 or 800/547-8010, with stunning views of the river and the **Shilo Inn** in Warrenton, west on Harbor Drive off Highway 101, 800/222-2244, an all-mini-suites motel with covered pool.

CAMPING

Camping at the state parks here offers wonderful options, particularly if you make friends with the rain. Some Oregon and Washington state

ASTORIA

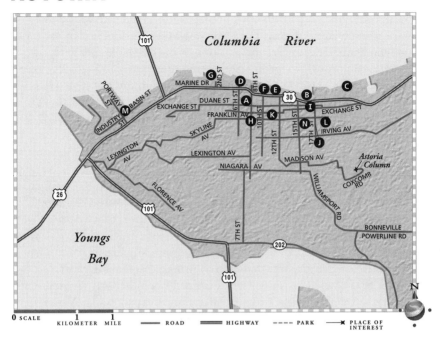

Sights

- **Ⓐ** Captain George Flavel House
- **Ⓑ** Columbia River Maritime Museum
- **Ⓒ** Heritage Museum

Food

- **Ⓓ** Cannery Cafe
- **Ⓔ** Columbian Cafe
- **Ⓕ** Pacific Rim Gallery
- **Ⓖ** Ship Inn Restaurant & Pub

Lodging

- **Ⓗ** Clementine's
- **Ⓘ** Captain's Inn
- **Ⓙ** Columbia River Inn
- **Ⓚ** Franklin Street Station
- **Ⓛ** Martin & Lilli Foard House
- **Ⓜ** Red Lion Inn
- **Ⓝ** Rosebriar Hotel

parks offer yurts, a convenient camping option for those who don't want to carry a lot of gear. **Fort Stevens State Park** is one of the most popular state parks in Oregon and one of the largest (3,500 acres). It has 596 campsites, five group camps, and nine yurts, $14 to $20, reservations advised, 800/452-5687. It's off U.S. Highway 101 near Hammond and Warrenton junction. **Fort Canby State Park** (see above) has about 250 campsites, $11 to $16. For information, call 360/642-3078; for reservations, 800/452-5687.

HELPFUL HINTS

The Astoria-Warrenton Crab & Seafood Festival, a three-day food, wine, and arts and crafts celebration, packs the town every April. The Astoria-Warrenton Area Chamber of Commerce is located at 111 West Marine Drive, 503/325-6311. Harbor Air has daily flights from Portland and Sea-Tac airports that land at Astoria Regional Airport.

Cruising the Columbia from Portland is another way to experience Astoria. Extensive cruise trips are offered by companies like Alaska Sightseeing/Cruise West, 800/888-9378; American West Steamboat Company, 800/434-1232; and Special Expeditions, 800/397-3348.

SIDE TRIP: LONG BEACH PENINSULA AND WILLAPA BAY

The southern coast of Washington—**Long Beach and Willapa Bay**—has long been a destination for Portlanders. Long Beach is the state's oldest coastal resort. It has a restored downtown, a new boardwalk, and 26 miles of sandy beach. And as home to the **World Kite Museum & Hall of Fame**, Third Street Northwest and Pacific Highway, 360/642-4020, it's obviously one of the world's best places to fly kites. Two hundred thousand high-flyers gather here the third week in August to celebrate the kite. The small museum's special exhibit of fighter kites—ranging from huge Japanese models used in team fighting to small ones from Java, decorated with ground glass for a competitive edge—shows a tiny portion of its 1,200-kite collection. Admission is $1 for adults. Open through August daily 11 to 5. **Willapa Bay** is a large saltwater inlet created by Long Beach peninsula. Preserved as Willapa National Wildlife Refuge, it is also home to well-known oyster farms. There are canoe and kayak put-ins here.

18
PORTLAND

Portland, like Paris and New Orleans, has a river running through it. And like those famous cities, it has both a bustling business side and a "village within a city" personality—an intimacy of scale and experience that draws you in and makes you feel very much at home. Half a million people live within the city limits, and well over a million and a half in the metro area, but unless you're here during a big event or caught in a traffic jam, it doesn't feel like a big city. Short city blocks have something to do with this feeling, as do the village green–like South Park Blocks and Pioneer Courthouse Square, spots where Portlanders go to gather and be entertained or relax.

An active arts and theater scene, vigorous restaurant offerings, a reputation as the microbrew capital of the Northwest (perhaps the country?), wonderful parks and public gardens—such as the Japanese Garden and Portland's International Rose Garden (Portland is known for its June Rose Festival)—and lots of recreation options add to the rich and delectable fabric of life here. With Portland State University near the heart of downtown you have a mix of business folks and students producing an offbeat creative energy that makes Portland so appealing.

The Columbia River defines Portland's (and the state's) northern limits and adds a vagabond seaport dimension to this city. Ships and boats leaving here have access to the Pacific Ocean and the world to the west and to the Snake River and Hell's Canyon to the east. ◼

DOWNTOWN PORTLAND

Willamette River

Tom McCall Waterfront Park

South Park Blocks

I-84
I-5
99W
I-405
I-26

STEEL BR
BURNSIDE BR
MORRISON BR
HAWTHORNE BR

NW 1ST AV
SW 1ST AV
SW NAITO PARKWAY (FORMERLY FRONT AV)
SW 2ND AV
SW 3RD AV
SW 4TH AV
SW 5TH AV
SW 6TH AV
BROADWAY
SW PARK AV
SW 9TH AV
SW 10TH AV
SW 11TH AV
SW 12TH AV
SW 15TH AV
SW 18TH AV

NW 4TH AV
BROADWAY
NW 10TH AV
NW GLISAN ST
NW EVERETT ST
NW COUCH ST
BURNSIDE ST
NW 12TH AV
NW 18TH AV
NW 21ST AV
NW 22ND AV
NW 23RD AV

SW ASH ST
SW ANKENY ST
SW PINE ST
SW OAK ST
SW STARK ST
SW WASHINGTON ST
SW ALDER ST
SW MORRISON ST
YAMHILL ST
TAYLOR ST
SALMON ST
MAIN ST
MADISON ST
JEFFERSON ST
COLUMBIA ST
CLAY ST
MARKET ST

HARBOR WAY
HAWTHORNE ST
MORRISON ST

SUNSET HWY
SW CANYON RD
SW VISTA AV
TUNNEL

N

0 SCALE
.3 KILOMETERS
.3 MILES

----- PARK BOUNDARY
—— ROAD

Sights

Ⓐ Oregon History Center

Ⓑ Oregon Maritime Center and Museum

Ⓒ Oregon Museum of Science and Industry

Ⓓ Portland Art Museum

Ⓔ Pioneer Courthouse Square

Ⓕ Pioneer Place

Ⓖ Saturday Market

Ⓗ South Park Blocks

Ⓘ Tom McCall Waterfront Park

Food

Ⓙ Hamburger Mary's

Ⓚ Heathman Restaurant and Bar

Ⓛ Il Fornio

Ⓜ Jake's Famous Crawfish

Sights (continued)

Ⓝ Jake's Grill

Ⓞ London Grill

Ⓟ McCormick & Schmick's Seafood Restaurant

Ⓠ Oba

Ⓡ Pazzo Ristorante

Ⓢ Red Star Tavern and Roast House

Ⓣ Zefiro Restaurant

Lodging

Ⓞ Benson Hotel

Ⓢ Fifth Avenue Suites Hotel

Ⓤ Governor Hotel

Ⓚ Heathman Hotel

Ⓡ Hotel Vintage Plaza

Ⓥ The Mallory

A PERFECT DAY IN PORTLAND

Portland is a breakfast town, so start with a huge glass of fresh-squeezed orange juice at the Heathman restaurant. Then stroll through South Park Blocks, visit the Portland Art Museum and the Oregon History Center; or, if you're in the mood to buy, buy, buy, indulge in tax-free shopping at favorite stops like Nordstrom, NIKE-TOWN, and Pioneer Place. To get a panoramic view of the city, drive to Pittock Mansion or the Japanese Garden. A perfect day in Portland ends with a warm summer stroll along the riverfront, stopping in for a drink or dinner at a riverfront restaurant. But take note: you shouldn't leave the Portland area without seeing the Columbia Gorge—so cut the above short if you have to and take an easy half-day driving tour of the amazing waterfalls and views east of the city along the Columbia River.

SIGHTSEEING HIGHLIGHTS

★★★ **The Grotto**—Portland's forested, glade-like Grotto was established as a Catholic sanctuary in 1924. It's named for the rock cave hewn from the base of a 110-foot cliff rising over the central plaza. Explore the 62-acre grounds enjoying reflection ponds and sculptures. The 550-seat chapel has cathedral-like acoustics; nearby is the natural stone grotto. In December, a "Festival of Lights at the Grotto" with choral performances runs nightly except for Christmas Day.

Details: Located a mile south of the Portland airport on Sandy Boulevard (Highway 30) at Northeast 85th Avenue, 503/254-7371 Admission is free. Small charge to ride the elevator to the upper garden. (1½ hours).

★★★★ **Japanese Garden**—Five gardens make up almost six acres of serenely beautiful gardens overlooking Portland. They are particularly awe-inspiring in spring when the cherry trees are in bloom. Adjacent find the **International Rose Test Garden**. The Japanese Garden is also near **Hoyt Arboretum**.

Details: In Washington Park, at 611 SW Kingston; 503/223-1321. Open June through August 9 to 8; April, May, and September 10 to 6; and the remainder of year 10 to 4. Admission: $5, seniors and students $2.50. (1–2 hours)

★★★★ **Oregon History Center**—The three-dimensional mural on the outside of this building catches your eye first; inside, explore the history of Oregon and the Northwest. There are changing exhibits. A special souvenir suggestion—you can order copies from the large collection of archival photographs that are suitable for framing.

Details: At 1200 SW Park Avenue; 503/222-1741. Admission $6. (1–2 hours)

★★★★ **Oregon Maritime Center and Museum**—Stop by this museum in the historic iron-fronted Smith Building in the Skidmore/Old Town district. View ship models and exhibits, or tour the *Steamer Portland*, moored at the seawall across waterfront park.

Details: 113 SW Naito Parkway, 503/224-7724; call for hours. Admission is $4. Handicapped access is available. (1–2 hours)

★★★★ **Oregon Museum of Science and Industry**—With six exhibit halls, an OMNIMAX theater, and the Murdock Sky Theater, OMSI, on the east bank of the Willamette River, is one of the largest science museums in the country. Visitors can tour the USS *Blueback* submarine that appeared in *The Hunt for Red October* and even beam a message into space. A great place for kids.

Details: 1945 SE Water Avenue; 503/797-4000; www.omsi.edu. Call for hours and admission prices. (2 hours)

✮✮✮✮ **The Oregon Zoo**—This wonderful zoo has major exhibits that simulate the animals' natural environment, such as the African Rain Forest, which features forest rainstorms for authenticity. The zoo lies against the hills with the rose test gardens and Japanese gardens nearby (a visit to all three would be a full day's outing). A train offers excursions of the zoo and park. In December the ZooLights Festival with over 300,000 lights draws visitors.

Details: West of downtown on U.S. 26 about 3 miles; 503/226-1561. Open daily at 9:30; closing varies. Admission $5.50. (2–3 hours)

✮✮✮✮ **Portland Art Museum**—This hundred-year-old museum on the South Park Blocks has an impressive painting collection that includes masters like Monet and Renoir. Enjoy the permanent collections of Asian, European, and American works, and special exhibits.

Details: 1219 SW Park at Jefferson; 503/226-2811. Open Tuesday through Sunday 10 to 5, and until 9 p.m. on Wednesday and first Thursday. (1–2 hours)

✮✮✮✮ **South Park Blocks**—This is a beautiful tree-studded strip of green space in the heart of downtown, surrounded by the city's cultural stalwarts like the Portland Art Museum and the Oregon History Center, and with Portland State University at one end. People gather here to talk, play chess, or watch the world go by.

Details: Between Park Avenue and Ninth Avenue. (20 minutes)

✮✮✮✮ **Tom McCall Waterfront Park**—Sweeping lawns and jogging paths along this downtown waterfront make it a particularly wonderful spot on a warm summer night. Stroll by the Waterfront Story Garden, a granite and cobblestone tribute to storytellers in the midst of **Japanese American Historical Plaza**, where 100 cherry trees commemorate the Japanese American internments of World War II.

Details: This three-mile long downtown riverfront runs between the Willamette River and Naito Pzrkway (formerly Front Street). The sternwheeler **Cascade Queen** *departs from* **River Place Marina** *and tours the Portland harbor area, 503/223-3928. The* **Portland Spirit** *offers sightseeing and meal cruises on the Willamette; call 503/224-3900 or 800/224-3901.*

★★★ **Pioneer Courthouse Square**—This is Portland's outdoor living room, an open brick courtyard where people gather to take in the sun and brown bag it for lunch, and where special events, including floral displays, are often featured. It's a great spot to people-watch.
Details: SW Broadway Avenue and SW Morrison Street. (10 minutes to 1 hour)

★★★ **Saturday Market**—From March to October, several hundred craftspersons and food purveyors gather each weekend to sell hand-made goods, including woodcrafts, leather items, and clothing.
Details: Beneath the Burnside Bridge at SW First Avenue, 503/222-6072. (1–2 hours)

★★ **Pioneer Place**—In the heart of downtown, this fashionable four-level shopping mall is adjacent to Saks Fifth Avenue, with Williams-Sonoma, Anne Taylor, and many other shops and eateries. Underground tunnel connects to parking.
Details: 700 SW Fifth Avenue; 503/228-5800. Open Monday through Friday 9:30 to 9, Saturday 9:30 to 7, Sunday 11 to 6.

★★ **Pittock Mansion**—This restored French Renaissance house was built by Henry Pittock, the founder of the *Daily Oregonian* in the early 1900s. It's filled with antiques and is a beautiful house to tour, but just as wonderful—and as good a reason to come here—is the incredible view of the city A good spot to have a sandwich picnic.
Details: Off Burnside at 3229 NW Pittock Drive; 503/823-3624. The house is open daily noon to 4. Admission is $4.50. It's free to tour the grounds, open daily from 7 to 9. (1 hour)

★★ **World Forestry Center**—This museum in Washington Park contains exhibits on the old-growth forests of the Pacific Northwest, fire-fighting, and on tropical rainforests. A tall "talking tree" at the entry captures the attention of children. Outside exhibits also featured.
Details: 4033 SW Canyon Road, 503/228-1367. Open 9 to 5 daily. Admission $3.50, $2.50 for seniors and students. (1–2 hours)

KIDS' STUFF

Kids particularly like the earthquake and tornado simulators at OMSI; the "talking tree" at the World Forestry Center; the roller coaster at Oaks Park Amusement Park, 503/233-5777, and the large elephant exhibit at the Oregon Zoo. Young children especially relate to the playful, interactive exhibits at the Children's Museum, 503/823-2227, and the cool old advertising signs, commercials, and videos at the American Advertising Museum, 503/226-0000.

FITNESS AND RECREATION

The Portland area boasts 37,000 acres of parks. The Willamette River Trail offers walkers, joggers, bicyclists, and inline skaters miles of scenic riverfront to explore. A doubledecker trolley serves this area as well. Indoor ice skating is available at Clackamas Town Center and Lloyd Center. In 1960 the Lloyd Center was the "world's largest shopping center." Although there've been a lot of shopping centers since then, there are still 200 stores here including Meier & Frank and Nordstrom. Its skating rink was recently redeveloped into a state-of-the-art facility.

There are numerous neighborhoods to explore. For fun shopping and liveliness there's **23rd Avenue** in Northwest Portland. South of here is the **Pearl District**, a lively mix of restaurants, galleries, and antiques shops in a former warehouse area. **Old Sellwood Antique Row**, further south still, was settled in the 1850s and named for Reverend James Sellwood. This unique neighborhood has become a top antique shopping district; it's along SE 13th Avenue, six blocks east of the Sellwood Bridge. The hip 60s-style **Hawthorne District**, in Southeast Portland, is another area popular with shoppers.

And by all means, make a stop at **Powell's**—one of the Northwest's most famous bookstores—on Burnside, 503/228-4651, to book-look till you drop.

SPECTATOR SPORTS

The best sporting event in Portland is a **Trail Blazer** game. NBA action is hard to beat. Go early to the **Rose Quarter** and choose from numerous eating venues that include a sports grill. The people watching is as

GREATER PORTLAND

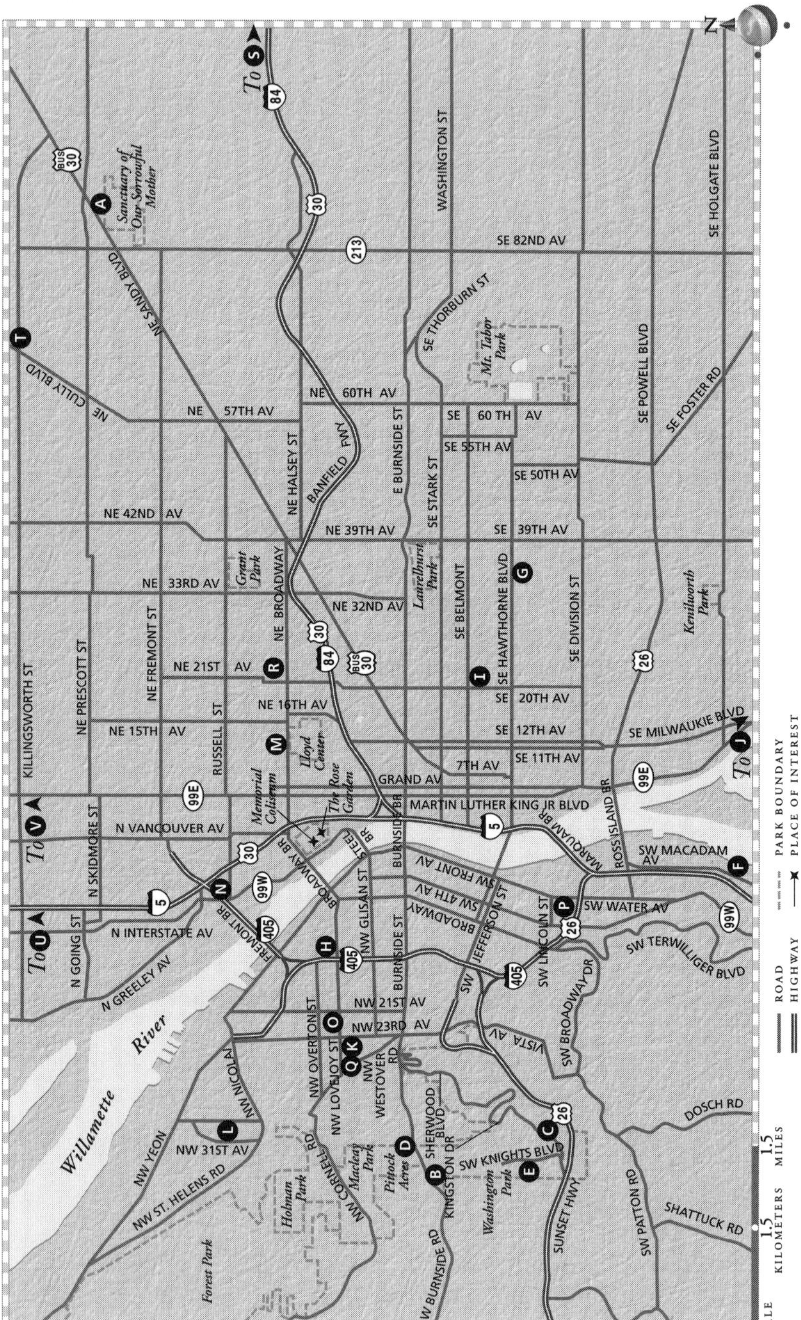

Sights

- **A** The Grotto
- **B** Japanese Garden
- **C** Oregon Park Zoo
- **D** Pittock Mansion
- **E** World Forestry Center

Food

- **F** Avalon Grill and Cafe
- **G** Bread and Ink Cafe
- **H** BridgePort Brewing Company
- **I** Genoa
- **J** Papa Haydn East
- **K** Papa Haydn West
- **L** Portland Brewing Company Taproom & Grill

Food (continued)

- **M** Ron Paul Catering and Charcuterie
- **N** Widmer Brothers Gasthaus
- **O** Wildwood

Lodging

- **P** DoubleTree
- **Q** Heron Haus B&B
- **R** White House

Camping

- **S** Ainsworth State Park
- **S** Cascade Locks Marine Park
- **S** Crown Point RV Park
- **T** Fir Grove RV and Trail Park
- **U** Jantzen Beach RV Park
- **V** Portland Meadows RV Park

Note: Items with the same letter are located in the same town or area.

much fun as the game itself! Half-time at the games features the very athletic Blazer Dancers.

In the mood for some arena football? The **Forest Dragons** will hike up just what you are looking for. And if soccer is your game, you should give the **Portland Pythons** a try. And if you crave the excitement of hockey, the **Winter Hawks** will have you up on your feet. Don't overlook some great minor league baseball played by the **Rockies**. Individual tickets can be purchased through Ticketmaster, 503/224-4400.

FOOD

The **Bijou Cafe**, 132 SW Third Avenue, 503/222-3817, is a funky gathering spot and a great breakfast start. Even simple scrambled eggs are great here. Near NW 23rd, **Il Fornio** offers Italian countryside charm and great French toast. **McCormick & Schmick's Seafood Restaurant**, First and Oak Streets, 503/224-7522, offers an updated version of traditional seafood. At **Dan and Louis' Oyster Bar Restaurant and Museum**, 208 SW Ankeny Street, 503/227-5906, oyster and crab stews, clam and salmon chowders, and oysters on the half shell have kept folks coming back since 1907. To sample Portland's "brew madness," visit one of serveral brewpubs for a tour and a meal. **BridgePort Brewing Company**, 1313 NW Marshall Street, 503/241-7179, has brewery tours daily at 2 and 5. **Portland Brewing Company Taproom & Grill**, 2730 NW 31st, 503/228-5269, has tours on Saturday by appointment. **Widmer Brothers Gasthaus**, 929 North Russell, 503/281-3333, has tours Fridays at 2 and 3 and Saturdays at 1 and 2. Several Portland-based tour companies offer microbrewery tours or transportation to and from pubs; these include: **Custom Tailored Tours**, 360/245-0536 or 800/391-5761; **EcoTours of Oregon**, 503/245-1428 or 888/868-7733; and **Van-Go Tours**, 503/292-2085.

    Avalon Grill and Cafe, at John's Landing, 4630 SW Macadam, 503/227-4630, is a romantic spot with dramatic, contemporary styling, overlooking the Willamette. There's casual dining and a cigar room upstairs, formal dining downstairs, and delicious food with Asian-style preparations. **Genoa**, 2832 SE Belmont Street, 503/238-1464, while expensive, has served top-rated classic Italian food for more than a quarter of a century. Its seven-course fixed-price dinner has seatings on the hour and half-hour from 5:30 to 9:30 p.m. Four-course dinners are an option Monday through Thursday. Reservations are a must here.

    Bread and Ink Cafe, 3610 SE Hawthorne, 503/239-4756, is a friendly neighborhood hangout in the Hawthorne district. Breads baked fresh daily here are a specialty, as is their eclectic menu of American classics, Mediterranean and Mexican specialties. This is a good spot for a late-night dessert. Around since 1892, **Jake's Famous Crawfish**, 401 SW 12th Avenue, 503/226-1419, is Portland's best known seafood restaurant. Nearby, **Jake's Grill**, 611 SW 10th Avenue, 503/220-1850, the corner of SW 10th and Alder in downtown Portland, does for steaks what the original Jake's does for seafood in an old-fashioned dark wood and tile-floored saloon atmosphere.

Hamburger Mary's, on Broadway, 503/223-0900, is an offbeat downtown place to go for soup, salads, or sandwiches. The **Heathman Restaurant and Bar**, on Broadway at Salmon, 503/241-4100, is a great spot to dine before or after attending a performance nearby at Portland Center for the Performing Arts. Breakfast here is great and brunch on Sunday is tops. The **London Grill** , Benson Hotel, 309 SW Broadway, 503/295-4110, is a legendary Portland gathering spot. **Macheezmo Mouse** (several outlets), serves healthy Mexican food, so no guilt when you nosh on the cheesy, black bean tortillas drizzled with fresh salsa in a high-tech, high-energy environment. Great for kids. **Oba**, in the heart of the Pearl District at 12th and Hoyt, 503/228-6161, is a richly colorful restaurant serving up tasty Brazilian-style food to match its energetic interior—the cheese dip, coconut prawns, and volcano cake are worth the trip. The chef uses lots of lime and different flavors. **Papa Haydn East**, 5829 SE Milwaukie, 503/232-9440, is known for fresh local produce—Hood River pears, Oregon raspberries, Dungeness crab. **Papa Haydn West** is at 701 NW 23rd Avenue, 503/228-7317. **Ron Paul Catering and Charcuterie**, two locations, 1441 NE Broadway, 503/284-5439, and 6141 SW Macadam, 503/221-0052, showcases Northwest regional cuisine. On Macadam it's a European-style café in the open market. The downtown Ron Paul Express conveniently offers carry-out; both offer reasonable prices. **Pazzo Ristorante**, at Hotel Vintage Plaza, 627 SW Washington Street, 503/228-1515, has both a soothing and energizing feel and is open daily for breakfast, lunch, and dinner. Like the **Red Star Tavern and Roast House**, 503/222-0005, on the premises of another Kimpton Hotel, 5th Avenue Suites, it mixes menu items that comfort or challenge.

    Zefiro Restaurant, 500 NW 21st Avenue, 503/226-3394, in Northwest Portland, is hip, fashionable and attracts serious connoisseurs. Call for reservations or dine at the more casual bar. The eclectic mix of dishes changes every couple of weeks. Good standby bets are oysters on the half shell and the Caesar salad. **Wildwood**, 1221 NW 21st Avenue, 503/248-9663, is known for the trend-setting talents of chef/owner Corey Schreiber.

LODGING

The **Benson Hotel**, 309 SW Broadway, 503/228-2000, is a distinguished and historic luxury hotel in downtown Portland offering 286 rooms. The **Governor Hotel**, 611 SW 10th at Alder, 503/224-3400 or

800/554-3456, is another historic Portland hotel in the heart of downtown. The **Heathman Hotel**, 1001 SW Broadway, 503/241-4100, has
direct access to the Arlene Schnitzer Concert Hall. The **Hotel Vintage
Plaza**, 422 SW Broadway, 503/228-1212, is a Kimpton Hotel with a
small inn feel. Rooms are named after Oregon wineries, and wine is
offered to guests late in the afternoon. **Fifth Avenue Suites Hotel**, 506
SW Washington at Fifth Avenue, 503/222-0001 or 800/711-2971, is
another Kimpton boutique-style hotel, with cheery and sophisticated
one-bedroom suites, an on-site Aveda Spa, Red Star Tavern, and Roast
House restaurant. The **Mallory**, Yamhill and SW 15th, 503/223-6311 or
800/228-8657, offers well-kept, old-style rooms at reasonable rates, just a
few blocks' walk to the heart of downtown. Several **DoubleTree** hotels
are in good locations, downtown, at the airport, and at Jantzen Beach
along the Columbia River; the Jantzen Beach DoubleTree is at 909
North Hayden Island Drive, 503/283-4466.

There are numerous B&Bs. **Heron Haus B&B**, 503/274-1846;
www.innbook.com/heron.html, is in a large home in a residential area
near lively NW 23rd. The **White House**, 503/287-7131, is in a historic mansion on NE 22nd. For a brochure from Portland Metro
InnKeepers Association, call 800/955-1647.

CAMPING

Three camping parks near the Columbia River about four miles north
of downtown offer convenience to sights and recreation: **Fir Grove
RV and Trail Park**, 503/252-9993; **Jantzen Beach RV Park**,
503/289-7626, with shady spots and a golf course nearby; and **Portland Meadows RV Park**, 503/285-1617, close to the Portland Meadows race track that operates October through April. Rates are about
$20 per night. Other camping options take you east along the Colum-
bia River Gorge: **Crown Point RV Park**, 503/695-5207, near the historical Vista House (see Columbia Gorge, below); **Ainsworth State
Park** 503/695-2261; or **Cascade Locks Marine Park**, 541/374-8619,
on 200 acres of waterfront park.

NIGHTLIFE

The heart of Portland's arts scene is the **Portland Center for the
Performing Arts**, which is comprised of several buildings, including
the **Arlene Schnitzer Concert Hall** ("the Schnitz"), 1111 SW Broad-

way, 503/248-4335, home to the Oregon Symphony Orchestra. The **Pearl District** is lively at night, hopping with restaurant goers—Oba and Paragon are here—and lots of galleries; first Thursdays art walks here are fun. The **Candlelight Room**, 2032 SW Fifth, 503/222-3378, is a good spot for jazz.

HELPFUL HINTS

Portland's numerous one-way streets and its bricked transit mall (parts of which are blocked to drivers) running along SW Fifth and Sixth Avenues make for some confusion in getting around. Walking is a good option, as is Portland's well-planned public transportation. **Tri-Met** transit is convenient and inexpensive; and **MAX** (Metropolitan Areas Express) light rail runs from downtown 15 miles east across the Willamette to the Lloyd District and Gresham. New in 1998 is a westside route that services the zoo, World Forestry Center, Washington Park, and Hillsboro. Both services are wheelchair accessible and free in "Fareless Square," a 300-block downtown area bordered on the west and south by Interstate 405, on the east by the Willamette River, and the north by Irving Street. **Gray Line** offers guided bus tours of the city and to Mt. St. Helens, the Gorge, and Mt. Hood; call 800/422-7042 for schedule information.

SIDE TRIP: COLUMBIA RIVER GORGE LOOP

Both a fabulous day trip from Portland and a destination in itself, the **Columbia River Gorge National Scenic Area** is a don't-miss sight, particularly the view from **Crown Point Vista House**, a truly top-of-the-world experience on the **Historic Columbia River Highway**. You reach it off Interstate 84, exit east of Troutdale or increase your speed and follow Interstate 84 east of Portland. Dozens of waterfalls enrich your drive. The most stunning is **Multnomah Falls**, which drops 620 feet to the historic lodge below. **Hood River** is the windsurfing capital of the world. Go up the **Hood River Valley** in spring as it transforms into a blanket of apple and pear blooms set against Mt. Hood, or in summer to sample the berries and other fruit here.

    Skamania Lodge, west of Stevenson on SR 14, 509/427-7700, offers panoramic views of the Columbia from the park lodge–style inn and golf course.

    Maryhill Museum of Art, 509/773-3733, is 100 miles east of Portland on SR 14 on the Washington side of the river. It was built by eccentric railroad tycoon James Hill early in the century and is now home to an amazing collection of small Rodin sculptures and many personal possessions of Queen Marie of Rumania. It's open daily 9 to 5. Admission is charged. Be sure to look at the copy of Stonehenge that Hill had built nearby.

Several cruise lines operate trips up the Columbia, most embarking from Portland. More than a relaxing cruise, more than a great getaway, a trip up the Columbia River offers you a journey through incredible geology. Witness the moody, misty beauty of the Columbia Gorge and the dry hills near Maryhill, the moonscape-like basalt flats along the Snake River and the deep cut of Hell's Canyon, where you can take a thrilling jetboat ride.

SIDE TRIP: MT. ST. HELENS NATIONAL VOLCANIC MONUMENT

This Washington mountain blew 1,300 feet of its top off in May 1980, spewing volcanic ash for hundreds of miles, changing lives, and reconfiguring the mountain and surrounding area. Though much of the landscape within the blast zone is haunting and stark, there's regrowth with wildflowers and wildlife evident. Over 70 miles of trails have been constructed for viewing the volcanic destruction and regrowth. For the best perspective, visit all four interpretive centers. **Coldwater Ridge Visitor Center**, east of Castle Rock on SR 504 about 40 miles, 360/274-2131, has stunning views of the Upper Toutle River Valley, Coldwater Lake, and the crater and lava dome of the mountain that lies seven miles away. To reach **Forest Learning Center at Mount St. Helens**, take Exit 47 from I-5 and go east on SR 504 about 33 miles. The Weyerhaeuser-sponsored center looks at the reforestation of the area, 360/414-3439. Viewing platforms offer mountain panoramas. **Hoffstadt Bluffs Visitor Center** (Exit 47 from I-5; go east on SR 504 about 25 miles) overlooks the Toutle River and the valley that leads to the mountain, (360) 577-3137. A short trail from **Mount St. Helens National Volcanic Monument Visitor Center**, (Exit 49 from I-5) east on SR 504 about five miles, 360/274-2100, overlooks Silver Lake. This center has a walk-in model of the volcano. All four centers offer free admission. The exits to the visitors centers are only about an hour's drive north of Portland on I-5.

APPENDIX

METRIC CONVERSION CHART

1 U.S. gallon = approximately 4 liters
1 liter = about 1 quart
1 Canadian gallon = approximately 4.5 liters

1 pound = approximately 1/2 kilogram
1 kilogram = about 2 pounds

1 foot = approximately 1/3 meter
1 meter = about 1 yard
1 yard = a little less than a meter
1 mile = approximately 1.6 kilometers
1 kilometer = about 2/3 mile

90°F = about 30°C
20°C = approximately 70°F

Pacific Northwest

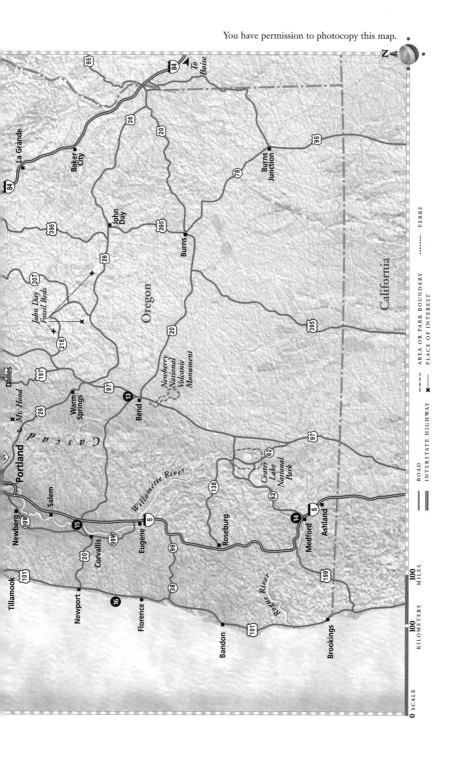

INDEX

Map Index

ABOUT THE AUTHOR

Jena MacPherson's roots run deep in the Pacific Northwest. Her ancestors were pioneers on Orcas Island in the San Juan Islands and homesteaders near Kamloops, B.C., and Prosser in the Yakima Valley in Washington, where she was born and raised on the family mint farm.

Her grandfather collected automobiles and loved to drive, and her British mother wouldn't fly, so Jena's earliest memories are of travel—along the backroads of the Northwest and on cross-country trains and trans-Atlantic cruise ships; it was an experience that whetted her appetite for adventure,and cultivated her interest in foods and fine cuisine.

For more than 10 years Jena has reported on the Northwest for *Sunset* Magazine. She has also contributed to *Odyssey* and *Journey* magazines and to a book on the West by *Sunset* Books.

Jena loves to hike, golf, kayak, and cross-country ski and follows the work of Northwest artists and artisans. She lives in Seattle, on the shores of Puget Sound, with husband, Jim, and dog, Molly the Magnificent.

You'll Feel like a Local When You Travel with Guides from John Muir Publications

CiTY·SMaRT™ GUIDEBOOKS

Pick one for your favorite city: *Albuquerque, Anchorage, Austin, Calgary, Charlotte, Chicago, Cincinnati, Cleveland, Denver, Indianapolis, Kansas City, Memphis, Milwaukee, Minneapolis/St. Paul, Nashville, Pittsburgh, Portland, Richmond, Salt Lake City, San Antonio, St. Louis, Tampa/ St. Petersburg, Tucson*

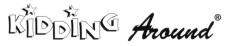

Guides for kids 6 to 10 years old about what to do, where to go, and how to have fun in: *Atlanta, Austin, Boston, Chicago, Cleveland, Denver, Indianapolis, Kansas City, Miami, Milwaukee, Minneapolis/St. Paul, Nashville, Portland, San Francisco, Seattle, Washington D.C.*

TRAVEL✦SMART®

Trip planners with select recommendations to: *Alaska, American Southwest, Carolinas, Colorado, Deep South, Eastern Canada, Florida Gulf Coast, Hawaii, Illinois/Indiana, Kentucky/Tennessee, Maryland/Delaware, Michigan, Minnesota/Wisconsin, Montana/Wyoming/Idaho, New England, New Mexico, New York State, Northern California, Ohio, Pacific Northwest, Pennsylvania/New Jersey, South Florida and the Keys, Southern California, Texas, Utah, Virginias, Western Canada*

Rick Steves' GUIDES

See *Europe Through the Back Door* and take along guides to: *France, Belgium & the Netherlands; Germany, Austria & Switzerland; Great Britain & Ireland; Italy; Russia & the Baltics; Scandinavia; Spain & Portugal; London; Paris;* or the *Best of Europe*

ADVENTURES IN NATURE

Plan your next adventure in: *Alaska, Belize, Caribbean, Costa Rica, Guatemala, Honduras, Mexico*

JMP travel guides are available at your favorite bookstores. For a FREE catalog or to place a mail order, call: 800-888-7504.

John Muir Publications • P.O. Box 613 • Santa Fe, NM 87504

PACIFIC NORTHWEST
TRAVEL ✦ SMART®

Mt. Shuksan behind Picture Lake

© John Elk III